3343148
324.70973
BRO

Mississippi Valley Library District

0 00 35 0298501 7

DEC 0 6 2016

# KILLING
# THE MESSENGER

SO-AIM-956

ALSO BY DAVID BROCK

*Blinded by the Right:*
*The Conscience of an Ex-Conservative*

*The Republican Noise Machine:*
*Right-Wing Media and How It Corrupts Democracy*

# KILLING THE MESSENGER

*The Right-Wing Plot to Derail Hillary
and Hijack Your Government*

~

## David Brock

MISSISSIPPI VALLEY
LIBRARY DISTRICT
408 WEST MAIN ST.
COLLINSVILLE, IL 62234

TWELVE

*New York    Boston*

Copyright © 2015 by David Brock

Cover photos © Narvikk/Getty Images (White House), Chris Clor/Getty Images (elephant)
Cover copyright © 2016 by Hachette Book Group, Inc.

Hachette Book Group supports the right to free expression and the value of copyright. The purpose of copyright is to encourage writers and artists to produce the creative works that enrich our culture.

The scanning, uploading, and distribution of this book without permission is a theft of the author's intellectual property. If you would like permission to use material from the book (other than for review purposes), please contact permissions@hbgusa.com. Thank you for your support of the author's rights.

Twelve
Hachette Book Group
1290 Avenue of the Americas, New York, NY 10104
twelvebooks.com
twitter.com/twelvebooks

Originally published in hardcover and ebook by Twelve in September 2015
First Trade Edition: July 2016

Twelve is an imprint of Grand Central Publishing. The Twelve name and logo are trademarks of Hachette Book Group, Inc.

The publisher is not responsible for websites (or their content) that are not owned by the publisher.

The Hachette Speakers Bureau provides a wide range of authors for speaking events. To find out more, go to www.hachettespeakersbureau.com or call (866) 376-6591.

ISBNs: 978-1-4555-3375-6 (trade), 978-1-4555-3374-9 (ebook)

Printed in the United States of America

RRD-C

10  9  8  7  6  5  4  3  2  1

To my colleagues and staff at Media Matters,
American Bridge, Correct the Record,
and the Franklin Forum

# Contents

# Return to Little Rock

The bar at the Capital Hotel serves Moscow Mules in copper mugs to the power brokers who run Little Rock. Set a block from the banks of the Arkansas River, it's where lobbyists, legislators, and miscellaneous political operatives have gathered for decades to talk shop and hatch plots.

"Rules," the hotel bar's website asserts, "are made at the Statehouse; laws are made at the Capital Bar."

I spent a lot of time at that hotel bar as a young man in the 1990s. But I wasn't there to make laws. I was there to make trouble.

And now, fifteen years after I'd last stepped foot in Arkansas, I was back to make amends.

If you'd told the younger me that, a few blocks east of my old stomping grounds at the Capital Bar, there would someday stand the Clinton School of Public Service...just up the street from the William Jefferson Clinton Presidential Library...on President Clinton Avenue...I would have had a stroke.

And if you'd told me that I'd someday find myself back in Little Rock to appear on stage at the Clinton School of Public Service as a guest speaker...I would have had another.

When the United States won the Cold War, the right lost its raison d'être—its organizing principle and its most effective argument for why conservative ideas should hold sway and Republican politicians should hold power. Ronald Reagan was exiting the stage, and the young ideologues who had enthusiastically followed him into the conservative movement were left scrambling to define a cohesive vision for the country's future.

I was one of them. During my college years at the University of California, Berkeley, I'd become a right-wing iconoclast, a crusading campus journalist bent on destroying what I saw to be a corrupt, politically correct liberal establishment. After graduation, I moved to Washington, where I joined a generation of young writers who gained prominence as the ideological (and, in many cases, biological) heirs to modern conservatism.

We inherited our predecessors' clubby social connections, and, in many cases, their affectations (at twenty-five, I was known to stroll around the offices of the *Washington Times*, the crusading right-wing paper owned by cult leader Sun Myung Moon, with a pipe and even a walking stick).

But while we all adored Ronald Reagan, reviled communism, and believed *liberal* was a dirty word, we never really got around to articulating what, exactly, we were for.

Instead, we found agreement on what we were against. Or, rather, who. Absent a clear ideological end, the demonization of our opponents became an end unto itself. The politics of personal destruction wasn't only something we did to further the conservative movement— it *became* the conservative movement.

I wasn't just a practitioner of this new kind of politics; I was a pioneer. In 1991, law professor Anita Hill accused Supreme Court nominee Clarence Thomas, her former boss, of sexual harassment. My fellow conservatives and I couldn't believe her. And, in fact, we made it our mission to discredit her—not just so that Thomas would

be protected from what we saw as outrageously unfair and false allegations, but because we saw Hill as an avatar of the liberal effort to attack
everything we stood for, whatever that was.

Thomas, of course, was narrowly confirmed. But we still had a job to
do: burnishing his legacy. And I was assigned to do it. I wrote a twenty-
two-thousand-word article for the March 1992 issue of the *American
Spectator* entitled "The Real Anita Hill," in which I attempted to take
apart Hill's story, characterizing her as part of a liberal conspiracy to
frame our hero, now Justice Thomas.

It was a hit piece, full of explicit (and, often, unsubstantiated) details
of Hill's personal life, innuendo, and pure hearsay—all capped with a
flatly racist caricature of Hill on the cover. Smugly labeling her as "a bit
nutty and a bit slutty," I used every nugget I could dig up, every allegation I was passed by Republican operatives in the Bush administration
and on Capitol Hill, and a healthy dose of imagination to smear Anita
Hill.

The *Spectator* proudly published it as "investigative journalism." I
turned the piece into a lucrative best-selling book. Rush Limbaugh
read from it on the air for three days straight. My career as a right-wing
hitman was born.

⌒

But even as I was making a name for myself on the right, the conservative movement found itself facing down a problem it couldn't solve: a
problem named Bill and Hillary Clinton.

As Governor Clinton campaigned for the presidency in 1992, it
quickly became clear that we couldn't compete with his message of hope
and optimism, much less his ambitious, positive agenda for the country.

(Later, I would learn that right-wing animus toward the Clintons
began even farther back in Arkansas, based in resentment among
the rear guard of Southern racists over then governor Clinton's early
embrace of civil rights and stoked by the nerve of his wife to build a
career and a public persona of her own.)

All we had were scandals, real and invented, that we hoped would stop the country from taking a chance on a young, dynamic, progressive Baby Boomer—and his ambitious, brilliant, accomplished wife.

It didn't work. The American people sent the Clintons to Washington. In a democracy like ours, that should have been the end of it. He won, we lost; better luck next time. But now that we were out of power in addition to being out of ideas, conservatives worried that it would be the end of *us*.

The problem with the Clintons wasn't so much who they were as what they represented. They were a threat to the established political and social order, serious agents of change who, if allowed to succeed, could make us look even more ideologically bankrupt, even more hopelessly irrelevant, than we already were.

So conservatives defied two hundred years of American history and set the stage for a coup. The Clintons barely had time to unpack in the White House before the threat of impeachment was being quietly bandied about in my circles. The right was determined to take down the Clintons. All they needed was an excuse. And I was sent to Arkansas to find one.

The *Spectator*'s publisher, billionaire Richard Mellon Scaife, believed Robert Penn Warren's famous line, "Man is conceived in sin and born in corruption, and he passeth from the stink of the didie to the stench of the shroud. There is always something." And he knew that if we were going to find that something, or, quite frankly, create that something, it was going to take a lot of money. So, long before the era of SuperPACs, this one lone billionaire was willing to shell out millions to propagandize the nation and wreck the Clintons.

His magazine—my employer—launched what became known as the Arkansas Project, a dirt-digging operation into the Clintons' past that eventually encompassed a kitchen sink full of allegations ranging from financial fraud to drug running and even murder.

That was how, as a young muckraker on the make, I found myself in

Little Rock, downing cocktails at the Capital Bar and swapping stories with a cast of eccentrics. On one trip, I was introduced by a Republican operative to a group of Arkansas state troopers who had served on then governor Clinton's security staff and who wanted to go public with stories scandalizing Bill and Hillary Clinton.

They painted a picture of the president as nothing short of a compulsive womanizer: picking up women at hotels, ushering conquests into the governor's residence for "personal tour[s] of the mansion," and even receiving oral sex in the parking lot of his daughter's elementary school.

As for Hillary, the troopers described her as cold, calculating, and cruel, a woman with a "garbage mouth" who "hated Arkansas" and "liked to intimidate men." The Clintons' marriage was, in the troopers' eyes, one of political convenience: "If he was dead politically, I would expect a divorce in 30 days."

If that strikes you as a little too perfect for the caricature of the Clintons the troopers were trying to draw, well, it struck me that way, too. As we talked, I became suspicious of the troopers' motives. I knew they wanted to use my article to cash in and sell a tell-all book. And, of course, I couldn't be sure if what they were saying was true.

But I had a job to do: Get dirt into print. So I did. I took the troopers at their word and published all of the above, plus plenty more, in the pages of the *Spectator*.

Nothing was too inflammatory to make it past the tissue-paper-thin fact-check at the magazine:

The troopers speculated that Hillary tolerated this behavior much as eighteenth-century aristocrats maintained marriages of convenience to suit the social and material needs of both parties. Hillary herself was intimately involved with the late Vincent Foster, a partner at the Rose Law Firm and later deputy White House counsel. Foster killed himself in July under circumstances that remain murky. "It was common knowledge around the mansion that Hillary and Vince were having an affair," said Larry Patterson, though he conceded that the evidence for this is more circumstantial than his first-hand knowledge of Clinton's behavior.

And nothing was too petty to be judged worthy of ink; even the Clintons' cat didn't escape unscathed (Socks, I revealed, "apparently retches with alarming frequency").

My "reporting" became national news, and the mainstream media soon followed up. This was no accident; turning the more respectable outlets against the Clintons was part of the goal of the Arkansas Project, and it worked. Soon, the troopers' allegations were printed in major newspapers and repeated on national television. The "scandal" even got a name: Troopergate. And the press now had license to chase all sorts of stories, even stories that were thinly veiled attempts to smear the Clintons for partisan purposes.

Troopergate, of course, was just such an attempt. On closer examination, it turned out that the lurid stories the troopers had told me belonged on the fiction shelf.

Other reporters, following up on the story for outlets that, unlike the *Spectator*, had fact-checking protocols in place, found gaping holes in the troopers' accounts. The troopers claimed that security gate logs had been destroyed as part of a cover-up; it turned out those logs had never been kept in the first place. The troopers described watching via surveillance camera as Governor Clinton and a supposed paramour engaged in sexual activity in a truck; it turned out that this was physically impossible, as the camera was incapable of capturing a clear image from inside a vehicle. The troopers recalled that Vince Foster had fondled Hillary at an event; it turned out that the event had never taken place.

The poisonous fruit from the tree of lies that I had planted by identifying a "woman named Paula" in my Troopergate piece prompted Paula Jones to come forward, she said, to clear her name, subpoenaed as part of Jones' sexual harassment lawsuit against President Clinton the troopers would reverse themselves, denying under oath much of what they had asserted to me in our interviews. Those depositions established that the troopers used their proximity to the governor to procure women for themselves.

It got worse: I later found out that an operative close to would-be House speaker Newt Gingrich had paid the troopers to talk.

This, then, wasn't just a false story. It was a setup, a deliberate and organized fraud perpetrated on the American people by wealthy conservatives and the Republican political establishment. It was, as Hillary Clinton was widely mocked for suggesting, the beginnings of a "vast right-wing conspiracy."

In the immediate aftermath of my *Spectator* piece, the mainstream media, suddenly transfixed by Arkansas, revived an old "scandal" from the 1992 Clinton campaign, one about quid pro quos and conflicts of interest involving a money-losing land deal called Whitewater that the Clintons had invested in. The feeding frenzy over Whitewater in Washington was such that President Clinton felt compelled to call for the appointment of a special prosecutor to investigate the matter. Eventually, a right-wing judge, Ken Starr, took over the inquiry and proceeded to go very far afield from his original mandate, probing the Paula Jones sexual harassment case, through which he found a former White House intern, Monica Lewinsky, with whom Clinton had had a consensual sexual dalliance.

After spending several years and $70 million investigating the Clintons, Starr turned up no wrongdoing. But the story of the president and the intern was enough for the GOP to open the impeachment proceedings in Newt Gingrich's House of Representatives that the right had lusted for since the Clintons came to Washington.

It was, in short, everything I went to Arkansas to achieve.

⌒

By then, six years into the Clinton presidency, I was disgusted with what I had wrought.

After the trooper story broke, a publisher commissioned me to write a book about Hillary Clinton, expecting a hit job that would be published on the eve of the 1996 elections. And why not? In addition to characterizing the president as a sex-crazed sociopath, conservatives thought they could gain political advantage by portraying his wife as a conniving, shrewish, unstable Lady Macbeth. And they were willing to pay me a million bucks to do it.

So I spent two years researching and writing, retracing every step of Hillary Clinton's life, doing more than a hundred interviews, and going back twenty years collecting virtually every piece of paper that had her name on it.

Contrary to what my patrons expected, I found no silver bullet that would stop the Clintons. What I did find was a woman with a steadfast commitment to public service, a clear political vision, and a deep well of personal integrity. I couldn't write the book conservatives wanted, not without betraying the facts as I saw them—and betraying myself in the process.

You see, in the aftermath of publishing my Anita Hill tract, while writing a review of *Strange Justice*, a competing book on the Senate hearings by Jill Abramson and Jane Mayer that provided fresh evidence for Hill's charges, I learned from my own trusted sources, the people who knew Clarence Thomas best, that they never believed he was innocent, despite what they had led me to think when I was reporting my book. Now I was part of their club, and these seasoned Washington players could let me in on their secret: Defending Thomas was never about bringing the truth to light; it was all about partisan politics. Thomas, not Anita Hill, had lied, just as *Strange Justice* suggested—in fact, he had perjured himself to get on the court.

And, for my part, I had been sold a bill of goods, which made me complicit in the monumental lies of Thomas and his supporters, even though I wrote my book in good faith. I made a private vow that as I reported on Hillary, I would not be used by the right again.

So I resisted the conservative spin on Hillary, sticking to the facts and being as fair as I could to my subject. And in struggling to find

Hillary's humanity, I gradually found my own. I didn't turn into a progressive or a Democrat overnight, but this period did mark the beginning of a political awakening that would play out in the years to come.

I ended up publishing a nuanced portrait of Hillary that exonerated her on the long list of charges that I concluded had been manufactured by her opponents: Whitewater, Travelgate, Filegate—there was nothing to any of it. And I also reached an affirmative judgment, based on my study of her prodigious talents, strong character, and bedrock American values: Hillary, I wrote, had the potential to be "an even more historically significant figure than her husband."

Predictably, the right wasn't interested. Their campaign of character assassination would continue without me. And by the time that campaign culminated in an unconstitutional power grab—the 1998 impeachment of President Clinton—I was ready to do everything in my power to help Clinton stay in office by blowing the whistle on the machinations of my ex-colleagues.

My divorce from the conservative movement came in a long piece I wrote for *Esquire* magazine, "Confessions of a Right-Wing Hit Man," and, later, a book called *Blinded by the Right,* in which I exposed what I had been involved in—a wrongful scheme to thwart a twice-elected president by throwing sand in the gears of progressive governance.

I apologized for smearing people. I confessed my sins to the public. And, in the years that followed, I'd find a way to make a different kind of impact on our political discourse, one that promoted honest debate and served to ferret out the kind of lies I'd once peddled.

But it took fifteen years for me to come back to Arkansas.

~

It was hard not to feel a bit like a rehabilitated convict returning to the scene of the crime.

I was nervous. And why not? The room felt more like a press conference than a college talk. Many of the reporters who had built careers at major national publications covering the "Clinton beat" flew down from New York and Washington, a mini-reunion of their own. Once again, my take on the Clintons would make headlines (including on the front page of the *New York Times*). And, of course, this being 2014, the press was also live-tweeting my remarks.

Also in the room were many of the Clinton associates I'd long done battle with, some of whom I'd even attacked personally. Up in the balcony, I could see Bruce Lindsey, a trusted counselor to the former president who had been on the front lines of the White House's legal defense efforts against the parade of phony scandals and Republican witch hunts.

And out in the crowd were countless local Clinton supporters whose names I'd never heard but who had been loyal to the former president dating back to when he was a young governor. Later, many waited in line to tell me they came to see for themselves if I understood the hurt and damage I had caused them.

Kicking off the program was Skip Rutherford, the dean of the school and an old Clinton hand from way back when who had valiantly attempted to defend the president from my attacks.

"In the 1990s," Skip told the room, "he certainly played a major role in this state, to the dismay of some." Standing offstage, I heard several people laugh nervously at the understatement.

Although Skip and I had known each other's names (and probably cursed them, too) for many years, we'd never met until the night before the speech, when we got together at the Capital Bar.

He was friendly and welcoming, but he made it clear to me how hard those days had been on Clinton supporters in Arkansas. Though the investigations my reporting had unleashed turned up nothing, they tormented innocent people, forcing them to ring up huge legal bills. It was important, he told me as we finished our drinks, not just for the sake of history, but for the future, that people hear my story.

And so, before a packed crowd—a mix of reporters, politicos, and young students looking to learn from my own strange journey in American politics and journalism—I told that story. I talked about the reclusive billionaire whose wealth funded a shadow campaign against the American president, about the right-wing publications that ignored any pretense of journalistic standards and chose instead to launder false accusations into print, about the way the mainstream media were unwitting accomplices to the crime of character assassination, and about the role I played in all of it.

It's a story that, as yet, lacks an ending. I didn't come back to Arkansas to settle some karmic debt, to find closure in a difficult, and at times ugly, chapter of my life, or to have one last Moscow Mule at the Capital Bar.

The real reason I came back—and the reason I wrote this book—is that the Clinton wars still aren't over.

Bill and Hillary Clinton remain the most important, perhaps the *defining* political figures of this generation. Hillary is the most likely candidate—and, in my opinion, the right candidate—to win the Democratic nomination for president in 2016. And the same reactionary forces that tried to drag them down in the 1990s are still at work today.

The Arkansas Project wasn't a relic. It was a rough draft. There remains what Hillary, back in 1998, called a "vast right-wing conspiracy" in this country. It even features many of the same participants. But it's become bigger, more focused, and better-funded than ever before. It's more like a "vast right-wing conglomerate," as the *Atlantic* magazine observed. And it's about to bring its considerable power to bear against Hillary Clinton.

Today, even more obviously than when I was involved, the conservative movement cannot compete in the marketplace of ideas. And when it comes to the 2016 election, the fact is that no Republican politician enjoys the widespread appeal, deep devotion, or impressive record of public service that Hillary does. The only way they can win is by using fear and sensationalism to undermine honest debate—and that's exactly what they'll do if we let them.

When I finished my speech at the Clinton School, I was relieved by the warm round of applause. And I wasn't surprised that, despite the radical personal transformation I'd detailed, a majority of the questions I got weren't about my story at all.

My questioners were concerned less with what I'd participated in back in the 1990s, and more about the ongoing right-wing campaign to distort the facts and destroy their opponents by any means necessary.

Today, conservative mouthpieces like Rush Limbaugh and his imitators are continuing to spread lies and spew angry rhetoric that deserve no place in our public discourse. One right-wing shock jock has expressed his wish to see Hillary "shot in the vagina."

Today, Fox News reliably recycles these lies onto cable news, creating an alternate universe in which facts are turned upside down and invective stands in for argument. Fox has accused Hillary of murder, compared her to a murderer, and suggested she commit suicide.

Today, Richard Mellon Scaife may be dead and gone, but he's been replaced by a pair of billionaire brothers, Charles and David Koch, whose motives are no purer but whose treasure chest of funding for right-wing causes is far deeper than Scaife's. They've pledged to spend close to a billion dollars to defeat Hillary.

Today, the *American Spectator* may no longer be the journal of record for the conservative movement, giving its most extreme elements a platform, but that's only because those extremists now have platforms of their own: a slew of new digital media properties from which conservatives slander their political opponents. They have Hillary squarely in their sights.

Today, the conservative movement has been co-opted by its rightmost fringe, blocking progress or even real debate on the issues that affect our country. The United States Senate is bullied and bossed by Tea Party types like Ted Cruz, who led a pointless government shutdown, and Rand Paul, a desperate presidential candidate who, as I pointed out in Little Rock, has already started recycling the same stale attack lines on the Clintons.

And, of course, today, it is still a Clinton who stands in the way of these forces. Well before Hillary declared herself to be a candidate for president, no fewer than eight conservative PACs had set up shop to try to tarnish her record and reputation before she had a chance to make her own case.

The market for such sludge is huge. Unprecedentedly, every major news outlet assigned a reporter to the Hillary beat three years before Election Day, while she was still a private citizen and unsure she'd even make the run.

This, then, is the dynamic in which events are unfolding, a dynamic I warned of in my speech: On the one hand, a voracious news media hungry for any Clinton crumb; and on the other, well-funded anti-Clinton mudslinging operations that feed the beast. This is the new reality of American media and politics, a sick and scary evolution from the world within which I operated back in the 1990s.

Fortunately, things have changed on the other side, as well.

Today, a network of progressive organizations exists to confront the right on the battlefield of public discourse, countering their lies and holding accountable those who spread them.

Today, Democratic politicians and their supporters embrace the idea that these smears cannot be ignored—they must be refuted and their sources exposed.

Today, Hillary knows that dedicated watchdogs have her back in the fight against conservative propaganda.

And, today, I'm one of them.

This book is, in part, the story of how Bill and Hillary Clinton, their enemies, and I have all evolved since the battles of the 1990s—how the Clinton Wars have become ingrained in the fabric of our politics, how the vast right-wing conspiracy has grown and changed, and how I came to take a leadership role in combating it.

Counterarguments and spin have long been a part of the normal give-and-take of politics in our democracy. But concurrent with the rise of the Clintons—and with the trajectory of my own time in politics—there arose a professional political class on the right, bankrupt of ideas and issues, whose sole and relentless preoccupation is slinging mud at the liberal alternative.

In my lifetime, the conservative message machine I was once an integral part of has grown into a formidable and treacherous leviathan. And my career has become a ceaseless (some might say Sisyphean) effort to counter the power of the organized right and restore some sense of truth and balance to the political arena.

That's what this book is all about. I wrote it not just to tell stories about the recent political past. I wrote this book to help shape the future.

I make no secret of the fact that I hope for the sake of the country Hillary Clinton is the Democratic nominee for president in 2016—and wins the presidency. And I know from my long experience on both sides of the Clinton Wars what it will take for that to happen—and what her opponents will do to try to stop her.

This, then, is more than a history of the new, vast right-wing conglomerate and the progressive infrastructure that has grown up to counter its influence. It's a handbook—a practical guide for Hillary supporters who want to help protect her from the dishonest conservative campaign already underway, for Democrats who are sick and tired of being bullied by the radical right and lied to by the press, and for plain old everyday Americans who want to see a real debate about their futures rather than a rerun of the stale scandal politics of the 1990s.

Hillary's candidacy means that 2016 will be the climax of a long struggle to determine America's purpose in the twenty-first century. The right will come at her with everything it has.

The good news is, I have their playbook. And I'm revealing it to you so that, together, we can be ready for what the right has coming and ensure our fellow Americans don't get tricked by it.

## Chapter One

# Building the Machine

*My phone was ringing.*

It was a blustery Saturday afternoon in January 2003, and I was walking through the front door of my townhouse on N Street in the Georgetown section of Washington, arms laden with groceries from the nearby Safeway.

Once upon a time, this townhouse—sometimes referred to as "the house Anita Hill built," since I had purchased it with the proceeds from my best seller, *The Real Anita Hill*—had been a social hub for conservative movement activists determined to destroy the Clinton presidency and have a rollicking good time doing it.

A typical cocktail party at my townhouse might feature appearances from bold-faced names like Grover Norquist, Ann Coulter, Laura Ingraham, Matt Drudge, and Tucker Carlson. You might bump into the conservative lawyers who represented Clinton accuser Paula Jones. You might run across the Republican Capitol Hill operatives investigating Whitewater. And no matter who was in attendance, you'd find plenty of booze, plenty of cigars, and plenty of braggadocio, as the leading lights of our movement celebrated and plotted.

On the night in 1994 when Republicans swept the midterm elections and Newt Gingrich rose to power, I'd hosted perhaps our most memorably raucous celebration, where we toasted again and again to the apparent demise of our enemies.

But it had been years since the house Anita Hill built hosted any right-wing bacchanalia. In fact, it had been a while since I'd had much company at all.

When I broke with the conservative movement in 1997, declaring in an *Esquire* article that "David Brock, the road warrior of the right, is dead," I wasn't just abandoning my professional network. I was turning my back on the only friends I had (or, at least, people who I thought were friends). In Washington, the personal and the political had always been intertwined, unusually so in my case. And in both respects, I was now adrift and alone.

That's how I spent much of the next four years—alone, in that townhouse, struggling to understand the journey I'd been on, let alone figure out a way to explain it.

The resulting book, *Blinded by the Right*, was an anguished endeavor. It also ended up becoming a critical and commercial success. The first review, a long piece in the *New Yorker* by Hendrik Hertzberg, signaled the consensus line on the book in media circles—it was an incisive exposé on the inner workings of the conservative movement. Moreover, Hertzberg and other reviewers found the confessional aspects of my story authentic and sincere.

As for my former friends on the right, they never laid a glove on what I wrote, factually or otherwise. Instead, they endeavored to smear me personally, which shouldn't have surprised me; they were using the same playbook that had made my own career.

I was gratified by the positive reception to *Blinded by the Right*, but I was no less alone. While I had declared myself a refugee from a movement with which I no longer identified, I was still a man without a country. And, really, without a plan.

After *Blinded*, I began work on another book, one that would open a wider lens on conservative organizing in both politics and media since the late 1960s, tracing the architecture of the modern conservative movement as it had developed over more than thirty years. I wanted to explain how, through their dedicated efforts, conservative Republicans had moved the country's political discourse so far to the right that they had become a dominant force in American politics as a whole.

*The Republican Noise Machine*, I called it. I knew from the inside how conservatives had built that machine, enabling them to shape public opinion and thus shift the political landscape. But as I began to research and write the book, I began to see, as well, how someone could build a machine to counter that influence, and even reverse it.

To be clear, I didn't yet see myself as that someone, though as part of the conservative movement, I was never purely an observer—my writing was a form of activism, and I still felt the pull to make a political difference with my work. But becoming an activist on the other side, a serious partisan working in liberal Democratic circles, I couldn't yet fathom.

And it might never have happened had I not walked in the door that cold January day, set my groceries down on the kitchen table, picked up the phone that was ringing on the wall, and—for the first time in my life—spoken with President Bill Clinton.

◦

I'd be lying if I said I remembered every word of the conversation. It was unexpected, almost unbelievable.

I do remember him thanking me for writing *Blinded*. And he clearly wasn't doing so to be polite. He was well versed in its contents, generous in his praise, and intrigued by the details I'd laid out about how the campaign against him had worked, who had been involved, and why I thought they'd done it.

(Later, I discovered that he had purchased dozens of copies of the book, sending them across the country and urging friends to read it. I once visited his Harlem office, where an aide opened a big cabinet to reveal that it was filled with copies. I probably owe him some royalties.)

At times, the former president seemed almost bemused by the antics of his detractors, especially some of the more colorful nemeses from back in his Arkansas days. At times, he was intensely curious—the reclusive and powerful Richard Mellon Scaife, in particular, was an object of fascination.

And when we talked about the sections of the book where I had laid out the way the right-wing media had manipulated more mainstream outlets, using them to spread its anti-Clinton propaganda, the former president became especially animated.

Then he asked me what I was currently doing—and what I planned to do in the future. We talked a bit about the paperback edition of *Blinded* I was tinkering with in between work on my new book, and he suggested that I consider going out and speaking, particularly on college campuses, as a way of spreading the message.

Actually, *suggested* isn't the right word. President Clinton insisted that I go see his speaker's agent as soon as possible.

Eventually, I found myself describing my new book project in some detail. And then I mentioned my nascent idea of an organization that could counter the "Republican Noise Machine."

Here, the conversation shifted. The former president had been doing most of the talking, but as I described this idea (more or less making it up as I went along), he got quiet, listening as I riffed. If a group like that had existed when his presidency was under siege, he finally said, things might have played out a lot differently.

At the end of the call, he told me to write a business plan for an organization along the lines of what I was talking about, and send it to him.

That's how the story of Media Matters for America, and everything that came after, began: The right guy called at the right time.

Had my phone not rung that day, and had President Clinton not responded so enthusiastically to the bits and pieces of an idea that were then floating around in my head, the organization almost certainly wouldn't exist today. And I really don't know where I would have ended up in life.

But by the time I hung up the phone, I could see a path, a way to take my singular perspective, apply the skills that had built my previous career, and reengage in the political process—only this time, instead of fighting *for* the far right, I'd be fighting on the side of what *is* right.

It was an unanticipated turn in my life. But in retrospect, it seems like fate.

~

It was easy to make the argument for why Media Matters needed to exist (and hard to understand why Democrats hadn't already created it).

For decades, conservatives had complained about liberal bias in the mainstream media. And to help them complain effectively, they set up watchdog groups like Accuracy in Media (launched to protect the Nixon administration from being criticized on Vietnam and Watergate) and the Media Research Center (founded in 1987 by Brent Bozell, the nephew of conservative paterfamilias William F. Buckley).

By the time I found myself drafting the original Media Matters prospectus, these groups had become enormously powerful, thanks to generous funding from right-wing activists like my old benefactor, Richard Mellon Scaife. The Media Research Center alone had a $6 million budget and dozens of employees. By comparison, the only media advocacy organization on the left, Fairness and Accuracy in Reporting (FAIR) had a cash reserve of less than $25,000.

Moreover, the right-wing watchdogs had been enormously successful in cowing traditional outlets into catering to right-wing spin and promoting right-wing commentary. Nine of the top fourteen newspaper columnists were now conservatives, reaching more than two thousand newspapers. At a July 2004 symposium at Harvard's Kennedy School of Government, network anchors agreed that the right was in their ear. "There is a guy by the name of Brent Bozell," NBC's Tom Brokaw told the crowd, "who makes a living at taking us on every night. He's well organized, he's got a constituency, he's got a newsletter, he can hit a button and we'll hear from him."

And in addition to pushing traditional outlets to skew to the right, conservative watchdogs were creating a rationale, a justification, and a market for explicitly right-wing media that played to its audience's sense of grievance with the "liberal" press: Rush Limbaugh, his imitators on talk radio, and, eventually, the Fox News Channel.

In October 2003, Bill O'Reilly could write: "For decades, [liberals] controlled the agenda on TV news. Now that's over." My old buddy Matt Drudge hailed "the beginning of a second media century." And *Weekly Standard* columnist David Brooks described the conservative media as "a dazzlingly efficient ideology delivery system that swamps liberal efforts to get their ideas out."

Liberals who watched Fox News recoiled at the constant stream of conservative misinformation being served up around the clock. But Fox didn't care—because liberals weren't the target audience. A 2004 Media Vote poll found that 88 percent of daily Fox viewers strongly supported President George W. Bush.

Instead, the idea was to reinforce right-wing messaging for the conservative base and bully mainstream media into swallowing it whole. The hugely powerful right-wing media, unmatched by anything on the left, could say whatever it wanted to its growing audience—at the time, 22 percent of Americans got their news from conservative talk radio, according to Gallup—and putatively "neutral" mainstream outlets were afraid not to give credence to its claims.

Few progressives failed to notice that the media climate had turned hostile. And many wrote books thoroughly debunking Rush Limbaugh's claim to be a "truth teller," Sean Hannity's claim to be a "responsible journalist," Bill O'Reilly's claim to run a "No Spin Zone," and, of course, Fox News's insistence that it was "fair and balanced."

But as I surveyed the political landscape in 2003, I didn't see anyone doing what I thought was necessary to solve the problem, as opposed to simply describing and decrying it.

What we needed was a system by which right-wing media no longer operated with impunity and its false charges could be answered in real time. What we needed was a way for liberals to register their concerns in newsrooms to discourage them from recycling right-wing misinformation—not with lengthy critiques of conservative influence in the *New York Review of Books*, but by fighting it out in news cycle after news cycle.

What we needed was a watchdog group of our own—one that, in the words of my draft prospectus for Media Matters, would be "nimble, quick, sharp, and focused."

At the time, nobody was even systematically recording talk radio, let alone transcribing and archiving it, making it impossible to hold the hosts accountable. As far back as 1994, Democrats were saying publicly that they needed to monitor Rush Limbaugh in real time—but no one ever did it.

But I wanted to do more than just subject some poor intern to listening to Rush. I wanted to take on right-wing print outlets like the *Washington Times* and the *Wall Street Journal* editorial page, conservative magazines, books, columnists, and websites the same way: tracking everything these guys said, calling them out in real time when what they said wasn't true, and making sure the mainstream media didn't repeat their lies without hearing from us.

I wrote a plan to fund a team of five researchers—one for each area of focus: Radio, TV, Print, Internet/Books, and Pundit Profiles. We'd build a website to catalog our findings, designed to reach the media itself, progressive activists, top bloggers, and everyday news consumers who might write a letter to the editor or call their local TV outlet when they saw or heard something wrong. And we'd produce daily Web content so that we could help shape each news cycle.

I hoped to launch in the spring of 2004, as the presidential election heated up, create some early momentum with a small group, track our progress, and then grow to scale. And I needed to find some funding—$1.8 million, specifically—to make it happen.

⌒

As it happened, purely by chance, a personal friend knew a Democratic strategist named Rob Stein. He was quietly working to build the network of progressive megadonors that would become known as the Democracy Alliance. Rob seemed like a good place to start pitching, but he was skeptical. Progressives, he explained, don't like to fund permanent institutions the way my old friends on the right did. Instead, they funded from election to election, flitting from project to project based on whatever they thought the next important fight was. He thought I'd find the whole experience of trying to build a piece of progressive infrastructure frustrating—but I was thankful when he agreed to help me anyway.

At that time, Rob was thinking along some of the same lines. His pitch for the Democracy Alliance urged wealthy progressives to fund broad-based (rather than single-issue) progressive institutions on a sustained basis by illustrating how the right's willingness to do the same— building an architecture of money, message, and media—had been so effective politically. I was happy to help Rob fill in some of the backstory on the conservative machine, he advised me on my business plan, and I later joined his road show as he enlisted wealthy progressives to sign up for the alliance. I was a firsthand witness to how the right had built up its network, including the ones who used to sign my paychecks.

Meanwhile, as requested, I sent President Clinton my prospectus, which laid out an ambitious plan to create "the leading media watchdog group for progressives in the United States," one that would "identify, expose, and correct media malpractice—wherever it's found, in every news cycle."

I also sent it to Senator Tom Daschle, the Democratic Senate leader, whom I'd met the year before, when he invited me to discuss *Blinded* at the Senate Democratic Caucus weekly lunch. He was one of many people who had received a copy of the book from President Clinton, in Daschle's case, complete with Clinton's own margin notes.

That lunch had been my first real journey into the heart of the Democratic establishment I'd spent so many years harassing. It was held in the Capitol's ornate LBJ Room, where Majority Leader Lyndon Baines Johnson had held court. Dozens of powerful Democratic senators were in attendance. Still, I was less nervous than you might think. I relished the opportunity to tell my story. And I was ready to answer every question the senators might throw my way.

Being invited to this lunch was an early sign that there was an influential audience for my message. And I learned from the senators' questions that they were truly interested in knowing how the other side had accomplished all it had. Frankly, they didn't seem nearly as interested in my personal odyssey, or the shenanigans I'd helped to pull, as they were in understanding the right's decades-long institution-building effort.

I'm sure there was skepticism about me in the room, but it never made itself apparent. Instead, I fielded questions from Senator Joe Biden about a right-wing leadership institute that had a large campus in his home state of Delaware. Senator Dianne Feinstein of California asked about specific institutions like the Heritage Foundation, where I had worked. There were a lot of questions about the Federalist Society and its role in grooming the right-wing judiciary. I was beginning to feel less like a snitch and more like an expert witness.

But there was one juror who waited until the very end of the lunch to speak: the junior senator from New York, Hillary Rodham Clinton, whom I had never met except once back in 1995 at a book signing for *It Takes a Village*, where I had approached her for an interview for the book I was writing about her. (Understandably, she politely declined.) I imagine I wasn't the only person waiting for her take on my presentation. Speaking last, she reinforced what I'd said about the power of the right-wing media machine and urged her fellow senators to take seriously what I was saying. "Here are the three points David just made that you guys need to remember," she began, summarizing my case more clearly than I had.

That event meant a lot. That morning, Matt Drudge had published on his website the (false) claim that I had worked on *Blinded* from a mental ward. And to be well received by this room full of accomplished Democrats—including Hillary herself—made me feel a little less vulnerable.

I didn't yet know, of course, that this conversation would be a prelude to my future. I never expected to end up helping Democrats compete in the political media wars. I wasn't sure they even wanted to compete in those wars at all.

But after I sent my business plan for Media Matters to Senator Daschle, I was invited to a meeting in his office with Senator Harry Reid and a handful of aides and Democratic operatives. Democrats had just lost control of the Senate. There was widespread sentiment that the party had to start doing things differently, particularly in the area of media and communications.

Everyone at the meeting agreed that an organization like Media Matters should be formed. I explained that Media Matters would be a nonpartisan group engaged in media criticism, a form of public education, and therefore should be incorporated as a tax-exempt charity. So unfamiliar was the group with ideological infrastructure like the Heritage Foundation and the Media Research Center on the right, both 501(c)(3) charitable endeavors, that several aides expressed astonishment with my plan.

Finally Senator Reid, seated at the end of a long wooden conference table, spoke up. "Well, if theirs is c3, then ours is going to be c3," he declared, pounding the table with his fist.

The real question in the room was whether I was the right person to form the group, and I wasn't totally sure myself. Some raised the valid point that I might be viewed skeptically as a truth-squad leader given my checkered journalistic history—and the credibility of Media Matters would be of paramount importance. Meanwhile, there was the issue of liberal skepticism—could someone with my baggage really go out there and raise money from wealthy progressives?

At that point, I turned to Senator Daschle and offered to give the idea away.

But someone intervened. It was John Podesta—the former chief of staff for President Clinton who had recently formed the Center for American Progress, which would go on to become a powerhouse progressive think tank in Washington. John argued that it was precisely because I had spent so long inside right-wing media that I was just the person to fight it.

The senator said he thought John was right, and the matter was settled. John soon gave me office space at CAP while I worked to launch Media Matters.

Meanwhile, President Clinton had given a copy of my plan to Hillary, who immediately sprang into action, inviting me to pitch it to meetings of her national Senate fund-raising council at the Clinton homes in Washington and Chappaqua. I would now see that the Clintons were as committed to forcefully confronting the organized right as I was, and to building and funding the permanent ideological machinery that success would require. It was on the basis of this mutual understanding that an early bond was formed.

⌐

Going to dinner at Bill and Hillary Clinton's house felt like an out-of-body experience. These were, after all, people I'd worked hard to destroy.

But at dinner, the Clintons were warm, welcoming, and gracious. When the food had been served, I stood up and made my pitch to a hundred or so people sitting under a white tent on the back lawn of the Clintons' Chappaqua home. Throughout, Hillary sat at a head table directly in front of me, nodding affirmatively. President Clinton was doing the same at a table nearby.

When I finished, they both spoke in support of me and my project—Hillary joking that they were inviting the fox into the henhouse, and Bill speaking about the importance of forgiveness in life while assuring their friends that every word I had spoken was true.

Forgiveness. That was the gift the Clintons gave me.

The former president gave me a tour of the house before I left, showing off the memorabilia he'd accumulated in office. And as I was leaving, still a bit dazed, Hillary followed me down the driveway, listing the dinner guests who she said would be interested in financially supporting the new venture. She asked if I knew what my next move would be. I said I had no idea. She told me to be in touch with her staff for help. And she went to work, as well.

A few days after the Chappaqua dinner, I addressed a group of Hillary's supporters in Washington, including Susie Tompkins Buell, the founder of Esprit and a close friend of Hillary's, who quickly spoke up and said she wanted to host a fund-raiser for Media Matters in San Francisco. I didn't know who Susie was, but I was happy to have the help, even more so when I found out she was one of the most important progressive donors on the West Coast, and downright stunned when, led by major donors Steve Silberstein and Louise Gund, I raised $800,000 in seed money at one dinner party, nearly half what I thought I needed to get started.

A few days after I met Susie, Kelly Craighead, who had been one of Hillary's closest aides in the White House and had just left Hillary's political action committee, called and offered to work with me to launch the organization. With Kelly came a valuable Rolodex. Yet her first call, to long-time Democratic donor B. Rappaport in Texas, didn't bode well. Rappaport flat-out told Kelly she was crazy to be working with me and hung up the phone. Luckily, his response wasn't at all typical, and in time he became an enthusiastic financial supporter.

Our first task: Find that other million dollars. Rob Stein had cautioned me that he'd seen many promising initiatives on the left begin to operate with too little seed cash, living hand-to-mouth and invariably going under—he warned that we should avoid starting operations until we had fully funded the plan.

Kelly set up a meeting in New York with Peter Lewis, the Progressive Insurance mogul, and his son Jonathan. At the time, Peter was coinvesting with George Soros in a number of political committees they hoped would defeat President George W. Bush in the 2004 election. The two put more than $60 million into Americans Coming Together, an independent media advertising and field organizing operation.

Peter and Jonathan had both read *Blinded* (by now, I was coming to understand that the book was a pretty effective calling card). Peter thought that perhaps he and Soros would split the million dollars, giving me the chance to launch in time to have an impact on the 2004 election. But Soros passed, saying he'd already funded a project at the Columbia Journalism School to fact-check the media, so Peter stepped up all by himself. (Soros later became a donor, as well.)

All of a sudden, we were a real organization—and one operating on Peter's sped-up election-year timetable. Kelly took the helm as chief of staff and lead fund-raiser. And we were off to the races: On May 3, 2004, Media Matters for America opened its doors.

Within days, we were monitoring Rush Limbaugh, and, sure enough, he didn't disappoint. Less than a week after our launch, Rush compared the horrific abuse at the Abu Ghraib prison in Iraq to a college fraternity prank. It was exactly the sort of thing he'd been saying for years—but now, there was a system in place to make sure that the world found out about it, and that he faced consequences for saying it.

We acted fast, posting the transcript on our website so he couldn't wriggle off the hook. And to show we were serious about getting his comments noticed, we ran a cable TV ad featuring them. Once upon a time, Rush's most inflammatory remarks provoked nothing but guffaws from his "dittohead" audience. This isn't my insult, by the way—Rush's listeners were famously so devoted in their allegiance to everything their hero said that they referred to themselves as "dittoheads," and callers often greeted him with a hearty "Megadittoes!" But now, for the first time, Rush's words were coming back to haunt him. The story made international headlines, with Limbaugh coming in for a wide round of condemnation.

With this early victory, we had proof of concept—clear and convincing evidence that a professional watchdog operation that always got its facts right could make lying a liability for the right if we could catch them in the act.

That operation was housed in a rented space in downtown Washington that looked every bit like the start-up it was. Researchers sat at rows of desks tucked along a narrow corridor, recording and watching cable news or plugging in headphones to monitor right-wing radio. Two of them were devoted to nothing but Rush. Other staffers toiled away updating the website. Our press team stayed on top of mainstream outlets, prodding them to acknowledge the right-wing misinformation we were finding.

The days began at 5 a.m., and they were powered by caffeine, youthful energy, and the victories we quickly began to rack up. In the same month we brought Rush's Abu Ghraib comment to light—our first month in existence—we highlighted the fallacy of Bill O'Reilly's talking points on income redistribution; exposed Matt Drudge for peddling talking points word for word from the Republican National Committee; and called out Fox News contributor Linda Chavez for labeling John Kerry a "communist apologist" and then, in what would emerge as a pattern, lying about having done so.

We felt good about our launch. Progressives were excited to see someone taking it to the right-wing bullies who haunted the airwaves. Some of the more fair-minded conservatives shrugged, acknowledging that it couldn't hurt to have another fact-checker in the game. And, of course, many of the leading lights of the far right went entertainingly berserk at finding themselves called out for what they were saying on the air, inevitably punching down at our upstart organization and helping us attract more influence (and more funding).

Media Matters quickly became a force to be reckoned with. In April 2007, Don Imus, the shock jock whose popular show was broadcast nationwide on MSNBC, made a racially loaded remark about the Rutgers University women's basketball team, calling the players "nappy-headed hos." Before Media Matters, the remark might have gone unnoticed, coming as it did at 6:14 in the morning. But a Media

Matters researcher caught it, and we quickly posted the video and transcript to our website.

By the next day, MSNBC had come out against the remark, condemning its own host's "offensive comments." Imus himself grudgingly apologized, as well. And in a previous era, that might have been the end of it.

But as the *Washington Post* reported, we were able to show that "the comments [were] 'just the latest in a long history of racial slurs made on the show by Imus, his guests, and regular contributors.'" This was someone whose executive producer once said, on the air, that Hillary Clinton was "trying to sound black in front of a black audience" when speaking at a civil rights event in Selma, Alabama. "Bitch is gonna be wearing cornrows," he mused, adding that Hillary would be "giving Crips signs during speeches." The shocking development wasn't that Imus had said something so offensive, it was that he had been given airtime on a national cable news network for so long.

After several days of public outcry, MSNBC and CBS Radio said they would suspend Imus for two weeks—a second attempt to distance themselves from their host without having to fire the man who brought in millions of dollars in ad revenue and who was the toast of much of the Washington media establishment he featured on his show. But the public pressure kept up, and advertisers kept fleeing. Finally, just a week after Imus insulted the Rutgers players, MSNBC announced that it would no longer broadcast Imus's show. A day later, CBS Radio canceled it. Imus was finished—and national media credited Media Matters with taking his scalp.

The same thing happened when we outed Lou Dobbs, a CNN regular since the network's launch in 1980, as a "birther" who doubted President Obama's eligibility to hold office. Far from the "Mr. Independent" image he worked hard to propagate, Dobbs routinely used his show to broadcast particularly skewed conservative political opinions—and when he talked about immigrants, which was often, he frequently crossed the line.

We had been cataloguing and debunking Dobbs's comments for years—such as his 2005 claim that "the invasion of illegal aliens" had caused an increase in leprosy—and when he plunged headfirst into the right-wing fever swamps, suggesting on his radio show there were unanswered questions about the circumstances of Obama's birth, we were ready. We bought airtime to highlight "CNN's Lou Dobbs Problem," and worked with a coalition of Latino and progressive groups to press Dobbs's advertisers to boycott the show. After weeks of pressure led by the National Council of La Raza, Dobbs abruptly resigned from the network that had been his home for nearly three decades. Like Imus, he ended up on the Fox Business Network—a refuge of the discredited, where both belonged.

Of course, while we continued to accumulate more and more of these victories, we weren't in it just to play "gotcha." Cable news was a better place without the likes of Imus and Dobbs, but Media Matters had never been only about discrediting individual miscreants. It was about fundamentally changing the media landscape so that trafficking in right-wing misinformation was no longer a good business model. It was about bringing accountability to the airwaves—not just accountability for the mouthpieces who spewed lies, but for the outlets that offered those mouthpieces microphones, for the advertisers who paid for them, and for the mainstream media that still uncritically passed their nonsense along.

～

Media Matters had grown enormously in its first five years. No longer anything resembling a start-up, by 2009, we were well established, well funded (with an annual budget above $10 million), and increasingly looked to as a top media watchdog.

But the stakes had grown, too. With President Obama's election, it was clear that progressives would now have a chance to lead—and that, committed as ever to doing the conservative movement's bidding, the right-wing media would represent a serious threat to the new president's agenda.

During the campaign, Americans were treated to a constant stream of false accusations about then Senator Obama's alleged connections to radical black activists and even domestic terrorists, not to mention the assertion that he had been born in Kenya and was ineligible to serve. And as he took office, the right's rhetoric reached a boiling point, as hosts warned of the demise of American democracy and even urged their audiences to hoard guns and food in preparation for some kind of Obamapocalypse.

Some of the attacks were silly, the kind of thing you'd get in an e-mail forwarded from your crazy uncle. More than a few were downright racist. But all of them, taken together, represented a serious threat to Obama's ability to govern. We couldn't afford to sit back and let the far right try to take down another Democratic president with a campaign of lies and distortions. It was time for us to go on offense. And we decided to start by attacking the heart of the beast.

So we declared war on the Fox News Channel.

For years, we had tried to contain Fox's influence. We knew that its hosts were strictly in the business of spreading right-wing misinformation, and we saw our job as quickly calling it out so as to discourage more credible outlets from repeating it—the same strategy we used with any right-wing media mouthpiece.

But now, in a campaign spearheaded by Media Matters President Eric Burns, we would attempt to go from ring-fencing Fox to actually assaulting it directly, going after what was said on its airwaves but also hitting the network where it really hurt: in the wallet. We wrote an eighty-five-page plan to focus our organization's efforts against Fox—and geared up to put it in place.

We hired researchers and reporters to help put together an investigative report on Fox's operations, which we published in 2012. We dug into the sketchy professional backgrounds of Fox executives. We set up legal support to help people file suit against Fox when their privacy had been invaded or their reputations harmed. We increased our pressure campaigns against Fox advertisers.

We published internal e-mails, like the one in which Bill Sammon, the managing editor of Fox's Washington bureau, told reporters when covering health care reform not to use the phrase "public option" when they could use the more loaded term "government-run health insurance." We aired secret recordings, like the one of Sammon on a conservative cruise revealing that he intentionally ran "what I guess was some rather mischievous speculation about whether Barack Obama really advocated socialism, a premise that privately I found rather far-fetched."

We even looked up the corporate ladder to take on Fox's parent company, News Corporation, and its CEO, Rupert Murdoch. At the time, Murdoch was moving to take over a British broadcaster—so we established a presence in London to bird-dog him every step of the way. We hired Ilyse Hogue, an executive from MoveOn.org to organize among News Corporation shareholders. We worked to pressure regulators to hold the company's feet to the fire. As a publicity stunt, I even bid in, and won, a charity auction for a chance to have lunch with Rupert Murdoch. (Murdoch refused and returned my money rather than sit down face-to-face.)

"Fox News," as we wrote in our battle plan, "is not a news organization. It is the de facto leader of the GOP, and it is long past time that it is treated as such by the media, elected officials, and the public."

Our first major success was our offensive against Fox News star Glenn Beck, the ringleader of Fox's effort to discredit the new president and sow fear, even paranoia, among conservatives about Obama.

Beck had been hired for this task by Roger Ailes—the Republican political consultant and former Limbaugh producer who ran the Fox "news" operation and whose own history was a rich tapestry of race-baiting. One of the architects of the Willie Horton attack that invoked the specter of a furloughed African-American convict to portray Michael Dukakis as soft on crime, Ailes reportedly said, "The only question is whether we depict Willie Horton with a knife in his hand or without it."

It came as no surprise, then, that the network's attacks on Obama had a decidedly racial tinge, with Fox hosts using Obama's former pastor, Reverend Jeremiah Wright, and outright inventing links between Obama and radicals like Louis Farrakhan in order to depict Obama as some kind of modern-day Black Panther.

Beck was the star of the show. And, frankly, he was good at what he was hired to do: playing to conservative fears. If, today, he's mostly remembered as a clown, tearfully ranting in front of inscrutable chalkboard diagrams, it's also worth recalling that, for a time, he was a clown who got results. It's largely because of Beck's exertions that Van Jones, a progressive African-American activist who had been tapped as a White House environmental advisor, was transformed in the eyes of the right into, in Beck's words, an "unrepentant Communist revolutionary" and, after a massive pressure campaign, forced to resign.

With Jones's media lynching, Beck turned his sights to an official at the Department of Education named Kevin Jennings. A former high school history teacher who had started the country's first Gay-Straight Alliance student club, Jennings had later gone on to found the Gay & Lesbian Straight Education Network (GLSEN), an organization that fought against bullying in schools, before being named to the Obama administration to coordinate antibullying efforts.

Between the right's general paranoia over the administration's "czars," Jennings's career exposing the harsh realities of discrimination against gay and lesbian students, and his status as an openly gay man, he was a natural target for Fox and its allies on the right. Jennings was falsely accused of "encouraging" and "covering up" statutory rape, of being a "pedophile," of having "personally pushed books that encouraged children to meet adults at gay bars for sex." Karl Rove even uttered the particularly vile lie that Jennings had engaged in "high-profile, in-your-face advocacy of things like NAMBLA"—the infamous pedophilia apologist organization.

Not knowing the facts, the White House was slow to defend Jennings. That was why a group like Media Matters was so essential. We closely examined the allegations and soon found the evidence to disprove them; for example, in one case, where the right was claiming that Jennings had covered up the sexual abuse of one of his students, we found the alleged victim, who told us that nothing of the sort had taken place.

In the end, CNN aired a report laying out the true facts of the Jennings case. Fox acknowledged its false reports. And Jennings himself would go on to keep his job and have an enormously successful tenure, including putting together a historic antibullying summit in the East Room of the White House.

Defeating the attacks on Kevin Jennings did stop the political targeting of Obama officials by Fox, but Beck nonetheless continued to conjure up a sinister conspiracy afoot in the White House. Nothing was too inflammatory: Beck routinely used violent rhetoric and even invoked the specter of the Holocaust and slavery to illustrate the alleged dangers of President Obama, whom he called "a racist" with "a deep-seated hatred for white people."

Beck's last rant was the spark behind an advertiser boycott that led to more than twenty companies pulling their spots from his program in the summer of 2009. Over the next year, working with allied progressive groups like ColorofChange.org, we helped sustain the drumbeat of criticism. We hired the organizer who had been leading the ad boycott effort, and that number of lost advertisers would grow to nearly three hundred.

In August 2010, *Washington Post* columnist Dana Milbank called attention to Beck's extremism. "Most every broadcast has some violent imagery," Milbank wrote. " 'The clock is ticking.... The war is just beginning.... Shoot me in the head if you try to change our government.... You have to be prepared to take rocks to the head.... The other side is attacking.... There is a coup going on.... Grab a torch!... Drive a stake through the heart of the bloodsuckers.... They are taking you to a place to be slaughtered.... They are putting a gun to America's head.' "

By making sure that Beck's advertisers didn't miss these gems, we made Beck toxic to the network. He helped undermine himself, of course. As we ramped up the pressure, he responded by becoming even more unhinged, and his frequent incitements to violence became even more thinly veiled. When Sarah Palin went on Beck's radio show to defend him, we hit back—and Palin's fans responded, menacingly, by posting the home addresses of our young research staff online. It was one of the lowest and most personally upsetting acts of retaliation we had endured over the years.

We beefed up security in the building, but we were undeterred—and eventually successful. Beck ultimately lost virtually every national advertiser he had, and Fox executives who could never have been persuaded by appeals to their sense of journalistic integrity were finally convinced by the effect on their bottom line.

In what turned out to be his last days on Fox, Beck became increasingly fixated on Media Matters. We became a featured player in his chalkboard conspiracies. At one point, he even tapped on the glass, as if to reach through the screen to where our researchers were watching, to brag that despite our best efforts, he was still in business. It got pretty intense; as Beck got closer and closer to going over the edge, we got more and more focused.

Three weeks after Beck addressed us directly on camera, I was getting ready to go into an event with some prospective donors when my phone rang with the news that Fox was declining to renew Beck's contract. Talk about a great way to break the ice with new donors. For Beck's last show, we threw a huge party at our new office space to celebrate our biggest victory yet.

At the height of his influence, Glenn Beck was celebrated on the cover of *Time* magazine as the face of a new conservatism. By the time Media Matters and our allies were done exposing him, he was just another crank on the Internet.

By 2013, three years after we'd declared war on Fox, the network itself, while still the outlet of choice for conservatives, had lost much of its ability to influence the broader political and media landscape.

In a January 2014 feature story in *New York* magazine, Frank Rich wrote, "Fox News *has* been defeated on the media battlefield—and on the political battlefield as well." Rich noted that the network's audience is disproportionately old and white, arguing that very few Americans "do not already know that Fox News is a GOP auxiliary and view it, hate-watch it, or avoid it accordingly." He attributed the network's damaged reputation in part to "Media Matters, an aggressive and well-financed watchdog operation."

The network was still selling its version of reality to a rabid audience, but Fox could no longer credibly claim to deserve recognition as a legitimate journalistic enterprise, a "fair and balanced" arbiter of fact. The conventional wisdom had changed, the mainstream media had become much more skeptical of Fox's reporting—and thus far less apt to pick it up.

It was time to declare a victory of sorts. We would continue to monitor Fox's programming, debunk its misinformation, and hold its hosts accountable, but the proliferation of new right-wing outlets online, which we'll investigate in a subsequent chapter, meant that Fox was also losing influence as the gatekeeper between the far right and the mainstream media. So we redeployed our troops to meet these new challenges as we recommitted to our core mission: taking the fight to the right, wherever they are, and speaking truth to their lies.

⌒

Today, our Media Matters staff has grown to eighty people, working from our newsroomlike open offices near Capitol Hill. Also residing there are servers that, as of this writing, store five hundred thousand gigabytes of archived material, forty times what the entire Library of Congress would take up if it were digitized. Instead of relying on an external cloud, we built our own, essentially a gigantic DVR, one that also tracks radio broadcasts and web traffic. We take a lot of precautions (including keeping tape backups offsite), because we're constantly facing denial-of-service attacks—although our IT department would proudly relate that, apart from one incident where our office Internet ran a little slow for a few hours, we've successfully fended off each one.

Our diligent researchers are still at the core of what we do. They still sit in long rows, listening and watching and occasionally raising a ruckus when they spot something really egregious. But we now have dozens of them, trading off eight-hour shifts so we can be up and running, rotating in teams, from 5 a.m. until after midnight most days.

One team monitors incoming material—anything from cable news to right-wing radio to conservative activists on social media. When someone on that first line sees or hears or reads something we could potentially go after, they send a brief report out flagging it (say, "Allen West just accused Obama of providing aid and comfort to terrorists on Neil Cavuto"). A second team is responsible for reviewing the tape, making sure we have the full context. Conservatives would be surprised how often we debate whether we're being completely fair to the likes of Rush Limbaugh. And they do whatever research needs to be done to debunk the lie. Then a third team generates published content based on that work, beginning with clipping the video and writing up our findings.

To answer an often-asked question: Yes, our researchers can take bathroom breaks. We build redundancy into the system to make sure we don't miss anything. But, still, you might find yourself wondering what kind of people would choose to do this sort of thing for a living. Fox's late night show, *Red Eye*, once broadcast a mock "interview" with an actor pretending to be one of our employees:

> It is the saddest place I have ever seen in my life. I think about it, and I want to throw up.... I get to work and I take off my clothes, and they strap me into a chair in front of a TV with [Fox News Channel] on. They keep my eyelids propped open like in *Clockwork Orange*, and I sit and type all day.

The truth is, Media Matters is actually a fun place to work. And rest assured that our staff is fully clothed. Sure, everyone hits a wall once in a while; it can be frustrating to listen to people lie all day. A show like *Fox and Friends*, which features a roundtable of conservative talking heads gleefully making things up, can be especially difficult to get through. But our researchers are passionate about what they do. Indeed, it's not uncommon for a researcher to have had his or her own watchdog blog before coming to work with us. They understand that truth telling is critical to advancing progressive priorities. They know that caring about the environment, or gender equality or economic justice means caring about the way these issues are refracted through the media.

But, yes, researchers also have to have a pretty high tolerance for listening to Rush Limbaugh. That said, it pays off. In time, Media Matters would succeed in marginalizing the once-invincible king of the dittoheads—not just by discrediting him, but by putting pressure on advertisers to withdraw their support of his show. Rush was always generous enough to give us a steady stream of material to work with. But in early 2012, he would finally cross the line once and for all.

Georgetown law student Sandra Fluke had become the face of a legislative fight over birth control. Ostensibly, it was a fight about the Affordable Care Act's mandate that employers cover prescription birth control for employees. But you didn't have to scratch too far beneath the surface to understand what conservatives were really mad about.

Rush made the mistake of saying what so many in the conservative movement were really thinking, calling Fluke a "slut" and a "prosti-tute." We caught the smears in real time, of course, but decided to hold off on spotlighting them. While Rush's vilification of a private citizen was disgusting, we weren't sure there was much to be gained by pick-ing a fight over a few nasty words. But Limbaugh wasn't done; over the next three days, he continued his smear campaign against Fluke, launching, by our count, forty-six separate personal attacks against her, each of which we recorded and catalogued. It was exactly the sort of offensive material that had given us our first major victory over Limbaugh back in 2004; now, however, we had eight years of Rush's vitriol archived and ready to display, allowing us to put his attacks on Sandra Fluke in their ugly context.

When we struck back, we struck hard, publishing a background piece highlighting Limbaugh's long history of extremism, misogyny, and personal attacks, and clearly demonstrating that his three-day smear campaign was no anomaly. It was a perfect example of our multifaceted approach (and talented staff) in action.

Our media team created a series of narrative-building videos which quickly amassed tens of thousands of views online. Our messaging initiative armed allies in the progressive community such as Planned Parenthood with talking points, and graduates of our pundit training program hit the airwaves, making dozens of appearances on cable networks. Our spokespeople joined them, driving the conversation in major national media. Fluke herself referred people to our website when she made appearances. And our online engagement team launched a radio ad campaign in key markets to urge local stations to give Rush the boot. And our outreach folks organized allies to pressure advertisers to abandon the show, collecting nearly a million signatures overall.

Today, Rush Limbaugh still has a radio show. But his program has lost hundreds of millions of dollars in revenue for the radio companies that carry it. Moreover, the show has become so toxic it is hurting all of talk radio. Indeed, a right-wing radio show ain't worth what it used to be. Despite the fact that so-called "news talk" radio remains the industry's second-most popular format (behind country music), advertising on those stations now costs about half what it does on stations that play music. In other words, while right-wing radio may still be popular, it's no longer so lucrative—because, as the *Wall Street Journal* reported in February 2015, advertisers want to "avoid associating their brands with potentially controversial programming." Rush may have been the father of right-wing talk radio, but, with a little help from Media Matters, his mouth turned out to be its undoing.

To be sure, our targets hated any scrutiny. Bill O'Reilly called Media Matters a "guttersnipe organization," "very fascist," and "vicious," and likened us to the Ku Klux Klan. Republican leader Mitch McConnell of Kentucky told a gathering at a conservative think tank: "Now on the outside there is a well-documented effort by a number of left-wing groups like Media Matters to harass and to intimidate conservatives with the goal of scaring them off the political playing field and off the airwaves as well." And Fox host Eric Bolling exclaimed, "Hey, Media Matters...I'd love to waterboard you for the truth!"

We took it all in stride. In fact, there was no better evidence that Media Matters really mattered.

## Chapter Two

# How Democrats Got in the Game

We celebrated a lot of wins in our first decade at Media Matters, but we didn't go undefeated. The conservative institutions we were racing to catch up with, and the falsehoods they were so prolific at infusing into the mainstream political debate, remained a serious threat to an honest debate. And even as we were beginning to build a truth-telling machine to counter that influence, we got an early reminder of how far we had to go.

Media Matters launched on May 3, 2004. The next day—May 4—the *Wall Street Journal* published an op-ed by a Vietnam War veteran named John O'Neill. That afternoon, a group of O'Neill's associates, calling themselves the "Swift Boat Veterans for Truth," held a news conference.

The coordinated message of the day was simple, direct, and devastating: Sen. John Kerry, a decorated Vietnam vet whose heroic service was the key to his biography and a major reason he was about to become the Democratic presidential nominee, was, in fact, a liar, a fraud, and a coward.

Claiming to have served with Kerry—and thus to have firsthand knowledge that he had not, in fact, performed the heroic feats that led to him being awarded three Purple Hearts, the Bronze Star medal, and the Silver Star—the Swift Boat Vets authored a book (published by a right-wing publishing house), appeared in television ads, and succeeded in sowing doubts not just about Kerry's heroic acts, but about his very honor.

They were lying the whole time.

At Media Matters, we were still unpacking—but we immediately saw the Swift Boat attack as a serious problem for Kerry. John O'Neill was no impartial observer—he was a longtime Republican who had been deployed by President Richard Nixon to publicly counter Kerry back in the 1970s, when as a young veteran, Kerry had become an outspoken opponent of the conduct of the war. Since then, he had worked for a variety of Republican judges and politicians. We smelled a rat and quickly got a post up on our new website exposing O'Neill's past. Some of the initial news reports mentioned O'Neill's partisanship, but most did not.

The next day, we highlighted some discrepancies in the Swift Boat Vets' accounts—including reports written by members of the group during Kerry's service that praised his conduct, and indications that other members had not, as they claimed, actually served with Kerry. And we continued to go after the Swift Boat Vets as they became mainstays on Fox News and game changers in the presidential election. In the end, their claims largely fell apart—they were wrong about so many details of the incidents they claimed to witness that, today, the very term *swift-boat* means "to destroy someone's reputation with lies."

But it didn't matter back then. Without an explicitly progressive media echo chamber to pick up on our work and debunk the Swift Boat Vets' claims for a larger audience (that would come years later), we couldn't be of much help. Nor did we have the delivery system yet in place to push responsible media outlets to do their own investigation before uncritically reporting on the book's contents.

Worst, and perhaps most telling, of all, the Kerry campaign itself remained silent as those accusations spilled from right-wing media onto the front pages of the nation's newspapers and across all TV news channels. After the election, Bob Shrum, the campaign's top political advisor, told me the campaign had missed the charges as they bubbled up from right-wing media and onto cable TV. The Kerry campaign only considered responding when the allegations were reported on the broadcast evening news—and by then the damage had already been done.

Today, this sounds like political malpractice. But the Kerry campaign was simply following standard operating procedure for the Democratic Party in 2004. They thought of cable news as an alternate dimension in which nothing that happened really mattered, because well-informed citizens got their news from Peter Jennings, Dan Rather, or Tom Brokaw. And they didn't understand that the distortions on cable news, if not confronted, could easily bleed onto the nightly news and directly into the consciousness of millions of voters, which is exactly what happened.

The story raged for weeks before, to our lack of surprise, it began to dominate the mainstream media. Only then was the Kerry campaign finally ready to push back. At that point, Kerry's stepson called my cell phone. He had noticed our early efforts online and wanted my advice. Should they dignify these false accusations with a response?

I offered the view that, in the era of 24-7 cable news, every charge needed an answer. But I also said that I thought it was too late. The lie had already traveled halfway around the world—and here we were, debating whether the truth should start to put its boots on.

Over time, we'd prove that a Swift Boater could be sunk with an aggressive defense. By the time Barack Obama emerged in 2008, we were ready for a command performance by Jerome Corsi, one of the right-wing operatives who had smeared Kerry and was preparing to do the same to Obama in a book called *The Obama Nation: Leftist Politics and the Cult of Personality*. Instead of waiting for Corsi's wild accusations to make news, Media Matters scored a copy before it even went on sale, and we published a list of dozens of falsehoods, which we got into the hands of every TV host interviewing the author. Right out of the gate, MSNBC's Contessa Brewer confronted Corsi with our research and he never recovered. The book soon sank with barely a trace. What a difference four years made.

⌒

There's an old saying in the legal profession: When the law's against you, pound the facts. When the facts are against you, pound the law. And when they're both against you, pound the table.

When it comes to the court of public opinion, both Republicans and Democrats are confident advocates, believing that they are right on the law and right on the facts. They walk into every political skirmish fully expecting that their ideas will win the day. And both sides do their share of table pounding when they lose cases (be they elections or policy debates) they feel they should have won.

The difference is that when it happens to Republicans, they smear the judge, the bailiff, the stenographer, and the guy who delivered lunch to the jury. They've built an entire cottage industry on (often imagined) grievances against actors whose impartiality they call into question—everyone from the news media to the scientific community.

But when it happens to Democrats, they turn their ire on the other attorneys sitting at their table. You hear it all the time from frustrated progressives who just don't understand how the likes of Karl Rove always seem to win: *What's wrong with us?*

Ironically, it was Democrats who, in the eyes of many analysts, set the standard for effective political communication in the modern era. In 1992, the Clinton campaign famously adopted a take-no-prisoners approach to rapid response, answering Republican charges aggressively and in real time, a winning effort chronicled in the documentary *The War Room.*

Perhaps lulled into complacency by the fact that they had won the White House, in the years that followed Democrats began to feel that they were being outgunned in the political trenches. The right had its well-funded infrastructure of talk radio hosts, gray-market pseudo-journalists, and scorched-earth operatives, not to mention an increasingly strong foothold in the mainstream press. And time and time again, Democrats found themselves sputtering in protest as Republicans shaded the truth, bent the rules, and got away with it.

When I was starting Media Matters back in 2003, this sentiment was at a fever pitch.

Democrats had worked hard to win two presidential elections in 1992 and 1996, only to see the man they elected hounded by a wave of scandals that turned out to be either grossly inflated or outright invented. Then they'd watched a presidential campaign in 2000 in which Al Gore was covered in mud by a mainstream media that misportrayed him as a diffident elitist and a serial liar, neither of which reflected his actual record. And while Gore was being savaged, George W. Bush's right-wing policies and deeply sketchy personal history somehow largely escaped press scrutiny. To this day, we know much more about what Gore said about being the inspiration for the movie *Love Story* than we do about Bush's actual service in the Texas Air National Guard.

As frustrating as the 2000 campaign was for progressives, the outcome was doubly so, coming down to an undemocratic recount in Florida that featured plenty of right-wing dirty tricks. At a pivotal moment, for example, Republican operatives staged phony demonstrations to give partisan election officials cover to stop counting votes. These "Brooks Brothers riots" were ridiculous on their face, featuring as they did a horde of well-scrubbed (and compensated) lobbyists and political staffers in nice suits posing as outraged local citizens.

In the end, of course, George W. Bush benefited from Republican control over Florida's electoral system, rigged through his brother, Jeb, the governor, and the conservative majority of the Supreme Court. As he was ushered into office by a 5–4 Supreme Court vote, Democrats roundly criticized Republicans for their willingness to win at all costs.

But hidden in their outrage was frustration. Even as the recount and its aftermath deteriorated into farce, it seemed that at every turn, Republicans were willing to do whatever it took to come out on top, while Democratic leaders seemed more concerned with maintaining decorum than winning the damn election.

Of course, when Democrats had found themselves a real, live war hero to puncture the phony flight-suit macho patriotism of a president who had lied us into Iraq, Karl Rove and his allies found a way to turn John Kerry's biggest strength into his biggest weakness—thanks to the Swift Boat Veterans for Truth propaganda campaign.

So it was no wonder that Democrats began to feel as if there was something that prevented them from fighting as hard—or, more accurate, as effectively—as Republicans. And they were right.

For a long time, both in the political arena as well as in the media, the Democratic Party behaved like a victim, handing over its lunch money day after day and going home despondent and hungry instead of standing up to the bully—which, of course, is the only response that a bully will ever understand.

Having spent much of my life on the outside of the left looking in, I feel I can say with the appropriate level of dispassionate detachment that the fundamental decency of Democrats, their altruistic desire to "win clean," can often be a liability. You don't always win just because you have the best ideas—and, more important, you don't get extra points by relying solely on the strength of your ideas to compete. Campaigns may be battles of ideas, but they're also battles of strategy and tactics—battles in which there may be rules, but there are rarely serious penalties for bending them, and there is never a reason to count on your opponent following them.

By that, I don't mean that Democrats suffer because they don't cheat. I mean that Democrats suffer because they tend to be surprised when the other side does. Time and again in the 1990s and early 2000s, the Republican Party proved that it was brazen and unscrupulous—and

Democrats were shocked into disorientation and even paralysis. By the time they shook off their astonishment, it was too late to fight back.

That's a generous explanation: that Democrats were simply too nice to do battle with the right. A less generous take might be that Democrats were naïve, and perhaps even a little bit smug. Most Democrats didn't consume right-wing media, they didn't know anyone who did, and they assumed that Rush and his ilk were self-discrediting. How could anyone ever believe these guys? And then a right-wing talking point would cross over to CNN, and Democrats would have no idea where it had originated or how it had come to be accepted as fact, and thus no idea of how to knock it down.

Even when some Democrats began to realize what they were up against, many still resisted the idea of fighting back against the right-wing media. Widespread among Democratic communications experts was the belief that led the Kerry campaign to slow-play its response to the Swift Boat attacks—that to answer a charge was to elevate it, an axiom that may have been true in a previous media age. But their reluctance to dignify the attacks with a response didn't earn Democrats any credit for declining to lower themselves to their opponents' level. What they saw as a principled refusal to play in the mud simply left more mud available for the right to hurl.

Then there's an explanation that takes us out of the psychology department and into the poli-sci lounge. The "war room" approach that worked so well for the Clinton campaign didn't work for the Clinton White House, simply because a campaign is by design a different, more nimble operation. And there were no independent watchdog groups on the left like Media Matters to pick up the slack.

During the presidencies of Richard Nixon, Gerald Ford, and especially Ronald Reagan, conservatives focused their energy on developing independent but party-aligned outside groups to supplement, bolster, and sometimes even perform many of the functions of a political party: developing policy ideas and circulating them in sympathetic publications, training young people to run for office and manage campaigns, maintaining message discipline among surrogates, and more.

When Barry Goldwater went down in flames in 1964, the Republican establishment decided that his famous maxim—"Extremism in the defense of liberty is no vice"—made for a better bumper sticker than it did a political strategy. The resulting conflict between party elders who wanted to win elections and conservatives who treasured their ideological purity would end up a defining feature of the GOP, one that's still playing out today.

With the Republican Party itself inhospitable to movement conservatism, conservative leaders believed, correctly, that they could set up institutions like the American Legislative Exchange Council (which helped coordinate the activities of state-level conservatives in all fifty states) and the Heritage Foundation (my old home and a leading right-wing think tank) that would act as a sort of shadow party, pulling the actual GOP to the right and allowing them to eventually take it over.

Sometimes this independent apparatus caused pain for the party establishment, but it also provided a structure for developing new strategies in the kind of political trench warfare that Republicans became expert at over time.

Democrats, on the other hand, had no such independent apparatus—primarily because they hadn't needed one. While the influence of the liberal wing of the Democratic Party waxed (Walter Mondale) and waned (Joe Lieberman) with each presidential ticket, there was never an equivalent struggle for the soul of the party. Progressives for the most part continued to feel at home in the Democratic establishment, and, despite a few flameouts on the presidential level, that establishment had been successful, controlling Congress for four decades leading up to the Gingrich Revolution.

Indeed, to the extent that a faction of Democrats established an influential organizational presence outside the party, it was the centrists who created the Democratic Leadership Council in the late 1980s. And even the DLC focused more on policy development and advocacy than on pure politics.

In the 2000s, that began to change somewhat as new infrastructure sprouted up on the progressive side. Unlike its right-wing counterpart, this new infrastructure was not the result of ideological or party factionalism. To the contrary, these were broad-based groups operating within the mainstream of the Democratic Party and in support of widely-held progressive ideas and values. Groups like the Center for American Progress and Media Matters, funded in part by a growing network of donors under the auspices of the Democracy Alliance, were generally considered to be at the forefront of this new movement, with real successes to their credit in just a few years.

~

But compared with groups on the right, CAP and Media Matters were still fledgling efforts when, in January 2010, in the 5–4 *Citizens United* decision, the Supreme Court ruled that independent groups funded by corporations, known as "SuperPACs," could spend unlimited amounts of money in directly attempting to influence federal elections. And the Democrats' lack of deep experience with outside groups caused them to fall behind once again.

Suddenly, the financing of campaigns was the Wild West. The more money you could amass, the bigger the war chest, the more powerful you were.

In the wake of the ruling, Republicans spent the better part of a billion dollars to win the 2010 cycle. Karl Rove, never afraid to seize on an opportunity to gain advantage, formed a SuperPAC called American Crossroads, raising $100 million and pouring it into slashing negative ads—and two wealthy industrialists from Kansas, Charles and David Koch, began to emerge as serious power players. (More about them later.)

As expected, Republicans were able to unholster the biggest guns in the early days of the Wild West era of campaigns. What came as a surprise to me, although maybe it shouldn't have, is that Democrats chose to disarm. They spent a long time lamenting the ruling—and with good reason. But their well-founded concern that these outside big money groups would turn our democracy into an auction made them reluctant to play by the new rules. Regardless of what you thought of *Citizens United* (I certainly thought it was both a terrible miscarriage of constitutional jurisprudence and a serious threat to the sanctity of our elections), it remains to me almost inconceivable that Democrats didn't do something to try and compete on this new playing field.

Newly able to accept unlimited cash, SuperPACs and other independent expenditure (IE) groups—which could directly advocate for the election or defeat of candidates but could not directly coordinate with those campaigns on strategy—were clearly about to emerge as the most powerful players in American politics, more powerful perhaps than the parties themselves, which operate with strict limits on donations. Rather than simply looking at the strength of a candidate's campaign, analysts would now be looking at the IE support they would likely get as a key sign of success—and yet, Democrats essentially took a pass on working to establish their own IE efforts.

It was, I believed at the time, a recipe for defeat.

Sure enough, on Election Day 2010, Democrats were wiped out across the country. There were, of course, many reasons for the Red Wave: the campaign of misinformation on Obamacare, the emergence of the Tea Party as a political force, the Democrats' recurring midterm turnout problem—but what turned a bad year into a total disaster was the fact that Republicans capitalized on the new rules, massively outspending the Democrats in the closing weeks of the campaign.

As Election Day approached and outgunned Democratic candidates, supported by a late IE effort on their behalf, prepared their concession speeches, I began some discussions about what, exactly, we could and should do to even the advantage going forward.

For me, the question of whether the new rules were good (of course they weren't) had nothing to do with the question of whether Democrats should compete fully under those rules (of course they should). The law was the law. And unilateral disarmament, which seemed likely to become the official strategy of the Democratic establishment, would simply cement the Republicans' advantage, leaving us hopelessly outmatched and putting everything we cared about at stake.

So, I decided to do something about it.

⌒

To be honest, I didn't really have much of a plan. But I also didn't have much reason to think that anyone else would step up and catalyze the critical conversation of how Democrats could stay competitive in a post–*Citizens United* world.

Given the overall negative attitude of President Obama and most of his advisors toward third-party big-money groups, I had little reason to believe that they would take the lead. Their objections were partly principled—like most Democrats, they believed, and not unreasonably, that big money was corrupting democracy—but partly they were political. At this early juncture, most political people were, naturally, suspect of outside efforts that by law they could not control. And they believed that the new world of SuperPACs were superfluous to organizing progressive politics around President Obama's strong personal brand.

Though the term *SuperPAC* hadn't yet been coined, I became familiar with third-party groups, then known as 527s, back in 2007. Excited about the prospect that Hillary Clinton might be the Democratic nominee—and eager to help—I got involved with a 527 called Progressive Media. Launched a few years earlier as a progressive effort to end the war in Iraq, the organization had morphed into a media fund planning to do opposition research and TV advertising against the Republicans to help the eventual Democratic nominee in 2008, whoever it would be.

In late February, the major financial backer of Progressive Media, Hollywood producer Steve Bing, a longtime Clinton supporter, asked me to take over at the helm. I took a temporary leave from Media Matters and got to work reorganizing the group and writing a plan to help elect a Democratic president in 2008. It was no secret that I wanted Hillary to be that person. Some commentators and even some Democrats were already concluding that her chances had slipped away, but I wasn't hearing it.

A couple of months later, as they appeared to clinch the nomination, we learned that the Obama team wasn't interested in our help. At a meeting of Obama's national finance committee in Chicago, the committee's chair, Penny Pritzker, made it clear that the campaign didn't want its donors supporting Progressive Media—or any third-party group, for that matter. In May 2008, the campaign made a formal statement on the record disavowing such efforts, spelling the end of our attempt to raise money to help get Barack Obama elected.

Shutting down the development of independent expenditure groups in 2008 was probably the right decision for candidate Obama. He went on to raise an unprecedented amount of cash directly into his campaign—disappointing campaign finance reformers by refusing to accept federal funds and thereby blowing up the limit on how much his campaign could spend—and he went on to win without outside help. (In the case of Progressive Media, it was understandable that the Obama campaign didn't want to entrust our group, top-heavy with Clinton supporters, with its messaging.)

But with the rise of new groups like Rove's American Crossroads, the political landscape shifted in 2010—delivering to the Democrats a historic "shellacking." And yet President Obama seemed not to recognize what I saw as the clear reality of the situation. In fact, I knew that he had personally nixed the plans of some deep-pocketed Hollywood donors to come to the Democrats' rescue in the midterm by forming a group to counter Rove's. I wondered if the president just didn't get what it would take to hold the Democratic majority in Congress that had helped him score so many victories during his first two years in office.

But I also knew this: If we didn't want to see a Republican romp to victory in 2012 and start repealing those achievements, one after another, we simply couldn't afford to fight with one hand tied behind our back. Democrats were going to have to embrace SuperPACs. Anything else would be political malpractice. And regardless of how the powers-that-be felt about it, that just couldn't happen.

And so, whether anyone else was ready for it, I was going to start a SuperPAC. It was time for Democrats to get in the game.

As it happened, I wasn't the only person worried about the Democrats' failure to compete during the cold, harsh winter of 2010–2011. Shortly after the election, at a Democracy Alliance gathering of the progressive movement's biggest donors, we sought to harness their dissatisfaction by standing up and announcing the formation of a SuperPAC, American Bridge 21st Century. I chose the name, in part, to signify the metaphorical opposite of Rove's American Crossroads, and also as a conscious echo of Bill Clinton's "bridge to the 21st century."

We dedicated American Bridge to Obama's reelection. But what would this new SuperPAC do? How much would it raise? What would be its playbook? We really didn't know. We did know that something had to happen; the Democratic position of refusing to play by the new rules had contributed to a devastating loss in 2010, and we couldn't afford to let it cost us the White House in 2012.

The reaction to the announcement was mixed at best. The Democratic political class—especially donors—was frustrated with the midterm result, but they still weren't ready to embrace SuperPACs. In fact, we started to worry that our intention to start a SuperPAC—which had only the vaguest of missions and was actively opposed by some of my own donors—might fizzle.

But my team forged ahead, essentially willing American Bridge into existence. We soon decided on an approach for the new group that took advantage of what we knew best.

The success of Media Matters owed in part to our aggressive, take-no-prisoners attitude toward right-wing vitriol: We weren't afraid to stand up, and we never let an offender off the hook. But you can't hold your opponents accountable for what they say if you aren't keeping careful track of what they say.

When it comes to Fox's Sean Hannity, you can just hit Record on your DVR. But there's no DVR for politicians; they often speak in settings where there is no media coverage and, of course, those are the settings where they tend to really let loose.

That was why, in addition to opening a separate, massive opposition research shop for politics, we invested in an army of trackers. Trackers, as political junkies now know, are the mostly young staffers who follow around their opponents with video cameras and record every word they say. They're not there to cause disruptions or provoke anyone; they're simply there to document what happens so operatives back in the war room can analyze the footage and search for telling moments.

And that was exactly what American Bridge set out to do. We would send trackers to campaign events to look for gaffes. We would deploy researchers to check court files and police records for information on politicians. We would scour voting records to build the case against Republican candidates and highlight their flip-flops. And we would put together dossiers to help Democratic ad makers launch their attacks.

We would be a game changer for two reasons. First, simply by existing, we were ending the counterproductive internal debate among Democrats over whether to compete in the post–*Citizens United* world.

In 2010, eschewing the "dirty" politics of SuperPACs while Republicans spent big, hand-wringing Democrats savored the moral victory of remaining above the fray—while Republicans celebrated actual victories that threatened to undermine the entire Obama presidency. With the birth of American Bridge, Democrats' sense of moral superiority began to vanish—now we were entering the ring with the Republicans who had just kicked our butts.

The move was a wake-up call to the party. Within a few months of our announcing American Bridge, Democrats took even more steps to get in the game. Top Democratic operatives established another new SuperPAC, Priorities USA, which would raise money to run ads for the president's reelection, as well as two new SuperPACs to run ads in Senate and House races. (Though Priorities was established by two of his former aides, the president did not bless its activities for more than a year, and even then he held his nose, declining to appear on the group's behalf.)

As well as prodding the left to adapt to the new political reality, American Bridge would challenge long-held ideas about how to do political research. No, we wouldn't be the first people to hire a bunch of trackers, send them to record politicians, and look to make hay out of the footage, although our tracking operation would dwarf anyone else's. But we were proposing to consolidate essentially the entire progressive community's research efforts under one roof—an idea that met with plenty of resistance.

In addition to Priorities and the Senate and House SuperPACs, there was also big money on the left being spent by labor unions and an alphabet soup of advocacy groups. Each organization would, of course, have its own membership, its own issues and campaigns of interest, its own communications and political strategies, and so forth.

But did each organization really need its own research operation? We didn't think so. If four different organizations are interested in a Senate race, and pay four different research consultants to examine the Republican candidate's voting record, professional background, and personal vulnerabilities, then they'll end up with four largely identical reports (known as "books")—and at least three of those organizations will have wasted their money.

There was no good reason why Comedy Central, home to *The Daily Show* and *The Colbert Report*, on which obscure clips would regularly become comedic fodder, should continue to have the best video archive in politics.

American Bridge, we thought, could be a central clearinghouse for such information. We'd do the work, and in our shop the "books" wouldn't sit on a shelf gathering dust—we would analyze and update and action the research in real time, as well as adding the tracking component. We would share any newsworthy nuggets with the press. And we would make it all available to our valued partners—the other big progressive groups and SuperPACs—to use in their communications efforts.

You see, as Democrats prepared to enter the world of SuperPACs, if we tried to copy what Rove and the Koch brothers were doing, we would always come up short. The other side had a bottomless treasure chest that we would never match dollar for dollar. Instead, American Bridge would help the left do more with less. We would allow other organizations to eliminate duplicative research costs, leaving more money for their critical core functions, while, at the same time, incentivizing everyone to coordinate their work more closely, hopefully giving Democrats an on-the-field advantage.

As I mentioned, we ran into some early skepticism, to put it mildly. Some groups wanted to control their own research the way they always had. Some didn't really understand our rapid-response model. Others wondered how we would be able to ensure that everyone's priorities were respected when it came to decisions like when to release a newly discovered piece of information or in what order we'd complete projects.

In the end, we decided to simply get started and hope that, as we did with Media Matters, we would be able to prove the value of the concept early and earn the trust of our partners as we went. We would give them our research for free, avoiding potentially messy negotiations about how the model would work financially.

We even figured out a way to help Democratic campaigns make use of our work, even though the law prohibited us from directly coordinating with them. That is, I couldn't e-mail a campaign manager to say, "Check out what your opponent is saying on birth control—and take a look at this article he wrote for his college newspaper that says the opposite." There was no need to get sneaky about avoiding this roadblock: We decided to take the unusual step of making our "oppo" public. Once in the public domain, anyone, campaigns included, could stop by our website, see what we had published, and use it however they saw fit.

The operation went more smoothly than anyone had anticipated. Despite concerns on the left that we wouldn't be able to simultaneously service a range of competing organizations with different priorities, we rarely if ever had any problems coordinating among our important progressive allies, who worked together seamlessly. And despite some flak from old-school operatives who preferred to do things "their way," it turned out that this new way was pretty effective.

For example: As Washington gossiped about who Mitt Romney might select as his running mate, we worried about a repeat of the Sarah Palin fiasco from 2008—not the part where John McCain was humiliated as it was revealed how dangerously unqualified she was, but the part that came immediately after her announcement, when Democrats scrambled to figure out what to say about this obscure governor no one had ever heard of.

Veteran political strategist Paul Begala, who was working with Priorities USA, had a great idea: Why not research some leading contenders, and put all the research up on a website in advance? We sent our researchers out to compile comprehensive reports on five Republicans we thought were the most likely finalists: Governors Tim Pawlenty of Minnesota and Bobby Jindal of Louisiana, Senators Rob Portman of Ohio and Marco Rubio of Florida, and Representative Paul Ryan of Wisconsin. We bought a website domain—VeepMistakes.com—and published all the research there, thousands of pages in all. The website got hundreds of thousands of hits in the first twenty-four hours.

The night before Romney's selection, Twitter lit up with news that the choice would be announced at a rally in Virginia. I panicked, thinking that the nod would go to Virginia governor Bob McDonnell—and we'd be totally unprepared. Fortunately, of course, that didn't happen.

Romney picked Paul Ryan. Our MeetPaulRyan.com website went live immediately. And even during the initial coverage of his selection—one of the easiest media cycles for a presidential campaign to dominate— our research on Ryan made it into the first news stories.

In the eight years I'd been pitching Media Matters, I'd learned a lot about the donors I'd be relying on to fund American Bridge.

Back then, Rob Stein had warned me about the tendency of progressive donors to flit from one cause to the next. Rob was right, of course, but at Media Matters we had shown that if you had strong content and measurable results, donors could be convinced to build and sustain permanent institutions.

I also learned that unlike, say, the Koch brothers, most progressive donors were not transactional, which was fortunate, because I had no favors to trade or access to grant. In any case, no one ever asked. (And the next person I meet who writes a check just because they want to have their picture taken with David Brock will be the first.)

But now we had another hurdle to jump—Democratic donors just didn't like SuperPACs. And we needed to raise millions of dollars to make American Bridge a reality.

We were fortunate that, by this time, Media Matters was a thriving $10-million-a-year enterprise. It was to these donors that I would naturally turn to seed American Bridge.

As a group, Media Matters donors are a fearless bunch. Many of them, it turned out, didn't want to disarm. They were up for the fight. At our first prospecting dinner in Boston, we raised $700,000 from a dozen people. Once American Bridge started scoring some victories, it became as hot a commodity in the donor world as Media Matters was. And in the end, our donor pool, including supporters of both organizations, would end up consisting of some four hundred generous people giving between $10,000 and $1 million every year—with an unheard-of annual renewal rate of more than 90 percent.

This was, of course, another step in my journey toward being what I never imagined I'd become: a Democratic operative.

But, to be honest, I never really felt like I was making a big transition as I looked to add American Bridge to the portfolio of work I was doing at Media Matters. Both organizations were in the business of promoting liberalism over conservatism simply by promoting facts over fiction.

I am, as you have probably figured out by now, much more of a practical person than I am an ideological one. To be sure, I never would have built these organizations if I didn't comfortably hold progressive views, or if I wasn't interested in seeing the progressive agenda prevail. But unlike the institutional builders on the right, and what may be a surprise to my critics, I am not an ideologue. In fact, my experience in the conservative movement made me alert to the dangers of sectarianism. I wanted to fight the right, not move my own party to the left.

I would make my contribution by eventually employing over one hundred people at American Bridge, researching the records of Republican candidates, showing up at their events to record everything they said, poring over position papers to look for inconsistencies or extremist statements—and then publicizing them. Together with our allied groups, we created a permanent capacity to go on offense against Republicans, launching missiles from our side in what Newt Gingrich described as "the information wars."

To be sure, Democrats were still outspent on the independent expenditure side in the 2012 election. But we were in the game. We made careful monitoring of the other side our top priority, we looked for opportunities to use conservatives' own words against them, we resisted the temptation to spin our own information instead of simply letting the facts speak for themselves, and we were fully transparent in our work. American Bridge became a Media Matters for politics.

And like Media Matters, American Bridge argued for its own necessity by winning some important victories.

Even with Democrats defending twenty-three seats in the 2012 election cycle (compared with the ten Republicans were defending), we were confident that Democrats could maintain their slim majority—in no small part because we knew that the Tea Party movement that had been so dangerous for Democrats two years earlier could easily end up being equally dangerous for Republicans.

When Republicans looked at Indiana's and Missouri's Senate races, they saw two Republican wins: an easy incumbent hold in Indiana, where moderate Republican Dick Lugar hadn't faced real competition since 1982, and a first-tier pickup opportunity in Missouri, where Democrat Claire McCaskill faced serious opposition in a purple-to-red state.

But when we looked at the field in those two states, we saw opportunity. In Indiana, a Tea Partier named Richard Mourdock was primarying Lugar from the right. Mourdock quickly revealed himself to be exactly the kind of Republican who could lose a race even in deep-red Indiana: Early in his campaign, our trackers caught him questioning the constitutionality of Medicare and Social Security. We filed it away. Meanwhile, when we looked at the crowded Republican primary field in Missouri, one candidate stuck out: Rep. Todd Akin, who had said in the summer of 2011 that "at the heart of liberalism really is a hatred for God." We hoped that Mourdock and Akin would win their primaries—and we did what we could to help.

In Indiana, we got to work making up for three decades in which nobody had bothered to run a real race against Dick Lugar (meaning nobody had bothered to do any opposition research against him). We highlighted parts of his record that might fire up Tea Partiers to oppose him, and even tweeted at Mourdock to show him a video we put together challenging Lugar's residency—he had sold his Indiana home in 1977 and lived in McLean, Virginia. Later, we discovered that Lugar had violated Senate rules by billing taxpayers for hotel stays in Indianapolis while claiming he still lived in the state, causing a series of embarrassing stories.

We executed the same strategy in Missouri, keeping our knowledge of Akin's extremism to ourselves and focusing instead on helping to undermine the two somewhat more moderate candidates. In truth, we didn't have to do as much here; Akin's two opponents spent the campaign attempting to destroy each other, and mostly doing a pretty good, if ultimately self-defeating, job of it.

The day after Todd Akin won the Missouri primary, we caught him telling a radio interviewer that he wanted to ban the morning-after pill, which he considered to be a form of abortion. A little over a week after that, our Missouri tracker was watching a local political TV show when Akin said the words that would make him nationally famous: "First of all, from what I understand from doctors, [pregnancy from rape] is really rare. If it's a legitimate rape, the female body has ways to try to shut that whole thing down."

The interviewer didn't seem to get what Akin had just said—the show had been taped a couple days earlier, and nobody had raised a ruckus. But our tracker practically leapt out of his seat, sending a report back to our DC war room immediately and setting our operation in motion. We quickly got the story moving through press outlets and on social media, and by that evening, it was national news.

It could have been just a very bad day for the Akin campaign, except for two things. First, his team bungled the response, attempting to defend and explain the offensive comment. Second, and most importantly, we were able to show that Akin's "gaffe" was no gaffe at all, but rather a reflection of what he truly believed—and the way he would vote in the Senate. We had hours of tracking footage in our archive that we deployed to illustrate that Akin was a true extremist, and we put it all online on a website we created (AkinTV.com). And we had plenty of research to illustrate that he wasn't an isolated example within the Republican Party: Paul Ryan himself had cosponsored legislation with Akin redefining "forcible rape."

With Akin's comments sparking months of conversation about Republican insensitivity to women's health care (and especially to survivors of rape), it would have taken a real lunatic to step in it all over again that fall. Fortunately, one had been nominated in Indiana. On October 23, at a debate with Democrat Joe Donnelly, Richard Mourdock said that "even when life begins in that horrible situation of rape, that it is something that God intended to happen." This drew national attention to the race, and we made sure reporters had plenty to see when they did start to look at Mourdock's record, dumping out all our research online.

In both states, we ended up using the Republicans' own words against them—literally. Voters received our talking mailers, much like singing birthday cards, that played Akin and Mourdock's offensive remarks when opened. And on Election Night, Democrats won in both states.

⌒

Of course, another Democrat won on Election Night 2012, as well: President Barack Obama. I'm sure that American Bridge's new model of research and communications played a role in his victory. And Priorities, the pro-Obama ad fund, made its own big impact on the race by turning a thousand-page Bridge research book on Romney's business record into a series of devastating TV ads highlighting the adverse impact on American workers.

The truth is that Democrats would never have been celebrating on Election Night if they had chosen to stay "pure" and let Karl Rove and his allies have the SuperPAC world to themselves.

If you think back on the 2012 race, your first thoughts are probably of Mitt Romney blowing it, showing the world that he was every bit the out-of-touch rich guy Democrats kept saying he was. Maybe it was when he said at the Iowa State Fair that "corporations are people." Maybe it was when he told reporters in South Carolina that "I get speakers' fees from time to time, but not very much"—and it turned out that "not very much" added up to nearly $375,000. Maybe it was the car elevator he planned to build at his giant mansion in La Jolla, California, allowing former Michigan governor Jennifer Granholm to quip at the Democratic National Convention, "In Romney's world, the cars get the elevator; the workers get the shaft!"

Mitt Romney was indeed the gift that kept on giving. But someone had to find the gifts, wrap them, and deliver them. That's what we did, whether it was capturing the "corporations are people" remark on a tracker camera, quickly doing the math on Romney's speakers' fees, or flying to California and digging through city records to find the plans for the Romney car elevator.

Time after time, we found raw material—an off-hand comment on the stump, a tense moment in a debate, a file from some dusty archive—and turned it into another liability for Romney and the Republicans. Our research found its way into ads, newscasts, and, sometimes, *The Daily Show* and *The Colbert Report*.

That summer, James Carville told me that he thought American Bridge was the biggest innovation in politics since the Clinton "War Room" of 1992—and that I should expect the Republicans to copy it in the next cycle.

Sure enough, they did. After President Obama won reelection, a group of former Romney officials launched America Rising, a Super-PAC explicitly meant to copy what American Bridge was doing. The Republican National Committee's postelection "autopsy" noted that the GOP had been outmaneuvered by us on the oppo research front, and that correcting the problem was a top priority—the first time, as far as I can tell, that Republicans had found themselves playing catch-up when it came to these tactics.

Today, Democrats no longer have a monopoly on the kind of aggressive research and communications approach we pioneered at American Bridge. For example, in 2014, Republican researchers discovered that Montana senator John Walsh (D) had plagiarized large sections of his senior thesis at the Army War College, forcing him to withdraw from the race, which was eventually won by a Republican.

While copying our tactics, the Republicans also sought to blunt them by training their candidates to avoid Akin-Mourdock moments on the stump. The *New York Times* described what sounds like a program of hazing for new Republican candidates, in which party operatives posing as trackers ambush them at airport baggage carousels and in other unguarded settings—a reminder that American Bridge is always watching. Indeed, in one memorable moment from the 2014 cycle, Republican Senate candidate Scott Brown decided to take a canoe out for a day trip; an American Bridge tracker was right behind him in another canoe, recording all the while.

Meanwhile, many of the same factors at play in the last midterm reared their heads once again; Democrats lost control of the Senate and fell even further behind in the race for control of the House.

But the defeat wasn't a permanent one. In politics, it never is.

At American Bridge, we did our own "autopsy." It's up to us to adjust to their adjustments—to stay smarter, more aggressive, and more creative in making sure that Democrats keep the edge we need to win. We're already developing new approaches to make our tracking more effective (although we still haven't made paddling a canoe part of the job interview for applicants), and working with all the power players on the progressive side to tune up other aspects of our own model, while also figuring out new ways to jam the other side's circuits.

Without tipping off our future plans to the Republican researchers who are no doubt scrutinizing this book, I'll just say that we're ready to roll out some innovations that have yet to be seen on the political battlefield—and that Republicans should indeed be running scared. But that's true of any candidate in this modern era of campaign warfare—and with the stage set for the climactic battle in 2016, the arms race is escalating faster than ever.

## Chapter Three

# The Party of Koch

One morning in 1994, I was summoned to the Four Seasons Hotel in Georgetown to sit down with the man who funded my anti-Clinton work at the *American Spectator*—my benefactor, my sugar daddy, the Wizard of conservative Oz: Richard Mellon Scaife. He was pleasant enough, but quiet; his aides did all the talking and, to me, seemed to be running the show. You wouldn't have known that the ruddy-faced man quietly listening to the conversation was one of the most powerful unelected people in America.

When Richard Mellon Scaife passed away in July 2014, I had occasion to spend some time thinking about his legacy. He was generous with his largesse. I vividly remember *Spectator* staffers sending off "Dear Mr. Scaife" letters to his office in Pittsburgh asking for six-figure sums for anti-Clinton research, requests that were generally granted quickly and with no questions asked.

But if you didn't share his commitment to conservative ideology, it wouldn't be hard to see him as some kind of comic book supervillain. After all, few people did more damage to the progressive project in the last quarter of the twentieth century. Scaife's banking fortune underwrote the work of powerful right-wing think tanks like the Heritage Foundation, and later funded the torpedoing of the Clinton presidency through his support of scandal-mongering publications like the *Specta-tor*, the *Pittsburgh Tribune-Review*, and *NewsMax*.

Scaife was an institution builder. Instead of getting ramped up to support candidates in one election cycle and then going on vacation until the next even-numbered year, he believed in the importance of conservative infrastructure: infrastructure to generate and spread ideas, infrastructure to constantly dig up dirt on anyone standing in your way, and infrastructure to get that dirt published.

Still, most of us aren't billionaires, and when we imagine what we'd do if we suddenly became billionaires, the answer usually involves beach vacations, private jets, or art collections, rather than plowing our time, our energy, and our fortune into political outcomes. Once you've made it to the top of the mountain, why not enjoy the view?

It can be hard to understand what really motivates people to do the things they do. In Scaife's case, I don't think it was a personal vendetta against the Clintons. Indeed, like me, he would later go on to befriend them and even support their work. His was, rather, a deep commitment to a pure libertarian vision for American society, one in which government played as small a role as possible and people were largely left to fend for themselves. Scaife was also something of an anti-establishment radical, which I thought was a little misplaced. After all, his middle name was Mellon—as in the Mellons who founded a bank, owned an oil company, built ships, and became one of the most influential families in America—and a good part of the fortune that he would use to shape our political landscape had been inherited. Horatio Alger he wasn't.

⌒

Scaife was also about winning by any means necessary. When I think back on his vast, relentless, and systematically funded enterprise, and its fueling of a doctrinaire, Manichean right-wing movement willing to do just about anything (including impeaching a president on partisan, made-up claims) to establish its political hegemony, the thing that still astonishes me the most is that, other than Hillary Clinton, nobody really believed he was doing it.

When Hillary pointed a finger at "the vast right-wing conspiracy" for working to destroy her husband's presidency back in the bad old impeachment days of 1998, people acted as if she had blamed the scandals on aliens from outer space or transmissions coming through Ken Starr's teeth. Not only was the press largely ignorant of what was going on, though they were being manipulated, many Democrats and progressives didn't really believe it either.

Of course, unlike most cases in which one person warns a skeptical audience about the pernicious intentions of powerful unseen forces, Hillary wasn't crazy. Hillary was right. There was, indeed, a vast right-wing conspiracy afoot in the 1990s. I know. I was part of it. And there is another one afoot today. The only difference is that, this time, the conspiracy is even vaster, and much smarter: more politically focused, more generously funded, more sophisticated in its approach. And, of course, thanks to *Citizens United*, it is not bound by much in the way of campaign finance laws.

Richard Mellon Scaife may be gone. He redeemed himself in the end by making up with the man he unjustly tried to destroy. But, as in any good comic book, the dark forces have emerged even stronger. Don't expect them to learn from Scaife's apology.

⌒

The day after I spoke at the Clinton School in Arkansas in March 2014, my phone rang. It was Senate Majority Leader Harry Reid, who had read about my speech in the papers. He told me he appreciated everything I'd done for the Clintons—but what, he asked, are you doing for me?

I didn't know how to respond. "What should I be doing?" I asked. The conversation would be the beginning of our fight against the dominant figures of the vast right-wing conglomerate, two wealthy industrialist brothers from Wichita, Kansas, named Charles and David Koch.

Reid, as he explained, had gone out on a limb, publicly and repeatedly blasting the Koch brothers, who by 2014 had emerged as the biggest threat to Reid's Senate majority, pumping what would end up being hundreds of millions of dollars into defeating Democratic candidates around the country.

Reid's attacks were enormously controversial among Democrats. For all the time they had spent *complaining* about the pernicious influence of big-money Republican SuperPACs, few on the left thought it would do any good to make the Kochs themselves an issue. After all, Democrats had plenty of wealthy backers, and they worried that Reid's strategy might come off as hypocritical and potentially offend important left-wing donors. Besides, most Democrats believed highlighting the Kochs' spending threatened to distract from their main messages: underscoring Republicans' extremist policies and promoting a middle-class economic agenda.

I certainly didn't think that campaign finance reform was going to be the issue that helped Democrats survive the ugly Senate map in 2014; indeed, as I described in the last chapter, I thought that Democrats had long overestimated the political value of being on the side of the angels when it came to SuperPACs.

But Reid didn't simply want to go after the Kochs because they were major contributors to the ongoing subversion of our democracy. He wanted to talk about what these guys believed, and why they were spending all this money, and what they planned to get in return, and, critically, what that would mean for everyday Americans. He wanted to focus less on the ugly *process* of turning campaigns into auctions, and more on the *outcomes* that would result if the Kochs ended up being the high bidders.

The majority leader wasn't just guessing. Private focus-group research that we had access to suggested that while voters did believe that there was too much money in politics, they weren't terribly alarmed, much less outraged, at the sheer magnitude of the Koch spending.

They had a much stronger, more negative reaction when told about the Koch agenda and how it would affect them.

The data showed that we could persuade voters to reject Koch candidates, but only if we showed them that the brothers were funding politicians who would help them greedily line their own pockets while undermining education, taking away health-care benefits, privatizing Medicare, and otherwise turning a cold shoulder to the concerns of the public. Two billionaires spending a bunch of money was one thing; two billionaires buying up political offices so they can increase their own bottom line at the expense, say, of clean water or workplace safety was something else entirely.

But with few other Democrats interested in making this argument, Reid was on his own. And drawing the link between the Kochs' spending, the right-wing agenda they were pushing, and the tangible impact those policies would have on their profit margins as well as on the lives of most Americans would take research, lots of it; Reid just didn't have the kind of operation that would allow him to prove the case.

But war rooms? We knew how to do that. I thought Reid was on to something important. And so we quickly launched a project called RealKochFacts, designed to educate voters about the threat posed by the brothers' self-serving political agenda.

It was an ambitious undertaking, and, as always, we started with primary source documents, the holy grail of all research efforts. Our team craves raw material. We once went through twenty-seven thousand pages of documents related to Scott Walker's corruption investigation in ten hours. We once sent a team to New Jersey to get 911 tapes from local police after Chris Christie shut down a bridge there, finding a computer café to send the audio back to headquarters, where forty people managed to listen to forty-five hours of tape in just an hour and a half. We once ventured to Massachusetts in search of old footage of Mitt Romney talking about health care; told that the relevant video archives were available only on VHS, we paid to digitize them all—a gift from us to the people of the Commonwealth; and it was a few thousand dollars well spent, as it yielded proof of his flip-flopping on the issue of the individual mandate for health-care coverage.

And now, as we began our investigation of the Kochs, we sent a researcher to the University of Virginia, where the Libertarian Party (the home of the Kochs' political activities during the 1970s and early 1980s) keeps its archives.

The files are stored in old boxes; the university's librarian told us that they hadn't been opened since the day they were put away. In a dark basement on the gorgeous UVA campus, our researcher spent two days inhaling dust and carefully sifting through the yellowing papers. We paid to digitize old reel-to-reel films that hadn't been touched in decades, worried that any attempt to play the reels in their current condition would cause them to disintegrate or burst into flames. And what we found would help to paint a gothic picture of the two most powerful unelected men in America.

As part of this project, I spend a lot of time speaking about the Kochs publicly, where audiences already cringe at the mention of the Koch name. But when I tell Democrats and progressives about today's vast right-wing conglomerate—when I show them how deeply the Kochs' influence has penetrated into our political system at the expense of the prosperity of everyday Americans—they seem shocked all over again, as if there's no precedent for the kind of coordinated, sinister effort the Kochs are mounting.

Progressives who want to win need to understand what we're up against. Richard Mellon Scaife was able to pump unlimited money into destroying Democrats without anybody in the mainstream media ever bothering to shine a light on the man behind the curtain. If the same mistake is made again, there's no telling how much damage the Kochs could do operating in the shadows. If we want to elect Hillary Clinton in 2016—indeed, if we want to move the progressive project forward at all in the years to come—we don't just have to beat the Republicans. We have to expose the Koch brothers.

When you imagine the Koch brothers, it's hard not to think of the 1983 film *Trading Places*, which featured as its villains a pair of brothers, commodity brokers named Randolph and Mortimer Duke. Bored with their millions, the Duke brothers decide to frame an employee for theft and drug dealing while offering riches to a street hustler—just to see what would happen.

The Kochs, of course, aren't in it for fun. They're in it for profit. Their family company, Koch Industries, is the second-largest privately held corporation in the country. And while there's little doubt that Charles and David are both sincere in their right-wing ideology, it helps to understand that the Kochs aren't spending their fortune attempting to sway elections simply because they see doing so as a contribution to their country. They're doing it because they see it as an investment in their company.

Back in the late 1970s, a federal audit found their company guilty of violating energy price controls (which Charles considered to be "socialistic measures"). A Koch subsidiary was ultimately faced with a $10 million fine.

When most people find themselves running afoul of the law, they might change their ways. When the Koch brothers found themselves running afoul of the law, David Koch decided to run for office so that he could change the law. And that was exactly what he did, joining the Libertarian ticket as its vice presidential candidate in the 1980 election. (One of the documents we found in the basement at the University of Virginia was a letter from Koch to Libertarian delegates pointing out a loophole in campaign finance laws that would allow him to bankroll the entire campaign if he was placed on the ticket.)

If you think back to 1980, you'll remember that conservatives really didn't have much reason to be upset with the Republican Party nominee, Ronald Reagan. For more than a decade, he had been a visible and vocal advocate for right-wing policies, a true believer who was now running on a platform of free-market economics, a militant foreign policy, and all the other things that make conservatives want to stand up and cheer. Even better, he was looking like a huge favorite to beat the pants off of Democratic incumbent Jimmy Carter.

But the Libertarian ticket, with a smooth-talking lawyer named Ed Clark at the top and forty-year-old David Koch riding shotgun, felt that Ronald Reagan simply wasn't conservative enough. Indeed, we found a letter they wrote to Reagan demanding that he stop describing himself as a "libertarian."

Reagan famously said that "government isn't the solution to our problem, government *is* the problem." But in the eyes of Clark and Koch, that just meant Reagan was soft on government. To them, government wasn't just the problem, it was the enemy, and these guys meant to crush it. As Charles Koch put it, "Our goal is not to reallocate the burden of government; our goal is to roll back government."

These weren't empty threats. The Libertarian platform (which was nothing more than the Koch platform) proposed to take a sledgehammer to the basic functions of government. They wanted to abolish the Federal Reserve, the Department of Energy, the Department of Education—and that was just for starters. Also on the hit list would be the Securities and Exchange Commission, which regulates Wall Street, and the Federal Election Commission, which regulates campaign spending. Gone as well would be the Small Business Administration, the Federal Trade Commission, and the Occupational Safety and Health Administration, because in David Koch's America, workers should be free to get sick and die from asbestos poisoning.

Oh, and they wanted to get rid of the minimum wage, zero out federal spending on highways, and abolish Social Security, which the Koch ticket called "the most serious threat to the future of stability of our society next to the threat of nuclear war."

David Koch campaigned on this platform in states across the country. And, to their credit, the American people recognized it for what it was: a radical and dangerous ideology that would have increased the power of America's wealthiest, blown up the safety net for America's poorest, and left the government completely unable to do anything to sustain and protect the middle class. Even in the big Reagan election when America cut its hair, put on a suit, and signed up for an experiment in conservative governance, the Libertarian ticket was able to earn just over 1 percent of the national vote.

"As a candidate," David Koch ruminated, "meeting only libertarians, it seemed to me that everyone was voting for us. We all got a little too optimistic." He was living in a bubble.

While the Koch brothers may have overestimated the popular appeal of taking a wrecking ball to the federal government, they weren't oblivious. They quickly came to understand that the American people weren't buying what they were selling. And if they wanted their ideas to win the day, well, then it was time for Charles and David to start buying—not acquiring other companies now, but instead taking over the Republican infrastructure. Instead of running as Libertarians, they would be Republicans—their version of *Trading Places*.

⌒

The brothers decided to make three tactical changes. First, instead of fronting their right-wing policies, the brothers would start funding them. Second, instead of attempting to run to the right of the Republican Party as Libertarians, they would simply try to pull the Republican Party to the right from the inside. Third, instead of plowing their money into any one campaign, they would follow the well-trod path of becoming conservative institution builders—one they had already begun to follow in 1977, when Charles founded the Cato Institute, which would quickly become one of the nation's premier right-wing think tanks.

It would be, in the words of Charles Koch, a "vertically and horizontally integrated" strategy, "from idea creation to policy development to education to grassroots organization to lobbying to litigation to political action." This would require the creation of a whole network of groups, each devoted to tackling a different piece of the Kochs' vision—and each fully committed to their right-wing ideology. As David put it, "If we're going to give a lot of money, we'll make darn sure they spend it in a way that goes along with our intent."

There's no way of knowing how much money the Koch brothers have spent on this project over the last thirty years or so, since so much of it has been and continues to be spent in secret. But if you look at conservative infrastructure, you see their fingerprints everywhere. Let's follow the money.

Take the Mercatus Center, a policy incubator at George Mason University that the *Wall Street Journal* has called "the most important think tank you've never heard of" and a recipient of at least $14 million in Koch funding.

When the Environmental Protection Agency announced new measures to reduce ozone pollution in 1997, it was a Mercatus economist who made the novel argument that smog-free skies might lead to more cases of skin cancer. A few years later, the DC Circuit Court actually ruled that the EPA had "explicitly disregarded" the "possible health benefits of ozone" and decided in favor of the polluters.

Now, you may think that the judges who bought the Mercatus economist's argument would have been concerned about the fact that the economist was funded by two brothers who, as owners of oil refineries that contributed heavily to ozone pollution, had a direct financial stake in overturning the proposed regulation.

But you'd be underestimating the Kochs.

You see, the judges who ruled in favor of the polluters had previously received trips to a ranch in Montana for what were essentially junkets. These vacations—excuse me, legal retreats—had been arranged by the Foundation for Research on Economics and the Environment (FREE). And you'll never guess who funded FREE. Yup: Charles and David Koch. But in Koch world nothing is really FREE. They get what they pay for.

The Kochs' think tanks weren't just there to harass Democratic policy makers. As they became more and more influential, they began to substitute for the policy-making apparatus of the Republican Party itself—and when Republicans took the White House in 2000, the Bush administration drew heavily on the brainpower of the Koch institutions to set the agenda.

For example, when the Bush administration began soliciting suggestions for regulations to eliminate, the Mercatus Center was ready with a list—and, in the end, fourteen out of the twenty-three regulations on the administration's "hit list" came straight from the Kochs' think tank. Again, the Kocus got what they paid for.

As vast right-wing conspiracies go, a wide-ranging, well-funded, and deeply influential network of think tanks and policy shops isn't a bad start. But what makes the Koch brothers uniquely threatening to democracy is that they didn't stop at building a mechanism to influence elites. They hired some foot soldiers, too. In 1984, they launched Citizens for a Sound Economy (CSE), their first attempt to foment a mass movement of antigovernment zealots. CSE would later branch off into a few different organizations.

One would be called Americans for Prosperity (AFP), which would become the grassroots army the Kochs had long lusted after. Indeed, AFP would go on to become the single most influential independent expenditure group in America, feared by Democrats who knew that the group could spend practically unlimited funds on negative ads and by Republican candidates who knew that falling out of favor with AFP was akin to losing your next primary.

Ask conservative true believers about the Tea Party, and they'll tell you that, as in 1776, America was in danger of succumbing under the boot heel of tyranny. Government had grown too large, too powerful, too, well, tyrannical. And the American people had had enough. Then, a prophet emerged: On February 19, 2009, a cable news talking head named Rick Santelli, outraged at President Obama's attempt to help struggling homeowners stave off foreclosure, went on a televised rant on the floor of the Chicago Mercantile Exchange—his own version of the "mad as hell" speech from the movie *Network*.

Channeling Santelli's outrage—and his suggestion that perhaps a "Chicago Tea Party" was in order to protest the president's actions—the Tea Party supposedly emerged as an authentic grassroots expression of the country's rage at Comrade Obummer's dastardly attempts to bail out the electric car companies, give free health care to illegal immigrants, and replace the Bible in every American hotel room with a copy of Chairman Mao's little red book.

This was the myth they told as the Tea Party became an ascendant force in American politics, and it was a complete fairy tale.

To be sure, conservatives were legitimately unhappy about the economic stimulus package that passed in 2009, as well as the Affordable Care Act enacted in early 2010. And much of the anger that got vented at Democratic officeholders during a series of tumultuous town hall meetings—in which angry citizens attempted to recreate Santelli's moment by screaming at their representatives about tyranny—was heartfelt. Conservatives really were mad that an (African-American) Democratic president was implementing a center-left agenda. Whipped up by the likes of Glenn Beck, some may have honestly believed that the individual mandate in the Affordable Care Act really was a prelude to an Orwellian society in which dissenters were ushered into FEMA camps.

But while the Tea Party may have been a reflection of authentic anger, that anger was funded, organized, channeled, and directed by Americans for Prosperity, along with FreedomWorks (another of the splinter groups that formed out of Citizens for a Sound Economy). Those organizations were responsible for many of the Tea Party's activities—organizing conference calls and rallies, writing and disseminating talking points, buying Web domains, and planning protests. In that way, the Tea Party wasn't a spontaneous outpouring of grassroots energy. It was the Koch brothers and their allies putting on a show—and finally building (or buying) their grassroots movement.

Of course, there's nothing wrong with political organizing—and the practice of "Astroturfing," or pretending that a well-organized and well-financed operation is really a grassroots groundswell—is common across the political spectrum.

But the Kochs work unusually hard to avoid public scrutiny—and the accountability that may come with it—hiding behind what the *Washington Post* calls "a labyrinth of tax-exempt groups and limited-liability companies" with cryptic names like POFN LLC and the TC4 Trust. And in the era of *Citizens United*, their ability to do so has only been strengthened. In 2012, they spent over $400 million trying to defeat President Obama and Democrats in Congress.

And they're really good at what they do. Forget for a moment that Obama managed to win reelection, and think of all those Democrats who lost their seats thanks to a flood of (generally misleading) negative ads from Americans for Prosperity—or look at the way they've succeeded in changing the Republican Party.

In 2007, when the House passed a minimum wage increase, eighty-two Republicans voted for it. When the bill went to the Senate, it passed with ninety-four votes—half of which came from the GOP. Today, with Americans for Prosperity warning that Republicans who deviate from their edicts will face the wrath of their activists, good luck finding one who will stand up for giving America's poorest workers a raise.

In 2008, the Republican platform acknowledged the impact of "human economic activity" on our climate, and their nominee, John McCain, campaigned on a cap-and-trade proposal. Today, membership in the GOP is equivalent to membership in the Flat Earth Society—because the Kochs haven't just made our air and water toxic for everyone, they've made holding a reasonable position on climate change toxic for Republicans.

⌒

But if you really want to see the Koch brothers' influence in action, take a trip to Columbus, Ohio.

The Columbus Zoo is widely regarded as the best zoo in Ohio, and one of the best in America. Its director emeritus, Jack Hanna, is familiar to late-night TV audiences as "Jungle Jack," the man who shows up to terrify Conan O'Brien with a komodo dragon or inspire *awww*s with a baby red panda. And with more than nine thousand animals representing nearly seven hundred species, it's more than a hub for conservation—it's one of the city's top tourist attractions, boasting upward of 2.3 million visitors every year.

In early 2014, the people of Columbus were set to vote on a ballot measure to increase funding for the zoo. It wasn't a big deal, just $31 million for capital improvements, the kind of measure that voters had approved time and time again. And there was no reason to believe that this time would be any different.

That was when voters started receiving flyers in their mailboxes featuring a gorilla hand holding a $100 bill, urging them to "stop the money grab." Soon, voters' doorbells were ringing—canvassers were going door-to-door to spread the same message, arguing against the funding increase. The pressure campaign was effective: When Columbus voters went to the polls, they vetoed the money for the zoo.

Who was behind the effort to stop the funding increase for the Columbus Zoo? Was it secret agents sent by jealous administrators at the Cincinnati Zoo? Had a group of orangutans evolved the capacity for political organization and used the referendum as a chance to protest their captivity?

None of the above, as it turns out. The organization behind the flyers and the door knocks was none other than Americans for Prosperity.

You've heard of the Matt Damon film *We Bought a Zoo*?

Well, in Columbus, Ohio, Charles and David Koch bought a zoo ballot initiative.

⌒

A zoo funding ballot initiative in Ohio. A city council race in Coralville, Iowa (population: 20,092). A Board of Supervisors election in Iron County, Wisconsin, where the Kochs helped elect a majority for around $10,000 a seat—a majority that promptly approved a controversial mining project.

The Koch brothers did not manage to buy the White House in 2012. But when you are as wealthy, as uninhibited, and as committed as they are, there's little limit on what you can buy when you shop in the state and local aisles. And the Kochs fund a wide variety of groups determined to wield influence over who gets elected to these down-ballot offices and what they do once they get there.

There's the American Legislative Exchange Council (ALEC), which drafts "model legislation" designed to benefit its corporate donors. ALEC bills were introduced in every state legislature in 2013—more than four hundred in all: bills to repeal renewable energy standards, protect big corporations from lawsuits, weaken public employee unions, require photo IDs at the polls, privatize education, and more.

There's the Susan B. Anthony List, which supports antiabortion candidates (not exactly in line with the Kochs' libertarian leanings). There's the State Policy Network, an umbrella organization for a network of mini Heritage Foundations that push conservative ideology in states across the country. Arizona has the Goldwater Institute, Louisiana has the Pelican Institute for Public Policy, South Carolina has the Palmetto Promise Institute, and the Koch brothers have a stake in all of it.

There's the Franklin Center for Government and Public Integrity, which trains right-wing think tanks to do "investigative journalism," although the fact that it was founded by a former Republican campaign operative with no journalism experience gives you a clue as to its true mission: harassing progressives with frivolous dirt-digging expeditions under the guise of news reporting and publishing right-wing blog posts about evil union bosses, Marxian senators, and the perils of renewable energy. The Franklin Center now has affiliates in most states; it claims to account for 10 percent of all daily reporting from state capitals nationwide, and its stories regularly filter up to local newspapers and TV.

And, of course, there's the granddaddy of them all, Americans for Prosperity, the Kochs' personal Astroturf group, ready to descend wherever someone wants a little more money for the local zoo.

⌒

One of the Kochs' allies is a man named Art Pope, a discount store magnate who has done in his home state of North Carolina exactly what the Kochs have done on a national scale. Pope has been working at turning North Carolina reactionary red for thirty years, bankrolling an entire network of think tanks and pressure organizations and funding sympathetic candidates for down-ballot offices. You might call him "Diet Koch."

North Carolina had always been a relatively progressive Southern state, with a reputation for racial tolerance and strong schools. President Obama carried it in 2008, and as the 2010 cycle began, Democratic governor Bev Perdue enjoyed a 30–20 Democratic majority in the state senate.

Then came *Citizens United*, and the end of North Carolina's ban on political expenditures paid for by corporations. In flowed the money—independent spending in 2010 more than quadrupled from four years earlier. Nearly three quarters of that money came from organizations tied to Art Pope (including, of course, Americans for Prosperity).

In 2010, Pope's groups spent $2 million targeting twenty-seven legislative races. They won twenty. Republicans turned their ten-seat deficit into an eleven-seat advantage in the state senate, and picked up more than a dozen additional seats in the House, flipping the majority there, too.

Then, in 2012, Republican Charlotte mayor Pat McCrory defeated Democrat Walter Dalton in an election in which 70 percent of the $14.5 million spent by outside groups went to benefit Republicans. Of the top ten outside groups accounting for 90 percent of the spending, seven were conservative.

In the span of four years, Republicans had seized full control of the North Carolina state government for the first time in more than a century. But like the Kochs, Pope wasn't just about electing his preferred candidates, but about setting their agenda—an agenda described through its slogans as "Scale Back Taxes," "Slice Away at the Social Safety Net," and "Reverse the State's Focus on Public Schools."

Indeed, with Pope himself newly installed as Governor McCrory's budget director, the new Republican establishment in North Carolina went on a right-wing rampage, passing more than three hundred bills in their first year in power.

They implemented drastic cuts in tax credits for low-income workers and slashed unemployment insurance. They reduced the number of openings available for children in state-run pre-K programs. They moved to cut college aid and teaching assistants, freeze teacher pay (it was already forty-sixth in the nation), and stop a minimum wage increase. They worked to flatten the income tax, expand the regressive sales tax, and eliminate the estate tax entirely. They rejected federal money for Medicaid and brought an end to tenure for teachers. They made it easier to carry guns onto school campuses and into bars. They adopted some of the most severe antiabortion and antivoting rights measures in the nation. They even passed a law to bar courts from applying sharia law (which hadn't really been an issue in North Carolina).

One GOP operative called it the "national Republican agenda on steroids." And none of it was an accident. During the campaign, the John Locke Foundation, a Pope-funded think tank, published a book laying out a series of proposals. Their president, John Hood, later crowed, "Virtually everything we proposed in the book in 2012 was enacted in 2013." And besides Art Pope's influence, the *Raleigh News and Observer* counted at least two dozen bills straight out of the ALEC playbook.

The lesson: When it comes to institution building, conservatives understand that you get what you pay for.

North Carolina isn't the only state to end up in the right's shopping cart. The Kochs themselves took an active interest in Wisconsin, home to "Fighting Bob" LaFollette and a progressive stronghold that had been the birthplace of policies like progressive taxation, workers' compensation, and collective bargaining.

In 2010, the Kochs and their cronies spent about $1.6 million targeting eighteen incumbent Democratic state legislators, defeating fourteen of them—a 78 percent win rate, and more than enough to hand Republicans a majority. Meanwhile, progressive stalwart senator Russ Feingold was defeated by Ron Johnson, an intellectually incurious businessman parroting the Koch party line. And Scott Walker became governor.

Overnight, the *New York Times* noted, Wisconsin "moved from Democratic dominion to total Republican control." The *Milwaukee Journal Sentinel* pointed out that Wisconsin was "the only state in the country where Democrats lost the governorship, a Senate seat, and an entire legislature."

As in North Carolina, the new Republican establishment in Wisconsin understood where its bread was buttered, and immediately set about implementing the Kochs' agenda. Governor Walker cut taxes for millionaires, and then took away unions' collective bargaining rights so he could slash their benefits to make up the shortfall. When that collective bargaining law was challenged in the state Supreme Court, Justice David Prosser—himself the beneficiary of $2.7 million in funds from the Kochs and their allies in his own campaign—was there to cast the deciding vote to uphold it.

Wisconsinites were outraged, forcing Walker into a recall election—but the Kochs stood by their man. Americans for Prosperity spent $1.5 million on TV ads during the recall alone, part of a $10 million effort to support Walker's career and agenda. They bused conservative counterdemonstrators to the state capitol. They even mailed absentee ballots with the wrong election date on them (calling it a "printing mistake") as part of a voter suppression scheme.

It was a sizable investment on the part of the Kochs. And Scott Walker knew it. One day, his office received a call from a man identifying himself as David Koch. You can imagine Walker straightening his tie and taking a deep breath before sprinting to the phone to take the call. They talked strategy for twenty minutes. Walker never realized that the call was a fake—it wasn't David Koch on the line, but rather a blogger executing a practical joke. But you don't ask questions when your sugar daddy calls. "I'll fly you out to California and show you a good time," the prankster "Koch" told Walker. "That would be outstanding," he replied.

In the end, the Kochs' investment paid off. In just a few short years, Walker and his allies in Madison were able to push through even more right-wing legislation: slashing $800 million from Wisconsin public schools, blocking a minimum wage increase, putting new work requirements on recipients of food stamps (which basically cut off support for thirty thousand poor people), enacting a blatantly unconstitutional voter ID law, passing new restrictions on abortion, allowing concealed weapons in parks and near schools, and, the Kochs being the Kochs, "streamlining" environmental regulations to allow for more mining.

If states are the laboratories of democracy, the Kochs and their allies have proven what it's like when a mad scientist is in charge of the lab.

⌒

In the 2010 elections, with the Koch brothers capitalizing on the *Citizens United* decision and Democrats shaking their heads in principled dismay, Republicans seized full control of twelve states. And it cost them less than you might think.

Between 2004 and 2012, the right spent around $120 million directly trying to elect Republicans in state races—most of it coming through the Republican State Leadership Committee, run in the 2010 midterms by former Bush administration figure Ed Gillespie. They spent another $100 million or so on policy and advocacy work—ALEC, the Franklin Center, and similar groups. That's a lot of money by the

standards of anyone not named Koch. But for the billionaire brothers and their allies, a couple of hundred million dollars to essentially
orchestrate a hostile takeover of a dozen states is an enormously successful investment—especially when you consider the timing.

In addition to being an election year, 2010 was also a census year,
meaning that the governors and legislatures elected in 2010 would be
in charge of drawing new congressional and legislative district boundaries for the next decade.

Like Astroturfing, gerrymandering—the intentional drawing of dis-
tricts to benefit one party over another—is common. Both sides do it.
But because Republicans did so well in state elections in 2010, they're
the ones who got to do it this time. And in 2012, Republicans retained
control of the U.S. House of Representatives—even though Democratic congressional candidates won a million more votes than their
Republican counterparts.

In six states where Obama won, Republicans still maintained a majority in the congressional delegation. Virginia, a state in which Obama
carried 51 percent of the vote, sent eight Republicans and just three
Democrats to the U.S. House of Representatives. Michigan, despite
giving 54 percent of its vote to the president, elected nine Republicans
and just five Democrats.

And because the next opportunity to redraw boundaries won't be
until after 2020, Americans are pretty much stuck with this ugly math
until the end of the decade. It doesn't really matter how good a year
Democrats have; winning the House back will be a nearly impossible task
thanks to the state-level GOP sweep in 2010 and their gerrymandering.

Meanwhile, the Koch brothers spent another $300 million in 2014,
and with Republicans watching out for American Bridge cameras (and
refusing to nominate more Todd Akins), they didn't blow their chance
to seize the Senate majority this time. Thom Tillis, the speaker of the
North Carolina House who ushered through so much of Art Pope's
legislation, defeated Democratic U.S. senator Kay Hagan in 2014
thanks to an insane $50 million-plus in outside spending, much of it

from Americans for Prosperity. And Harry Reid lost his majority leader position to Mitch McConnell, who promised at a Koch network summit to block "gosh-darn proposals" like raising the minimum wage.

If the Kochs and their allies are able to buy the White House in 2016, then they can look forward to full control of the federal government: a president who will owe everything to their support, a Senate majority consisting largely of Republicans who got there with the help of Tea Party energy and Americans for Prosperity's largesse, and a House majority that's largely bulletproof thanks to gerrymandering. And a Koch approved Supreme Court. They've promised to spend a billion dollars to make it happen.

And they won't just have the power to set the agenda—they'll have an agenda ready to go, one that's been developed at Koch think tanks and tested in Koch-bought states. They'll make Richard Mellon Scaife look downright small-time.

They also may succeed in making Scaife seem like a nice guy by comparison. Though the Kochs do what they can to avoid the spotlight and hide what they're funding, privately they're blunt about their objectives, sometimes brazenly so. Aside from politics, the Koch brothers are generous with their philanthropic dollars, funding major arts and cultural institutions and medical centers, with David Koch especially active on the New York City charity circuit. At one such glittery event that attacted a bipartisan crowd long before Hillary announced her candidacy, I learned that Hillary had bumped into her would-be nemesis. Hillary was her gracious self; Koch, not so much. While he expressed admiration for her service as secretary of state, partisan politics, not charity, was on his mind. "I'm going to spend a lot of money to defeat you," Koch gruffly told her, before turning on his heels and vanishing into the crowd.

⌒

So how the hell do we beat these power-mad plutocrats? We can't stop them from spending their billions; indeed, the more powerful they become, the less likely it is that we'll see the passage of campaign finance reform that would rein in their power. Nor should we bank on being able to match their financial resources; the only reason they didn't spend more in 2014 is that they didn't have to.

Part of the solution is to try to inoculate voters from being misled by the ads that money buys. Believe it or not, there are limits on what you can say in an attack ad. The law does, in theory, protect people from being libeled (although libel suits don't generally fare well in the political world—they're mostly filed for show by candidates who've been badly wounded by an attack to emphasize just how untrue the attack is and just how offensive voters should find it). More relevantly, TV stations can, and do, refuse to air falsehoods.

But does that mean you can't lie on TV? Of course not. For example: In an attack ad against Arkansas Democratic senator Mark Pryor, Karl Rove's Crossroads GPS claimed that the Affordable Care Act, which Pryor supported, "cuts over $700 billion from our Medicare." By any reasonable definition of the word *lie*, this is a lie. The Affordable Care Act, as fact-checkers have gone hoarse repeating over the years, does not affect benefits for seniors on Medicare.

What the law does is reduce future reimbursement payments to health-care providers under the Medicare Advantage program, which allows private insurers to compete with Medicare. This will put Medicare on sounder financial footing, extending the program's solvency by several years.

But the claim was a great way to scare seniors. And it was a great way to distract from the fact that Pryor's opponent, Republican congressman Tom Cotton, supported Paul Ryan's plan to eliminate traditional Medicare entirely, replacing it with a voucher that actually would have reduced health-care benefits for seniors. (Cotton ended up winning by double digits.)

The Affordable Care Act was a complicated piece of legislation. For example, it set minimum benefit standards for insurance plans; flimsy plans that didn't offer much in the way of actual benefits were canceled, and people who had those plans were given an opportunity to shop for better insurance in a regulated, subsidized marketplace. This allowed millions of Americans to improve their coverage—and it allowed Americans for Prosperity to run ads saying that "millions of Americans have lost their health insurance."

As Upton Sinclair, the muckraking journalist, famously observed, "It is difficult to get a man to understand something when his salary depends on his not understanding it." In 2014, the salaries of right-wing attack ad gurus—not to mention Republican hopes of winning the Senate—depended on these sorts of willful misunderstandings of the Affordable Care Act. In between the actual truth and the kind of lies that get you sued, there is a vast chasm, and Republicans love to operate in that space.

It would be great if this kind of dishonest politics didn't work—if the mainstream media reliably called out these falsehoods for what they are and forced Republican candidates to either answer for or disavow them, or if voters were able to easily discern truth from lies in slick political commercials. But until the day that our campaign finance laws are changed, it will be up to progressives to slug it out with the Kochs—running our own ads while aggressively fact-checking theirs.

In the next chapter, I'll talk about another process by which falsehoods are slid into the political debate: a sort of right-wing assembly line by which damaging stories are concocted out of thin air, given a patina of credibility by conservative operators posing as journalists, amplified by Republican politicians, and pushed into the mainstream media, where, without the kind of critical scrutiny that is often lacking in the press, they become legitimized as fodder for attack ads paid for by the Kochs.

But before I do, it's worth remembering that Harry Reid was right: Charles and David Koch did end up posing an insurmountable threat to the Democratic Senate majority in 2014—and making the Koch brothers themselves an issue did, in fact, work in one key contest.

The Kochs had high hopes for Republican Terri Lynn Land in her campaign against Democratic representative Gary Peters in Michigan's open Senate seat. She began the race six points up, and the Kochs spent millions hammering Peters on the airwaves.

As in other states, Democratic researchers worked to expose the facts about Land's backers: the American jobs they'd sent overseas, the environmental damage they'd caused, the havoc their business practices can wreak on local communities. But in Michigan, researchers dug up one special connection: a Koch-owned company was responsible for dumping petroleum coke on the shores of the Detroit River. The press jumped on the story. THE KOCH BROTHERS, one headline reported, HAVE BURIED AN AREA THE SIZE OF A CITY BLOCK UNDER 30 FEET OF OIL SANDS WASTE. The Peters campaign, backed by local environmentalists and Reid's Senate party committee back in DC, decided to run against the Koch brothers as hard as they were running against Terri Lynn Land—and, in the end, that connection proved to be as toxic as their refinery's waste.

By August, the Kochs pulled a million-dollar ad buy for Land, knowing their support for her was a liability. And polls were showing that the Kochs were overwhelmingly unpopular in Michigan; by the time the campaign was over, only 5 percent of voters had a favorable opinion of the duo, while 74 percent had an unfavorable opinion. On Election Day, Peters won a resounding victory, the only nonincumbent Democrat to win a Senate seat in the 2014 cycle.

⌒

The Koch brothers are clearly aware that sunlight is their worst enemy because it is, as Supreme Court justice Louis Brandeis said, "the best disinfectant." The president of Americans for Prosperity has taken to accusing American Bridge of engaging in "the politics of personal destruction," even though we've focused exclusively on their policy views and business practices. Koch PR operatives frequently warn reporters against using our research, even though they haven't been able to challenge our facts. And keen-eyed Super Bowl viewers in January 2015 might have noticed what must have been a hugely expensive feel-good ad for Koch Industries—part of an unprecedented positive PR campaign the brothers are running to restore their image.

When you're spending that kind of money on damage control—"Hey, we can't be all bad; we're the guys who make your toilet paper"—you know you've got a problem. In fact, the Republicans have become so anxious about our plans to shine light on the Kochs that in the spring of 2015, they engaged in a bit of espionage to find out more about what we are up to.

That April I was scheduled to deliver a talk in San Francisco to a conference of the Democracy Alliance—the big liberal-donor network—on the threat to democracy posed by the brothers' spending and our organizational plans to turn their influence against the 2016 candidates they fund.

Republican oppo research outfits and right-wing websites are known to stake out the DA conferences hoping to pick up political intelligence on its operations. For instance, in the café of the Four Seasons Hotel, a young tracker for America Rising followed me to a table where I was meeting with a potential donor and was able to film a short—and thankfully innocuous—portion of our interaction. Soon a video clip of me—in which I was seen and heard ordering a Diet Coke, of all nefarious things!—surfaced on the right-wing *Daily Caller* website.

More serious was a successful effort to steal a document that pertained to my presentation. The weekend before the meeting, I sketched out the text of my talk on index cards and carried them with me to San Francisco. Separately, my staff produced a standard "question-and-answer" briefing to prepare me for queries from the audience after the talk. The document was faxed to my attention at the hotel, where it was intercepted and copied before it was delivered to my room. How do I know? Two months later, it surfaced on *Politico*, billboarded as a "secret memo" detailing a new $3 million effort to go after the Kochs.

The memo was authentic, so I may as well let you in on all the trade secrets the Republicans were trying to pilfer. As I explained at the conference, in 2014 we only had six months to build and make our case against the Koch brothers; now, we're working on taking that case again to voters in 2016. We're hiring more researchers, launching new investigations, examining the brothers' finances, and looking at their business practices, such as their use of known carcinogens like formaldehyde and asbestos, their questionable workplace safety record, their international tax shelters, their history of outsourcing American jobs, and more. Most of all, we'll be looking at how the Koch agenda would affect voters in individual states where their network will try to win elections this cycle.

While exposing the Kochs isn't enough to win an election, I believe it's a critical component in creating a climate where Democratic candidates can win. And I look forward to seeing the Kochs' self-serving version of economic patriotism up against the progressive one on the ballot in 2016. Let the sunshine in!

⌒

Sometimes, even the Kochs' philanthropy has a political edge. Despite spoiling the Columbus Zoo's plans for expansion, they have a soft spot for animals—at least, extinct animals. And if you do, too, and you happen to find yourself in Washington, DC, then I have a tourist suggestion for you: the David H. Koch Hall of Human Origins at the Smithsonian National Museum of Natural History.

In addition to the usual assortment of saber-toothed taxidermy and such, the Hall of Human Origins has an interactive exhibit where your kids can learn to stop worrying so much about climate change. After all, the exhibit argues, humans have always adapted to environmental instability and will continue doing so.

Besides, the exhibit suggests, adapting to the new era of climate change won't be so bad. We can build "underground cities"! Maybe we'll develop "short, compact bodies" or "curved spines" so that "moving around in tight spaces will be no problem."

Here we are, at one of the nation's foremost institutions for the advancement of science, learning about how we shouldn't sweat global warming because we can always turn ourselves into mole people, scuttling around subterranean tunnels—in an exhibit financed by two of the men most responsible both for polluting our planet and for paralyzing our government's ability to do anything about it.

That's the Koch brothers' America. An American Hunger Games. But it's not a dystopian sci-fi vision of the future; it's a clear-eyed analysis of what they are doing to our country right now. And rather than letting them lead us to a future in which our salvation comes from our "curved spines," Democrats need to stiffen the spines we have now and face down the Kochs. Remember, they hate sunlight.

## Chapter Four

# The Scandal Launderers

The week I began making notes for this book, in the summer of 2014, Bill Clinton was accused of rape. Another story claimed that, in his postpresidency, he'd had an affair with a woman whom his Secret Service detail had code-named "Energizer." Meanwhile, Hillary Clinton was accused of being a falling-down drunk and a drug addict.

These allegations, all of them anonymous and none substantiated, were made in a trio of new anti-Clinton books, part of what Hillary shrugged off as a "cottage industry" of right-wing publications devoted to recycling discredited charges and peddling the familiar caricatures of the sleazy, womanizing Slick Willie and the ruthless, manipulative, even unstable Lady Macbeth.

In addition to being riddled with innuendo and inaccuracies, these books simply weren't very good. You could read all three of them (though I wouldn't recommend doing so, much less in a single sitting) and not learn a single new verifiable fact about the Clintons. But that wasn't the reason they were written, nor was it the reason people bought them.

Conservatives (and I say this with some affection, given that I have sold a lot of books to conservatives) don't buy books to be transported, or learn something new, or to open their minds. They seek to have their own prejudices reflected back to them. They want to see their political fantasies in print. They find comfort in knowing that someone else shares their suspicions about the liberal target of the day. And, most importantly for publishers and authors, right-wing audiences see buying the book as itself a political act.

If you take a look at the *New York Times* best-seller list, you'll often see a book or two you've never heard of about some conservative bugaboo of the day. There are two related reasons these books tend to be big commercial successes. The first is that conservative organizations often bulk-buy mass quantities of the books to help them make it onto that very list, an example of how conservatives see buying books as a form of activism.

The second is that, even if a right-wing book never successfully finds a mainstream audience, the right-wing audience is large and concentrated enough that major publishers are willing to cater to it. For a long time, these screeds were published by right-wing outlets; ignored by mainstream publishers and reviewers, they rarely gained traction with mainstream audiences.

But as talk radio and, later, Fox News, began to attract huge and homogenous audiences—and proved that they were willing to shill any idea that furthered the conservative cause—the big New York publishing houses began to see dollar signs, and established right-wing imprints to exploit this lucrative market. A publisher like Penguin Random House wouldn't risk its venerable brand by lending it to a book full of gossip about the Clintons, but by publishing it through its conservative imprint, Sentinel, it could reap the rewards from giving conservatives a chance to scratch their incurable anti-Clinton itch.

This business model helps to explain another unique feature of the conservative publishing industry, which is that nobody really cares if those books are true. The books themselves have far lower standards for accuracy than, say, the one you're reading right now. But the difference isn't just reflected in the fact-checking budgets of right-wing publishing imprints. Conservative authors, it seems, can get caught lying with absolutely no repercussions for their future viability among conservative audiences. Indeed, pretty much the only way they can lose their credibility among right-wing readers is to do what I did: Write something they don't like—the truth.

There is no better example of the right-wing book racket than the author of one of 2014's anti-Clinton books, Ed Klein (or, as his former editor Tina Brown used to call him, "Ed Slime").

Klein is a familiar character. Back in 2005, Klein wrote a book (published by Sentinel, the conservative imprint of Penguin) entitled *The Truth About Hillary: What She Knew, When She Knew It, and How Far She'll Go to Become President.* The lie began with the title—*The Truth About Hillary.* Given the author's credentials (he was a former editor of the *New York Times Magazine*) and the book's rollout (excerpted in *Vanity Fair*), it stood a good chance of breaking out of the conservative ghetto—and thus laundering Klein's tall tales into mainstream discourse. So, at Media Matters, we prepared to go over the book with a fine-tooth comb. As it turned out, we didn't need the comb; the inaccuracies in this book were visible from outer space.

Indeed, the very first revelation touted from the book turned out to be an embarrassing misfire. Two weeks before publication, the conservative website *NewsMax* issued a newsletter breathlessly previewing a bombshell from the upcoming tome: "The book will reveal Hillary's struggle with New York's Senator Daniel Patrick Moynihan to get his seat. Though a Democrat, Moynihan had little use for Hillary."

Klein's smoking gun for this claim? Moynihan's remarks at the 1999 press conference where Hillary announced her candidacy. "Oddly," the preview revealed, "Pat Moynihan never uttered Hillary's name—not even once—during this event. He could not bring himself to mention Hillary by name—but the press reported his 'endorsement' just the same."

In Klein's write-up of the event, Moynihan is quoted as saying:

God, I almost forgot. I'm here to say that I hope she will go all the way. I mean to go all the way with her. I think she's going to win. I think it's going to be wonderful for New York.

And in case that doesn't strike you as particularly strange, Klein helpfully offers his interpretation: "For Moynihan, apparently, it was easier to say 'she' than 'Hillary.'"

For Klein, apparently, it was easier to read the late senator's mind than to read the transcript—because here's how Moynihan actually introduced Hillary at the event:

> Now, I have the great pleasure to welcome Mrs. Clinton to the farm and turn over the microphone to our candidate.
>
> Before you do—before I do, and, my God, I almost forgot—yesterday, Hillary Clinton established an exploratory committee as regards candidacy for the Senate, United States Senate, from New York, a seat which I will vacate in a year and a half.
>
> I'm here to say that I hope she will go all the way. I mean to go all the way with her. I think she's going to win. I think it's going to be wonderful for New York, and we'll be proud of our senator and the nation will notice.

The next day, I wrote a piece for the Media Matters website debunking the claim. It wouldn't be the last time we had to correct Klein on something that only an incorrigible fabricator could have gotten wrong.

For example: Klein claimed that, after her 1999 embrace of the wife of Palestinian leader Yasser Arafat raised eyebrows (the reference itself an attempt to give new life to a manufactured, then six-year-old controversy), Hillary sought to "pander" to Jewish voters by "suddenly turn[ing] up a long-lost Jewish stepgrandfather"—except that the news about Hillary's Jewish ancestor had received extensive media coverage three months before the incident with Arafat.

It went on and on. The thing was just chock-full of falsehoods, and easily exposed ones, at that. At Media Matters, we published dozens of debunking research items. We also called on the publisher to withdraw the book. And we made sure that as Klein peddled the book, he was called to account for his hackery. At one point, Klein inexplicably agreed to appear on Air America Radio's *The Al Franken Show*, where the future senator, along with cohost Katherine Lanpher and liberal columnist Joe Conason, proceeded to tear the book apart, in one of the most excruciatingly awkward and hilarious radio segments you'll ever hear.

You would think that Klein, having been so thoroughly discredited in 2005, wouldn't have much of a market for more of his unsubstantiated Clinton scandalmongering a decade later. But you'd be underestimating not just the right's appetite for anything critical of the Clintons, but also the complete and total irrelevance of facts within the conservative media marketplace.

Conservatives bought Klein's book, *Blood Feud: The Clintons vs. the Obamas*, in droves. But the mainstream media, perhaps remembering our exhaustive debunking from a decade ago, ignored it. The book's far-fetched tales were pretty much confined to the gossip pages of Rupert Murdoch's trashy *New York Post*. You know you're in trouble if even Rush Limbaugh casts doubt on the accuracy of the quotes in your book. So while the right-wing nuts brought the book to the *New York Times* best-seller list, this time we stayed largely mum, so as not to give the book any unnecessary exposure to a regular readership.

We took pretty much the same approach with the other two anti-Clinton books, with the same results. *Clinton, Inc.*, written by a *Weekly Standard* editor, Daniel Halper, recycled old charges and repackaged them as a portrait of a ruthless and corrupt Clinton empire. We worked behind the scenes to debunk the book while depriving it of a public food fight that might have put Halper, a first-time, virtually unknown aspiring hack, on the map. When Bill O'Reilly canceled a planned interview, citing the book's heavy reliance on anonymous sources, we knew it would sink quickly.

The "Energizer" allegation came from a third book, *The First Family Detail: Secret Service Agents Reveal the Hidden Lives of Presidents*, written by former *Washington Post* reporter Ronald Kessler, who in addition to his mainstream credentials was at least at one time apparently well sourced in the intelligence community. But a little digging by Media Matters found that more recently Kessler had been a promoter of a series of wacky lost causes, ranging from Donald Trump's 2012 presidential campaign to the claim that Hillary had driven former White House lawyer Vince Foster to suicide. Kessler had even proven too scurrilous for the right-wing site *NewsMax*, which parted company with him.

A few days before Kessler's book hit the stores, the pages involving the "Energizer" story started circulating among Clinton beat reporters, who quickly concluded it was all just anonymous gossip. None of them touched it, and Kessler's book, too, disappeared.

～

At this point, you may be wondering: Who cares? Why not let conservatives have their fan fiction?

For the answer, let's go back to 1995, when a White House aide named Chris Lehane wrote a 332-page document that, for the first time, attempted to describe how "fantasy becomes fact" by charting the flow of information from the whisper campaigns of the far right all the way into the pages of the *New York Times* and onto the evening news. Lehane called it the "Communication Stream of Conspiracy Commerce," but it foreshadowed what Hillary Clinton meant when she described a "vast right-wing conspiracy."

Lehane described it this way:

First, well funded right wing think tanks and individuals underwrite conservative newsletters and newspapers such as the Western Journalism Center, the *American Spectator*, and the *Pittsburgh Tribune Review*.

Next, the stories are reprinted on the Internet where they are bounced all over the world.

From the Internet, the stories are bounced into the mainstream media through one of two ways: 1) The story will be picked up by the British tabloids and covered as a major story, from which the

American right-of-center mainstream media (i.e., the *Wall Street Journal*, *Washington Times*, and *New York Post*) will then pick the story up; or 2) The story will be bounced directly from the Internet to the right-of-center mainstream American media.

After the mainstream right-of-center American media covers the story, congressional committees will look into the story. After Congress looks into the story, the story now has the legitimacy to be covered by the remainder of the American mainstream press as a "real" story.

Take it from someone who was, at the time, skulking around Arkansas on Richard Mellon Scaife's dime, looking for dirt or rumors of dirt on the Clintons: Lehane was 100 percent correct. The stories I'd "report" in the *Spectator* (based on information I'd been passed by Republican operatives) would be planted in certain British papers where standards were lower. Then the item would ricochet back across the Atlantic to right-wing papers in New York and Washington. Then it would be amplified on talk radio. Pretty soon, Republicans would find a reason to raise "concerns" about the story, and mainstream outlets would have a reason to write about it.

I call it "scandal laundering": Just as the mob uses a series of front businesses like dry cleaners and olive oil importers to turn dirty money into clean money, Republican operatives use friendly right-wing outlets—from book publishers to bloggers—to push false allegations into the mainstream, and thus give them the patina of truth.

The original scandal launderer, of course, was Matt Drudge. Drudge was an insatiable gossip scavenger who cared about little but attention. He maintained close relations with Republican operatives who knew that they could send him half-baked opposition research and see it up on his site within the day—and that reporters at the outlets they really wanted to get into were clicking Refresh several times an hour, not wanting to be the last to a hot story. Tipped by the right, Drudge would also often report that a media outlet was planning to run a particular story (or, more frequently, that liberal bias was compelling it to sit on a story), forcing its airing before full vetting.

For the Clintons, this was a dangerous dynamic, one made worse by the fact that mainstream outlets, even those that actually were liberal in their editorial policies, were incentivized by the dynamic of scandal laundering to trash them. "Pro-Clinton" became an insult; reporters skewed to the right, fearful that conservatives would accuse them of being "in the tank." Those few journalists who refused to take the bait and resisted recycling the pseudoscandals were stigmatized as "Clinton defenders." And with so much organized conservative pressure to attack the Clintons—and such a large conservative audience eager to vote with their wallets for content that did so—all the mainstream media needed was an excuse. Drudge and his fellow scandal launderers provided that excuse by giving them a report to report on.

In the 1990s, of course, this was something of a ragtag operation. Puffing on my pipe and meeting with state troopers in shady Little Rock bars, I wasn't aware that I was pioneering what would become the dominant communications strategy of the Republican Party. But while the Arkansas Project may have begun on the fringes, the model worked—and it has been professionalized by today's conservative movement.

Opposition research has been mainstreamed, legitimized, and institutionalized. Young, enthusiastic operatives at the Republican National Committee—and at SuperPACs like America Rising—don't hand their scoops to friendly outlets in the shadowy back corners of parking lots; they trumpet them on Twitter.

The right has also pioneered a network of web magazines and blogs masquerading as news outlets that offer an important new media platform, one that progressives will never match. Sure, many left-leaning Americans choose to get their news from outlets, like *Talking Points Memo* or the *Huffington Post*, that share a progressive sensibility. But these websites actually practice journalism; they may pick up the phone when someone from, say, American Bridge calls to pitch something, but they ask tough questions and don't run stories unless they pass journalistic muster. (As in the book market, conservatives who are engaged online see it more as a form of political activism than information seeking.)

The new conservative sites I'm talking about—like the *Washington Free Beacon*, the *Daily Caller*, and the *Blaze*—exist to give right-wing propaganda a digital home—and rile up a new crowd of readers. They gleefully publish opposition research dumps that more credible outlets won't touch, often disguising them as original reporting. They provide something for Republican politicians and SuperPAC ads to cite. They create enough noise around false stories that the mainstream media feels obligated to follow up. And if the right wing's stories don't get the play they were hoping for, they complain that media bias is to blame—and then the media writes up the bias claim, slipping the faulty stories through the back door.

Today, faced with new online competitors, the *Drudge Report* has lost its edge, rarely breaking "news" anymore. But it remains a powerful news aggregator, incentivizing mainstream reporters to treat right-wing Orwellian "newspeak" as news. The *Drudge Report* was still the top referrer of traffic to mainstream outlets like the *New York Times*, CNN, and *Politico* in 2015. For the cottage industry of scandal laundering, the more things changed, the more they remained the same.

 

If anything, the right-wing media complex is much more powerful today than it was when Hillary Clinton described the "vast right-wing conspiracy" nearly twenty years ago—when Fox News was just gaining ratings traction and Rush Limbaugh was the only face of conservative talk radio. Now, Fox's Bill O'Reilly not only has the number-one-rated show across the cable dial but its nightly audience of 3 million viewers has become so dedicated over the years that it has direct political power, delivering tens of thousands of dollars to the website of a campaign or right-wing cause off even a short guest segment.

Right-wing radio has become a more sophisticated political machine, too. Eclipsing Limbaugh in influence through not in audience, syndicated talk show host Hugh Hewitt has become the GOP's "go-to pundit," according to the *National Journal*. You can listen to his show the old-fashioned way, stream it online, or get it through Hewitt's mobile app. Unlike his competitors, Hewitt, despite publishing a trashy anti-Hillary tome with the campy title *The Queen*, has made inroads with mainstream reporters who fall for his Harvard-educated, faux-cerebral on-air persona. As guests on his show, they give credence to the latest anti-Clinton conspiracies Hewitt is peddling, and thus taint themselves with anti-Clinton bias, whether they have one or not, simply by showing up and lending the credibility of their news organizations. In the first five months of 2015 alone, Chuck Todd, the host of NBC's prestigious *Meet the Press*, CNN's Jake Tapper, and Chris Cillizza of the *Washington Post* all appeared frequently on the show, a ten strike for the scandal launderers.

For the most part, however, the scandal-laundering action has moved online. Here are the prime actors:

- The *Daily Caller*: Run by Fox personality Tucker Carlson, the *Daily Caller* has become one of the most prominent, and often least scrupulous, scandal launderers around. Much of the funding for the site comes from Foster Friess, the Rick Santorum Super-PAC backer who famously said, "Back in my days, they used Bayer Aspirin for contraception. The gals put it between their knees." After the 2012 campaign, Friess decided to double down on fake journalism, and the *Caller* got even more cash. Much like Tucker Carlson himself, the *Caller*'s tone is smug and petty; they're one part tabloid, one part Internet troll—and one part right-wing smear factory.

- The *Washington Free Beacon*: Originally part of Bill Kristol's Center for American Freedom (which itself was intended to be the conservative answer to the Center for American Progress), the *Free Beacon* split off and became its own for-profit business with mysterious investors. The Beacon's editor in chief is Kristol's son-in-law, Matthew Continetti, but its guiding spirit is former Koch operative Michael Goldfarb, described by the *New York Times* as an "all-around anti-liberal provocateur" who delights in personal attacks against progressives. Their staff doesn't practice journalism—indeed, Media Matters discovered that they paid an oppo research firm to dig through the Clinton archives in Little Rock for dirt that they then passed off as real journalism.

- *Breitbart News*: In 2010, the late right-wing gonzo agitator Andrew Breitbart posted a video clip showing a USDA official and civil rights movement hero named Shirley Sherrod seemed to make racially charged remarks. The story bubbled up to Fox News, then into the mainstream press, and Sherrod was forced out—all before it was revealed that Breitbart had deceptively edited the video to frame her. Breitbart is deceased, but the site that still bears his name has continued his tradition of low standards. In November 2014, it alleged that President Obama's attorney general nominee, Loretta Lynch, had been part of the team defending President Clinton during the Whitewater scandal. I'll let their correction provide the punch line: "Correction: The Loretta Lynch identified earlier as the Whitewater attorney was, in fact, a different attorney."

- *RedState*: This blog's proprietor, Erick Erickson, a Fox News contributor and host of a daily Atlanta-based radio show, is on the leading edge of utilizing both old and new media platforms to pack a powerful punch. In fact, Erickson is "arguably the most powerful conservative in America today," according to the *Atlantic*. Erickson openly—and successfully—campaigns for Tea Party favorites running for office, and "his pronouncements can light up a congressman's switchboard," according to the *Cleveland Plain Dealer*, which also noted that Erickson was not known for his "sensitive tastes." Erickson questioned in a blog post whether President Obama was "shagging hookers" but decided he hadn't, because his "Marxist harpy" wife Michelle would "go Lorena Bobbitt on him should he even think about it," according to the paper.

In the media wars to come in 2016, look for even newer players using newer technologies to stir up trouble. One usual suspect is conservative rabble-rouser James O'Keefe. He specializes in running video "sting" operations designed to catch low-level employees at organizations like Planned Parenthood doing something made to look embarrassing on tape. O'Keefe tries to snooker the media by releasing only heavily edited—and totally misleading—portions of his videos, leaving the fact-checkers at Media Matters trying to beat the clock to publish the full context before a smear takes flight. Another is right-wing blogger Michelle Malkin, who originally founded Twitchy, a network that mobilizes outraged conservatives to harass real journalists on Twitter. Then there is Glenn Beck's online *Blaze* and the *Independent Journal Review*, one of the most highly trafficked websites in the world that you've probably never heard of. Finally, there is the America Rising SuperPAC, which uses a Tumblr account to further blur the distinction between oppo research and reporting.

It's all happening now at such warp speed that the opportunities for injecting misinformation into the bloodstream of the public conservation have dramatically increased since Drudge's heyday. Media Matters' watchdogs are constantly innovating with new techniques and technologies of our own to keep pace with the deluge. On some days we stop lies in their tracks; but in the flood of falsehoods, some lies inevitably seep through the cracks.

⌒

Soon after President Obama nominated Republican senator Chuck Hagel to be defense secretary, a story broke on *Breitbart*. It was written by Ben Shapiro, the website's editor at large and, as his byline notes, the author of the book *Bullies: How the Left's Culture of Fear and Intimidation Silences America* (published by Simon & Schuster's conservative imprint, Threshold Editions).

The first paragraph of the story:

> On Thursday, Senate sources told Breitbart News exclusively that they have been informed that one of the reasons that President Barack Obama's nominee for Secretary of Defense, Chuck Hagel, has not turned over requested documents on his sources of foreign funding is that one of the names listed is a group purportedly called "Friends of Hamas."

If the story was true—if the president's nominee to be defense secretary really had accepted money from a group called "Friends of Hamas"—then it was news, indeed. Shapiro made sure to create a sense of drama:

> Called for comment and reached via telephone, Associate Communications Director at the White House Eric Schultz identified himself, heard the question, was silent for several seconds, and then hung up the phone immediately without comment. Called back via the White House switchboard, Schultz's phone rang through to his answering machine. Called on his cell phone, Schultz's phone rang through to his answering machine.

That was the third and final paragraph. There was no evidence to support the claim that Hagel has been palling around with Hamas—if there was, the story would have been written in a real newspaper and Breitbart wouldn't have had its exclusive.

Writing in *Slate*, David Weigel tracked how the story "caught fire on the right in no time": from the conservative blog *RedState*, to the *National Review*, to Hugh Hewitt's radio talk show, and beyond. It was picked up by Fox News and appeared in the *Washington Times*.

Mike Huckabee, at the time a Fox News host, speaking in Israel, said that "rumors of Chuck Hagel's having received funds from Friends of Hamas" could "disqualify him." Jennifer Rubin, the shrill conservative blogger for the *Washington Post*, jumped on it with both feet, tweeting (with the hashtag #extreme) that Hagel had once spoken to a group that defended reporter Helen Thomas after she made a controversial comment about Israel (a real bank shot, even by conservative standards). And when Republican senator Rand Paul began making noises about it, Friends of Hamas was thrown into the media mosh pit—and became a potential endgame to Hagel's confirmation.

Weigel did note one little hiccup in the rush to condemn Hagel's ties to Friends of Hamas: there was no such organization as "Friends of Hamas." "Hint No. 1," Alex Pareene quipped in *Salon*, "should probably have been that a pro-Hamas front group *would not call itself 'Friends of Hamas'*" (emphasis in the original).

It eventually emerged that a reporter from the New York *Daily News*, fishing for leads on any controversial groups Hagel may have spoken to, jokingly asked a Republican Senate staffer if Hagel had received a speaking fee from "Friends of Hamas" (or the "Junior League of Hezbollah," which was funnier). By the next day, whether intentionally or unwittingly, the GOP aide was treating the joke as a real scoop, and the entire right-wing food chain was eager to gobble it up.

For his part, Shapiro didn't even pretend to have learned anything from the fiasco. "The story Breitbart News ran originally was accurate and clearly caveated," he wrote. Shapiro also accused the *Daily News* reporter of lying about being the inadvertent source, scoffing, "Welcome to the Obama media, where protecting Chuck Hagel and attacking any media who question Hagel is par for the course."

⌒

A week before the 2012 election, the *Daily Caller* ran a story by its "Investigative Reporter," Matt Boyle, making a similarly incendiary claim:

Two women from the Dominican Republic told The Daily Caller that Democratic New Jersey Sen. Bob Menendez paid them for sex earlier this year.

In interviews, the two women said they met Menendez around Easter at Casa de Campo, an expensive 7,000-acre resort in the Dominican Republic. They claimed Menendez agreed to pay them $500 for sex acts, but in the end they each received only $100.

Five years earlier, when Republican senator David Vitter was accused of visiting prostitutes, *Daily Caller* editor in chief Tucker Carlson venemently defended him, scolding the media for potentially destroying a public figure by digging into his private life.

Now, however, the *Daily Caller* was out in front on a big story that might end Menendez's career, and help give the outlet new credibility in Washington.

As it turned out, Republican operatives had also pitched the story to outlets ranging from ABC News (which also interviewed the women making the claim) to the *Star-Ledger* in New Jersey and even the *New York Post*. None found it credible enough to write. But based on a brief Skype interview with the women, the *Daily Caller* ran the story— which was quickly picked up by Fox News and the rest of the right-wing media, giving national Republicans an excuse to talk about the allegations.

And once that happened, the mainstream media followed up. Stories about whether or not Menendez had patronized prostitutes appeared in major publications across the country. But real reporters soon found that the women's claim simply wasn't credible. The *Washington Post* reported:

A top Dominican law enforcement official said Friday that a local lawyer has reported being paid by someone claiming to work for the conservative Web site the Daily Caller to find prostitutes who would lie and say they had sex for money with Sen. Robert Menendez (D-N.J.).

The lawyer told Dominican investigators that a foreign man, who identified himself as "Carlos," had offered him $5,000 to find and pay women in the Caribbean nation willing to make the claims about Menendez, according to Jose Antonio Polanco, district attorney for the La Romana region, where the investigation is being conducted.

In a Fox News media blitz that included at least twenty different segments, Tucker Carlson asserted on *The O'Reilly Factor* that the *Caller*'s sources have "received no money from anyone." Once the story fell apart, however, Fox went silent—and while Carlson kept being invited back on the air, he was never asked about his website's embarrassing failure. There was no price to be paid for faking it.

⌒

In early June, the Republican oppo group America Rising tweeted out a seven-second video from the campaign trail, hyped as showing Hillary telling a supporter who asked her to sign something to "go to the end of the line." The clip was meant to portray a cold and imperious Hillary blowing off a voter. It soon popped up on the *Drudge Report* with America Rising's framing. When I saw that I had two thoughts: There's probably something off about the video, and Hillary's in for a drubbing nevertheless.

Predictably, the video ricocheted through the right-wing online world, where a narrative was gelling and our researchers were capturing and noting every instance:

- The *Weekly Standard* promoted the video of Hillary Clinton telling a supporter to "go to the end of the line" outside a campaign event in New Hampshire.
- Moments later, Twitchy picked up the video, referring to Clinton as "Queen Hillary" and linking to several disparaging tweets.

- The *Daily Caller* also deemed Clinton "Queen Hillary," suggesting the video was evidence that Clinton wanted to be "coronat[ed]" rather than elected in 2016:

  "Most peasants are happy just to feel the breeze of Hillary Clinton's passage through their meager, insignificant lives. But every once in a while, a serf forgets his or her place. Every once in a while, Her Majesty must put the rabble back where they belong....

  "Honestly. Why is she being forced to put up with this sort of impertinence? Can't we just coronate her already?"

- The Western Journalism Center suggested that the seconds-long video of the interaction between Hillary Clinton and a supporter "could have long-lasting implications for a presidential campaign already suffocating at the bottom of a growing pile of scandals."

- The British tabloid *Daily Mail* pointed to Clinton's "blunt tone" while promoting the video in an article titled "Condescending Hillary Clinton tells autograph-seeker to 'go to the back [sic] of the line.'" The article also noted that some Twitter users were mocking Clinton's "royal-like demeanor, calling her Queen Hillary."

And Fox News followed suit:

- On Fox News' *Hannity*, conservative columnist Ann Coulter used the short clip of Clinton's interaction with a supporter in New Hampshire as evidence that Democrats "are waiting for old, white people to die off" so they can advance "the browning of America."

- On *Fox and Friends*, cohost Kimberly Guilfoyle pointed to the video as further proof that Clinton "is not known to be very friendly, or, you know, warm, or engaging" in person. Cohost Steve Doocy also claimed that the interaction was "a great moment in retail politicking" that would have created a "media freak out" if a Republican candidate such as Governor Scott Walker had said it.

- Later, on the same edition of *Fox and Friends*, Doocy claimed that Clinton is simply "not a good politician," pointing to America Rising's video as "exhibit A." Conservative radio host Laura Ingraham agreed, adding that Clinton would never send "influence peddlers in foreign countries, and big corporations... [to] the back of the line" the way she apparently did in the video.

- On *America's Newsroom*, cohost Martha MacCallum noted that the video "will get played over and over" throughout the 2016 campaign and is "not good for Hillary Clinton, regardless of what the circumstances exactly were."

But then the story took an unusual twist. It turned out America Rising released only 7 *seconds* of a 17-*minute* video. Guy Benson, an enterprising conservative blogger at the news aggregator site *Townhall*, explained after personally examining "the full 17-minute video" that there was "nothing out of the ordinary" about the scandalized interaction. According to his review, "the added context casts the awkward exchange in a far less damaging light" and "the short sound-byte contained in the tweet above isn't representative of her attitude or actions":

When I wondered about context on Twitter, one of the organization's representatives was kind enough to email me the full 17-minute video, which I've since examined. As I suspected, the added context casts the awkward exchange in a far less damaging light. Hillary emerges from the building and slowly makes her way down the line of well-wishers, taking photographs, shaking hands, and making small talk. She's not a natural politician, and many of the interactions feel stilted and perfunctory, but it's nothing out of the ordinary. When people start asking her to sign items (books, photographs, even baseballs), Hillary seems to make a snap decision that she'll accommodate their requests, but not until she's made it all the way through the crowd. Hence, the "end of the line" request.

Sure enough, the last four-or-so minutes of the complete video features Hillary Clinton dutifully autographing paraphernalia for all comers, asking questions like, "want me to make it out to you?" Mrs. Clinton appears ill at ease and not especially eager to stick around throughout much of this extended rope line-style interaction, but the short sound-byte contained in the tweet above isn't representative of her attitude or actions. She's slightly uncomfortable and less than enthusiastic; she isn't hostile or rude.

Media Matters flagged the *Townhall* post and raced to get it into the hands of legitimate news outlets, where the story died.

Opposition research works only when reporters can reliably cite it without fear of getting burned. In this case, America Rising deceptively edited a seventeen-minute video to seven seconds, and then used Twitter to hoodwink the media. It was a black eye for the group, though it remained to be seen whether the media it relies on to distribute its content would wise up and stop reflexively pushing the group's agitprop. There was some grounds for hope: Fox's Greg Gutfeld, not normally known for his journalistic scruples, announced to America Rising: "We no longer trust you!" Well, we'll see.

$\sim$

In the end, Chuck Hagel was confirmed, Bob Menendez was reelected (he was later indicted on unrelated corruption charges), Hillary Clinton remained the Democrats' front-runner, and none of these fables took down their intended targets.

But we at Media Matters learned a valuable lesson about the way the new right-wing food chain works. These examples illustrate how manufactured, planted, and outright false allegations can move swiftly and seamlessly from the fringes of the conservative media to the front pages of real newspapers unless they're caught in time—and how Republican politicians, opposition researchers, and conservative journalists work in cahoots to make it happen.

If spending eight hours watching Fox News sounds like a tough job, imagine spending eight hours scrolling through Michelle Malkin's Twitter feed or watching James O'Keefe in a ridiculous costume trying to convince some poor intern to say something politically inopportune. In this new media environment, when the right can count on a network of semiprofessional and totally in-the-tank outlets to help legitimize smear campaigns, nipping these things in the bud has never been more difficult—or more important.

Whether it was Fox News contributor Katie Pavlich taking to Twitter during the Benghazi hearings to impugn the State Department's impartial investigation of the matter; Republican pundit Ric Grenell tweeting "Remember: Hillary wants you to empathize with these people" during a terrorist attack in Paris; or the *National Review*'s Kevin D. Williamson tweeting a picture of a Chinese Communist Party meeting with the hash tag #ReadyforHillary, tracking—much less rebutting in real time—the flood of digital right-wing propaganda was no small feat.

And while the proliferation of new media outlets has made it harder for a story to rise to the top of the pile and gain a critical mass of attention, right-wing activists have many more online avenues to get their misinformation in front of voters—from *Politico* to *BuzzFeed* and beyond, there are many, many more legitimate reporters now monitoring these outlets in the hopes of finding a new lead to dig into. The rise of Twitter has only made a clubby media scene clubbier, as operatives, journalists, and those who are a little of each interact freely.

Today, understanding the pervasive reach of the right-wing means understanding the rhythms of social media. CNN's Jake Tapper, NBC's Chuck Todd, and Fox's Ed Henry—and many others of similar influence and reach in mainstream media—obsess over Twitter. They get information from it, they get ideas for stories from it. They focus on how people are reacting to the things they say—which of course influences how they cover future stories.

The reason this phenomenon matters is that it exposes a vulnerability. These major media influencers are susceptible to manipulation by political forces that are able to game them. A smart operative can create an online controversy, which can very well seem to justify covering a topic that would never get noticed or pass editorial muster otherwise. In this way, the massive right-wing noise machine online can expose illegitimate material to a broad audience of news consumers.

And their techniques for exercising this influence are constantly advancing. One aspect of the new media landscape is known as leap-frogging, which basically disrupts the older notion—first laid out by Chris Lehane back in 1995—of the media food chain. Previously, you'd need a right-wing outlet to cover something, and then it slowly worked its way up the chain before it became a big story. It just wasn't possible for information to really enter the zeitgeist unless it went through this food chain. This is partly why Media Matters' war on Fox was so important—for a period of time, Fox News was a key gatekeeper. They were a critical point in the chain, often making or breaking stories.

Leapfrogging changes all that. Leapfrogging is when a piece of information—or misinformation—spreads so far and wide through social media channels online that it doesn't matter whether news outlets cover it, because it's already spread and been ingested by the body politic. It's like one of those e-mail chains someone's wacky relative would send in the days of old, except on steroids and with more perceived legitimacy. Sure, established media outlets can ignore a lot of these viral stories, but in reality, the traffic potential is just too good to pass up, so oftentimes they pile on.

In this kind of media environment, the scandal launderers are free to launch as much, and as egregious, misinformation as they want. They rarely pay a price. They rarely lose their credibility with the mainstream press. They can pull the football away time and time and time again, and Charlie Brown will still come running, hoping that, this time, he'll get to kick it.

Meanwhile, even as it's gotten easier to introduce misinformation into the public discourse, it's gotten hard to ferret it out. This is due to a phenomenon known as a "filter bubble."

The news and information that people are served when they surf around online is, more and more, being determined by sophisticated algorithms designed to show you stuff you're likely to be interested in. So, if you're a right-winger, you're more likely to see more right-wing news. But if you're a media watchdog, it can be hard to identify the spread of misinformation—and much harder to ever reach these misled audiences with the truth. The more time people spend inside these ideological bubbles, the harder it is for fact-checkers to do their jobs—and the easier it is for extremism to fester.

By the spring of 2015, with the Clinton campaign officially under way, scandal laundering moved front and center in the Republican playbook, and the GOP thought it finally hit pay dirt with a book called *Clinton Cash* by GOP operative Peter Schweizer. I wish I could say that book was dead on arrival, but the catnip in it—which claimed that Hillary Clinton made decisions about U.S. security policy as secretary of state to curry favor with donors to the Clinton Foundation—proved irresistible to the entire political press corps.

I'll have much more to say about this in a later chapter. While we couldn't stem the tide of media interest, our fact-checkers manned the barricades and affected coverage, publicizing Schweizer's partisan background and history of botched reporting—and spoiling the book's launch.

We were ready for such right-wing attacks, because we'd been busy getting ready for Hillary ever since she left her State Department post back in 2013. Our organized pro-Hillary effort was unprecedented, fitting for what we hoped would be an unprecedented candidacy.

## Chapter Five

# Getting Ready for Hillary

Washington, DC, is a ghost town in the last month of even-numbered years, as losers clear out their offices, winners measure the drapes, staffers circulate résumés, and everyone tries to squeeze in a vacation before the next cycle begins in earnest. And I was away for the Christmas holidays when word came that Hillary Clinton was in the hospital.

~

In stark contrast to her 2008 campaign, when Hillary served as secretary of state, she enjoyed mostly fair and accurate press coverage. Playing a nonpolitical role, Hillary also got a respite from right-wing attacks.

But as she prepared to leave office, that all changed. In mid-December 2012, Hillary, who had been suffering from a stomach virus, fainted at home and ended up hospitalized with a concussion and a blood clot. The good news was that she was fine. The bad news was that conservatives were already using this health scare to spin a wild web of conspiracy theories.

Hillary's condition led her to cancel an appearance before the Senate Foreign Relations Committee, where she was scheduled to answer questions about the Benghazi tragedy. And the right began to question whether she was really sick at all, or whether they had finally found the missing piece they needed to turn Benghazi into a real scandal.

"I'm not suggesting she didn't get a concussion," said Megyn Kelly on Fox News less than forty-eight hours after Hillary was hospitalized. "But there is a legitimate question about, is—do we believe this is an excuse and that she really will show up to testify?" Her guest, Monica Crowley, a former aide to the disgraced Richard Nixon, responded by describing Hillary's illness as "this virus with apparently impeccable timing." And the race was on.

Over the next three days, nearly every program on Fox featured speculation about whether Hillary was faking it. Former U.N. ambassador John Bolton suggested that Hillary was suffering from "a diplomatic illness" that, he said, often afflicted those who "don't want to go to a meeting or a conference or event." Syndicated columnist Charles Krauthammer diagnosed Hillary as "suffering from acute Benghazi allergy which causes lightheadedness when she hears the word 'Benghazi.'"

The conspiracy theory spilled into the print press, with the *New York Post* running the headline HILLARY CLINTON'S HEAD FAKE and even the *Los Angeles Times* polling its readers on the question: "Did she fake it?"

Predictably, this malicious fantasy quickly fizzled. Hillary's doctors released a statement explaining that, no, Hillary was not faking her concussion—in fact, the blood clot that resulted from her injury was serious enough to require treatment to prevent lasting damage (which would later give rise to the opposite, if equally false, conspiracy theory that Hillary was, in fact, far sicker than she let on). And a month later, after she recovered, Hillary did, in fact, appear before two congressional committees to talk about Benghazi, appearances that proved she wasn't shrinking from a confrontation with the Republicans to dispel their conspiracy theories. To the contrary, even Brit Hume said on Fox that Hillary hit the ball out of the park with her testimony.

"Bengazhi flu" would go on to become a forgotten tributary of the mighty river of right-wing misinformation on Benghazi. But I was worried—first about Hillary's medical condition, and then, when it became clear that she would be okay, about what the episode meant for her political future.

Ironically, this early unhinged right-wing attack on Hillary helped catalyze an unprecedented effort by her Democratic supporters—me included—to build an early surrogate campaign apparatus around her potential candidacy.

With Hillary hard at work at the State Department, her political operation was in a state of suspended animation. But it was no secret that Hillary's political career was only sleeping, not dead. Many of us who had supported her in 2008 expected that once she left the State Department, she'd begin considering a second run for the White House in 2016. And, obviously, so were many on the right who had been savaging her for decades.

Benghazi, it seemed, would be their cudgel—and while there was no evidence that Hillary had anything to fear in a clear and fair examination of the facts, there was no reason to expect that a clear and fair examination was what the right had in mind.

Having failed to damage President Obama by inventing charges of negligence or mendacity, they were turning their sights to the 2016 election and hoping to pin the tail on the likely Democratic nominee.

No one should have been surprised that the Republicans would try to swift-boat Hillary in 2016, turning an accomplished diplomat into a feckless bungler who lied to cover up her own failures.

But the beginnings of the Benghazi hoax didn't remind me of the Swift Boat days as much as they did the Whitewater hoax from back in the 1990s. Republicans would never be able to point to actual evidence of wrongdoing on Hillary's part (and, despite myriad investigations, they haven't). But they wouldn't need to if they could create the appearance of scandal by confusing the public about what actually happened before, during, and after the attack.

Their strategy wouldn't be about proving a case. It would be about throwing up enough gorilla dust to frustrate the public and make people doubt they were getting the truth from the government. It would be death by a million questions, with the goal of fostering an impression of a politically motivated cover-up on the part of the Obama administration and Hillary herself.

They would use the same machinery they had used in the 1990s—only now it was better oiled. There would be countless congressional investigations that, even though they never seemed to turn up any incriminating evidence (or any new information whatsoever), kept the issue in the headlines. Republican investigators would strategically leak to sympathetic media outlets in order to create a sense of momentum. Right-wing lawyers would sign up "whistleblowers" and lie to the press about their testimony. Hillary and her aides would be drowned in a sea of depositions and document requests.

And whether or not the Republicans managed to make *Benghazi* a household word, I knew that a substantial element within the Republican base would respond to these conspiracy theories—and that whipping these activists up into a frenzy could be a formidable organizing tool in and of itself. I doubt that many of the prominent Republicans who dabbled in birtherism during the early years of the Obama administration really suspected that the president was born in Kenya; they simply basked in the attention they got from the right-wing base by giving voice to their fears.

Yes, this looked like it would be Whitewater all over again—and while, in the 1990s, the Clintons had been able to rely on the White House communications and research operation to help fight back, this time, Hillary was on her own. There was no Clinton campaign—indeed, there was no Clinton fact-checking operation at all. My political Spidey sense was tingling again.

I put Media Matters on the case right away, but hewing to our mission, all we could do was repel misinformation in the press—a useful and important role, to be sure, but the right's effort to blame Benghazi on Hillary was a full-scale political campaign, and it required a full-scale political response.

We needed to be able to go directly after the lies told by showboating Republican politicians looking for their fifteen minutes of fame (or, at the very least, for a couple of minutes on a Fox News show that might result in a bump in donations to their websites). We needed the research that could discredit them as finders of fact. We needed to contact the Democratic members of the committee, find out who the Republicans were planning to put up as witnesses, and assess the credibility of those witnesses.

In other words, we needed yet another war room: a round-the-clock political rapid response and intelligence-gathering operation of a kind that Hillary herself simply couldn't build until she had a real campaign around her. And if we waited for that to happen, it would be too late—Hillary could be damaged by the smear campaign before she was ready to fight it.

The hearings that took place that spring only deepened my concern. Hillary's State Department aides were roasted over the coals under the presumption that the only reason significant wrongdoing had yet to be proven was that they had covered it up. And Hillary herself faced a barrage of hostile questioning from Republican senators intent on catching her in a contradiction about any number of minute details—and thus proving that she was hiding something.

At that, they failed. But they eventually scored the gotcha moment they were looking for.

"With all due respect," Hillary said in response to one particularly redundant line of cross-examination about the State Department's early assessment of the motive behind the Benghazi attack, "the fact is we had four dead Americans. Was it because of a protest or was it because of guys out for a walk one night who decided they'd go kill some Americans? What difference, at this point, does it make?"

Ripped from any context, Hillary's rejoinder to committee Republicans trying to score cheap political points was replayed ad nauseum in the right-wing media—as proof of her supposedly callous attitude toward the victims of the attack. Hillary's actual point—that the debate about Benghazi should be forward looking—was edited out in the right-wing videos. As part of the exchange, Hillary also had said, "It is our job to figure out what happened and do everything we can to prevent it from ever happening again."

But that didn't stop Republicans from grossly misrepresenting Hillary's words. On ABC's *This Week*, John McCain even changed what Hillary had actually said to: "Who Cares? Remember when she said, 'Well, who cares how this happened' in a rather emotional way?" It was a neat hat trick, suggesting at once that Hillary was both unemotional and overly emotional.

In short, Benghazi was becoming a problem. Hillary was essentially defenseless against an onslaught of utterly false charges—charges that were beginning to draw blood.

⌒

When Hillary left the State Department in early 2013, she occupied an odd position as a presumed (some tossed around the word *inevitable*) nominee of her party for the presidency who held no office and employed no political staffers.

Meanwhile, no fewer than eight new SuperPACs had emerged on the Republican side with the explicit mission of tarnishing Hillary's reputation and distorting her record before the campaign even got started. Conservatives knew what we knew—that Hillary was the most formidable general-election candidate Democrats could field—and they hoped that attacking her early and often, even if they had to recycle or invent charges, would render voters skeptical about her candidacy, or at least weary of hearing her name. Or perhaps the strain of the scrutiny would wear Hillary herself out, remind her of the brutality of a presidential campaign, and cause her not to run at all.

It was a GOP strategy of preemptive disqualification—and an array of new groups soon emerged to aggressively pursue it.

Foremost among the new groups was America Rising, run by Mitt Romney's former campaign manager Matt Rhoades, who was outmaneuvered in that race by Democratic researchers, despite the fact that he was "seen as a pipeline" to Matt Drudge, according to news reports. Now, Rhoades seemed ready to get some revenge. "I am convinced," Romney himself said of the new effort, "that [Rhoades] will erase the disadvantage GOP candidates have had. And if I were a Democrat candidate, I'd sleep less soundly knowing that Matt is watching everything they have and will say and do." With Rhoades at the helm, Rising enjoyed support from the Republican Party establishment and its donors and set its sights on Hillary Clinton in particular (one early headline: HILLARY, FLANKED BY SECURITY AND ASSISTANTS, HAS PRIVATE SHOPPING SPREE AT BERGDORF GOODMAN).

But Rising wasn't alone. Just as a Hillary candidacy would be a stimulus package for journalists, there were plenty of conservative hucksters eager to make a buck off of the far right's loathing of the Clintons. There was Dick Morris (whose picture you might find when you look up "conservative huckster" in the dictionary) and his Just Say No to Hillary PAC.

There was the Stop Hillary PAC, which claimed to have a database of six hundred thousand activists who aimed to ensure that "Hillary Clinton never becomes president." They promised to target Hillary on "everything from Whitewater to Benghazi." It was chaired by a state legislator from Colorado, Ted Harvey, who once sponsored a bill to allow teachers to carry guns in school. Harvey's Twitter bio indentified him as "a conservative fool for Christ." The group's spokesman was quoted as saying, "If we could dissuade [Hillary] from running for office in the first place, then we'll consider our effort a success."

The Hillary Project was devoted to "wage a war on Hillary Clinton's image." It appeared to traffic largely in online video games that let players "slap" Hillary and childishly insulting Internet memes (like a picture of Hillary with the caption—"Favorite Movie: *Kill Bill*"—get it?).

The list went on and on. There was Women Against Hillary PAC.

Veterans Against Hillary PAC. And the Special Operations OPSEC Education Fund—a group of former special forces and intelligence operatives attacking Hillary on Benghazi.

And, of course, longtime Clinton antagonist David Bossie was still lurking in the shadows. Back in 1992, he had worked for the organization that promoted the original anti-Clinton book, *Slick Willie*, and went on to become an investigator for House Republicans looking into Whitewater, a position from which he was fired after getting caught leaking doctored recordings of Hillary's phone conversations with a former law firm colleague to falsely implicate her in a cover-up. Bossie's 2008 *Hillary: The Movie* described her as "a congenital liar," "not qualified," and "the closest thing we have to a European socialist." The movie featured a woman who claimed the Clintons had her cat assassinated.

Naturally, Bossie was planning a sequel for 2016.

By June 2013, Democratic operatives in Washington were starting to explore what an independent SuperPAC structure around a potential Hillary candidacy should look like. Buoyed by the 2012 election, the first in which Democrats had fielded a fleet of SuperPACs that clearly impacted the race, Democrats had come a ways since their early allergy to such outside groups. Hillary seemed open to their value. And I was eager to get involved.

First out of the gate was a grassroots organizing effort called Ready for Hillary—the brainchild of a young former Clinton staffer, Adam Parkhomenko, and a college professor, Allida Black. The idea was to marshal enthusiasm for a campaign by building an e-mail list, developing a small-donor network, and engaging in social media and other political outreach—in other words, doing the basic blocking and tackling that the Obama campaign had done so well.

In the early going, Ready for Hillary attracted its share of skeptics, both inside and outside the Clinton orbit. Some believed it was happening too early and could confer on Hillary an aura of inevitability that had not served her well in 2008. Others questioned the groups' strategy and its leadership. Longtime Clinton political advisor Craig Smith was soon brought on board to ensure that the PAC was in seasoned hands. Smith could see the value in having the energy around Hillary's prospective candidacy corralled under one roof; our side wouldn't have a dozen Dick Morrises running around operating fly-by-night groups—all claiming to be the One True Hillary Super PAC.

In the end, Ready for Hillary won wide praise for giving the candidate an important leg up in low-dollar fund-raising and signing up enthusiastic volunteers. The group built an e-mail list that dwarfed the size of the one Hillary had at the end of the 2008 primary—and it raised millions of dollars, with 98 percent of contributions coming in at $100 or less, the foundation of a valuable low-dollar donor base that was transferred to the campaign.

Meanwhile, Obama's 2012 SuperPAC, Priorities USA, backed by Hollywood mogul Jeffrey Katzenberg—who, in 2007, had become an early Obama supporter in the primary—was set to reorient itself around Hillary. The board was reshuffled, with the former Michigan governor and longtime Clinton ally Jennifer Granholm and Obama reelection campaign manager Jim Messina signing up as cochairs. Along with several other Clinton allies, I was named to the board, as well. The SuperPAC planned to raise several hundred million to back Hillary in the Democratic primary and take on her Republican opponent on TV in the general.

A part of progressive politics I've never quite gotten used to is the intense competition for money and credit—two things around which Priorities and Ready for Hillary soon clashed. By contrast, I had grown up in a culture on the conservative side where this dynamic was far less prevalent, simply because there was a lot more money—and therefore credit—to go around.

Ultimately peace was reached between the two, though some of the tactics the Messina group in Priorities used to try to bully Ready for

Hillary into folding foretold a very public skirmish I would later have with the same players over—you guessed it—money and credit. But that came much later.

One point of consensus in the "peace talks" between the two groups was that there was a missing piece in the pro-Hillary structure being put into place: Everyone involved in the early planning saw a need for a research and communications shop that would operate on Hillary's behalf until she had her campaign up and running. I'd been thinking along those same lines since the Benghazi "flu" outbreak at Christmas, so I dashed off a memo sketching out what such an effort would entail and made it known to the two groups that I was up for the challenge. I wasn't a moment too soon. The very next day, America Rising launched a "Stop Hillary 2016" push.

That July, I hired four veterans from Hillary's 2008 campaign and launched an effort we called Correct the Record. Although I forecast that the team would include a dozen or so staff, the volume and intensity of the attacks on Hillary were such that we soon had twice as many people devoted to this one project.

As with Media Matters and American Bridge, it didn't take long for Correct the Record to be pressed into service. The *Washington Free Beacon* had hired a Republican opposition research firm to rummage through the Clinton archives in Arkansas in search of anything that could be spun up into a scandal. Among other weak leads, they found tapes from the 1980s of Hillary discussing her legal defense of an accused child rapist in the 1970s.

The scandal launderers went to work, attacking Hillary for "choosing" to take such an unsavory client and arguing that she was "soft" on rape and gender issues because she had done what, as a lawyer, was simply her job: mounting an effective defense.

Correct the Record moved quickly to thwart the attack in a variety of outlets ranging from *Talking Points Memo* to CNN. But we didn't just speak in Hillary's defense—we went out and investigated the claims ourselves. We found the original prosecutor in the case, who still lived in northwest Arkansas and confirmed to us that Hillary didn't "choose" to defend the accused rapist; she had been appointed to the case by a judge over her objection. At our suggestion, he spoke with reporters to clarify how that process worked.

And while we were at it, we proved a link between Hillary's experience in that case and her instrumental role in founding Arkansas's first rape hotline. We published talking points online to arm Hillary's defenders with hard facts to show that the story was based on false claims.

Meanwhile, the University of Arkansas suspended the *Free Beacon* from continuing to access their materials; as documents from the library proved, the website had violated rules in publishing the tapes. It was through examining these documents that we were able to discover that the *Free Beacon* hadn't done its own legwork, farming out the job instead to hired guns from a GOP oppo shop. This revelation completed the circle: instead of landing a devastating blow against Hillary, the *Free Beacon* succeeded in embarrassing only itself.

Without an early, aggressive, and comprehensive response, this story—based on nothing—could have become part of a larger, more damaging narrative. We could have seen it pop up as a subject for discussion on Sunday shows, as Republican politicians tired of being called out for their association with the likes of Todd Akin and Richard Mourdock attempted to turn this into "Hillary's War on Women." It could have been featured in SuperPAC ads against her ("The *Washington Free Beacon* has reported that . . ."). But not with Correct the Record now on the case.

For eighteen months before Hillary declared her candidacy for president, Correct the Record staffers got up every morning and went to work, dispelling the falsehoods and negativity surrounding her potential candidacy.

By its nature, the project's work was partly defensive. With all the incoming attacks, defense was a vital part our mission, one that is still too often underappreciated by Democrats who think, "If we're playing defense, we're losing." What they don't understand is that without an aggressive defense, you'll never even get out of the gate.

But defense was only part of our approach. I learned long ago through my years as a right-wing warrior that the best response to an ambush is to attack. So I was always deliberate in constructing war rooms to build in offensive capacities as well.

Correct the Record went on to do more than five hundred on-the-record interviews with the media as we established ourselves as the go-to place for facts about Hillary's record. But we also attacked the attackers—going up against everybody from Rand Paul, to the Republican National Committee, to—yes—Dick Morris. We placed more than one hundred op-eds from a wide range of experts and leaders highlighting Hillary's accomplishments—while knocking down the lies that she was a "do-nothing" secretary of state or that she was a late convert to progressive priorities like addressing the gap in income equality. And we trained more than one hundred Hillary surrogates to go out and spread the truth—everywhere from national TV shows to local union halls.

During this critical precampaign period, we were pretty much all Hillary had to fend off the bad guys.

                                         ⌐

With the founding of Correct the Record, three organizations became part of what the media would call Hillary's "shadow campaign." With Priorities USA raising money to spend on paid advertising, Ready for Hillary building grassroots enthusiasm on- and off-line, and Correct the Record serving as a sort of ad hoc comm shop, we had built an unprecedented coordinated effort on behalf of a candidate who was perhaps two years away from formally declaring her candidacy—that is, if she decided to run. (I was once asked in an editorial meeting at ABC News what would happen if Hillary decided not to make the race, after all. "Well, then I was wrong," I joked.)

Once again, part of the story was that we were harnessing the dubious *Citizens United* decision to our advantage—but a bigger part of the story was that we were identifying and seizing on opportunities to gain strategic advantage in an era when we knew that, at the end of the day, we would be on the short end of the money stick. As Bill Clinton had always said, we didn't need to raise more than the other guys—we just needed to raise enough, and be smarter in how we used it. We now had a structure to raise enough money, and a multipronged apparatus that represented a truly new approach to preparing for a presidential campaign.

For my part, and I think this went for a lot of my fellow organizers who had been committed to Hillary in 2008, we were extramotivated by the knowledge that we'd been granted a second chance to help elect her, and by a desire not to squander that second chance. This time, we would get it right. This time, things would be different.

## Chapter Six

# How to Beat Hillary Clinton

After six years of single-minded focus, conservatives thought they had succeeded in destroying Barack Obama. As the 2014 election approached, his approval ratings were in the basement, and in November, dozens of Democrats met their electoral doom simply because they were tied to the president's agenda.

Thus, as they looked ahead to 2016, the right wished to believe that retaking the White House could be as simple as taking their 2014 attack ads and swapping out those head shots of Mark Pryor and Kay Hagan and Mark Udall and other losing candidates in exchange for pictures of Hillary Clinton; she, too, could be tied to the unpopular incumbent and dragged to the bottom of the sea.

"Hillary Clinton has a Barack Obama problem," read a missive from America Rising that hit reporters' inboxes in the summer of 2014. "No matter how many of her advisors whisper to reporters that she's different from Barack Obama, Americans still know who she is: Barack Obama Part Deux."

Republican politicians fell all over themselves agreeing. "She was part of his administration," Rand Paul told Fox News the week after the midterm election, "and I really don't know of many, if any, policies they disagree on."

Meanwhile, fellow presidential hopeful Bobby Jindal, making the conservative policy rounds in Washington, "painted a gloomy portrait of America's domestic and global standing in the Obama era, and in a nod to the upcoming race for the White House, he made sure to link Hillary Clinton to the policies of the president she served as secretary of state," according to the *Atlantic*.

"Hillary Clinton is very beatable," speculated Paul Ryan, "because a Hillary Clinton presidency is basically the same thing as an Obama third term. I don't think she'll be able to shake that."

"Hillary Clinton and Barack Obama," Mitt Romney told Fox News, "are two peas in the same pod."

As attempts at branding your Democratic opponent go, "Obama's third term" was an understandable choice. Conservatives who have spent Obama's entire presidency attacking him would love nothing better than for his perceived flaws to doom his potential successor; there might have been a certain satisfaction to be had from the idea that, like George W. Bush, Obama was such a failure that future nominees would still suffer from the damage he had done to his party's brand.

But this line of attack looked doubtful as we headed into 2016.

For one thing, President Obama's approval ratings had rebounded, rising back above 50 percent in early 2015. Presidents are generally regarded more favorably as their administrations fade into the rearview mirror; moreover, economic indicators continue to suggest that the mood of the country overall is likely to improve between now and Election Day. For all the chaos and controversy of his term, history is likely to judge President Obama kindly; he will leave the country in inarguably better shape than he found it.

For another, as Hillary begins to actually campaign for the presidency, she will outline her own policy priorities, making it more difficult for Republicans to simply project their least favorite Obama policies onto a blank slate and slap Hillary's name on it. She'll offer her own ideas for preserving and extending the progressive gains made since 2008.

And besides, while, historically, it has been a steep hill to climb for a party to retain control of the White House for a third straight presidential election (it has happened only once since the ratification of the Twenty-Second Amendment in 1951), Hillary Clinton won't face the same headwinds that Richard Nixon did in 1960, Gerald Ford did in 1976, Al Gore did in 2000, or John McCain did in 2008. She can break that precedent by virtue of the unprecedented nature of her candidacy. Hillary is poised to break the last, highest glass ceiling, and polls show that a clear majority of Americans are ready for a woman president.

Besides the history-making aspect of her candidacy, through her years in public service Hillary already has her own strong political brand, one that any candidate would envy and that her enemies fear (although they frequently deny it). On the Democratic side, one has to go all the way back to the candidacy of Lyndon Johnson in 1964 to find a putative nominee in such a commanding position, both within the party and in the electorate as a whole.

So, as they brushed the confetti from their hair in the wake of their 2014 triumphs, conservatives looking ahead to 2016 with clear eyes understood that defeating Hillary would be a much tougher task than their bluster about "third-term-itis" suggested.

～

Start with the fact that Hillary would enter the race more popular— and, critically, better known—than any other conceivable candidate. In fact, in December 2014, Gallup found that she topped notables like Oprah Winfrey and teen peace activist Malala Yousafzai as Americans' most admired woman on the *planet*—the nineteenth time (and seventeenth in the last eighteen years) that she had held that distinction.

Three months later, another Gallup poll illustrated just how difficult it would be to ruin Hillary's image. Asking Americans for their impressions of a variety of potential 2016 candidates, Gallup found that 50 percent viewed Hillary favorably, compared with 39 percent who had an unfavorable view. The difference between those two numbers—an 11 percent net favorability rating—must have worried conservatives; no Republican candidate enjoyed a net favorability rating greater than 5 percent.

But it was the sum of those two numbers that must have caused the most heartburn for the right. After twenty-plus years in the public eye, Hillary was a known quantity; 89 percent of Americans were familiar enough with her to have an opinion. By contrast, nearly a third of respondents didn't know enough about Jeb Bush to rate him favorably or unfavorably, and less than half knew enough to rate Marco Rubio. Even the sitting vice president, Joe Biden, had a "familiarity score" more than ten points lower than Hillary's.

Another challenge for Hillary's antagonists was that Democrats had united early, and strongly, behind her. A March 2015 CNN survey found that 62 percent of Democrats supported Hillary; no other candidate got more than 15 percent. Before the race had even begun, Hillary had majority support among liberals (59 percent) and moderates (63 percent), men (56 percent) and women (67 percent), whites (56 percent) and nonwhites (67 percent), those under fifty (59 percent) and those fifty and older (66 percent), those who earned under $50,000 a year (64 percent) and those who earned more (56 percent), those who had attended college (63 percent) and those who had not (60 percent).

With Democrats largely on board, conservatives worried, Hillary would be able to spend months patiently building her organization, honing her message, and raising money—all without the pressure of a heated primary battle, despite GOP efforts to stoke one.

It was a nightmare scenario for the right: A carefully orchestrated launch, a quick and bloodless scrimmage against token Democratic opposition, a coronation at the convention in Philadelphia, and Hillary could emerge in July 2016 tanned, rested, and ready—flush with cash, unmarred by friendly fire, and prepared to take it to whichever Republican ended up the last man standing in what would assuredly be a crowded, fiercely contested GOP primary.

And no matter who emerged as Hillary's Republican opponent, he would find himself standing on a debate stage next to a far more seasoned, inarguably more experienced candidate.

Indeed, one of the reasons America is so ready for Hillary is that she is so ready to lead. In her career, she has been a civil rights activist, a prominent attorney, an advocate for children and families, an influential and policy-focused First Lady, an accomplished senator with a legacy of bipartisan achievements, a dedicated philanthropist, and, of course, secretary of state.

Whether any presidential candidate has *ever* been more prepared for the office is a question for historians. But, to be certain, no 2016 candidate is even in Hillary's galaxy: not two-term governors Chris Christie and Scott Walker; not freshman senators Marco Rubio, Rand Paul, or Ted Cruz; and not Jeb Bush, who hasn't held elected office in a decade.

Experience, of course, isn't everything. But in an April 2015 poll, 55 percent of voters found experience a more important characteristic in a presidential candidate, compared with 37 percent who instead preferred a candidate who could offer a new direction—a clear advantage for Hillary.

If Republicans won't be able to beat Hillary on the strength of their nominee's leadership abilities, they certainly won't be able to beat her on the popularity of their platform. With the wedge issues that worked in the past—such as gay marriage and abortion rights—no longer dividing the electorate in a way that benefits Republicans, the terrain heavily favors the Democrats, who, polls show, enjoy an advantage on nearly every major issue, from immigration reform and infrastructure to tax reform and gun control.

This advantage is particularly pronounced on what seems likely to be the most important issue of the election: the economy—specifically, growing concerns about economic inequality as the middle class still struggles to recover from the Bush recession.

For all their rhetoric about being the party of growth, Republicans have no actual policy solutions that suggest any real departure from the trickle-down approach that Americans have seen fail time and time again. They have nothing to offer families struggling to pay for college or invest for retirement, moms and dads trying to balance career and child rearing, working people frustrated by the unfair treatment they receive from their employers, or any American who feels like it's gotten harder and harder to get ahead. Their economic "policy" is the same it's always been: Tax cuts for the rich, scraps for the rest.

Hillary, on the other hand, has a long and accomplished history of focusing on kitchen-table issues, especially those that affect women and children. As progressive economic theories gain more support her record shows that she is well positioned to speak with credibility to the needs of voters.

Then there is the Democrats' built-in advantage in the Electoral College, where Hillary as the Democratic nominee will begin the general election with a projected 247 votes. Adding Virginia and Colorado to her column brings her to 269—one vote short of the magic number, even conceding Florida and Ohio to the Republicans. That one vote could be picked up with a win in Iowa, New Hampshire, or Nevada.

Thus, from the moment she left the State Department in early 2013, Hillary Clinton was justifiably seen as the clear favorite to capture the White House in 2016. And conservatives would have to pull out all the stops in their attempt to defeat her.

⌒

So how do you solve a problem like Hillary Clinton? Over the remaining chapters of this book, I'll look at how conservatives plan to answer that question—and how they began to implement that strategy long before she even announced her candidacy.

Oddly, a key element of that strategy was the right's determined effort to cast doubt on whether Hillary would really be that formidable a candidate at all.

Given that, in the eyes of the right, Hillary has spent her entire adult life pursuing political power—that she is a Machiavellian manipulator who carefully cultivates her friends and revels in plotting the destruction of her enemies—it might seem strange that they also believe (or pretend to) that her campaign is doomed from the jump and that she, in the words of Reince Priebus, is "not really good at politics."

Yet it is a treasured talking point on the right that Hillary is a terrible politician. They sneer that she is wooden and ill at ease in public settings, and a tone-deaf disaster on the stump. They say she's tightly wound and thin-skinned, cold and distant, unable to connect with ordinary people, "as gaffe-prone as Dan Quayle and as awkward as Bob Dole," as neoconservative pundit John Podhoretz wrote in the *New York Post.*

Conservatives' evidence for all this is what Podhoretz calls the "spectacular incompetence" of Hillary's first presidential campaign in 2008. Overlooked is the fact that Hillary won a fiercely contested Senate seat from New York by more than ten points in 2000 and received 67 percent of the vote in her reelection campaign six years later. In those campaigns, Hillary proved herself a compelling and effective candidate, overcoming the initial hurdle of being new to the state with good, old-fashioned retail politics—she often happily bunked in people's homes while on the hustings—and also a mastery of voters' local concerns.

Indeed, Hillary's second-place finish to a once-in-a-generation political phenomenon by the narrowest of margins is all her critics can point to in trying to paint her as a bad politician. But even that is questionable proof that Hillary lacks what it takes to win elections. After all, she won 18 million primary votes, more than any candidate in history— Barack Obama included. Of the seven states with the largest populations, she won the popular vote in six (California, Texas, Florida, New York, Pennsylvania, and Ohio), losing only Obama's home state of Illinois. And, overall, Hillary won more votes from among women, seniors, Latinos, union members, and rural voters.

None of that should cause us to question that Barack Obama's victory was a spectacular political achievement—but neither is it grounds to conclude that Hillary Clinton's defeat was a spectacular political failure. Hillary herself committed no game-changing gaffe, exposed no fatal weakness; if she had a slow start in finding her voice on the stump, she fought through it, developing a resonant message that connected with voters both intellectually and emotionally.

In short, Hillary very narrowly lost a contest that she should have very narrowly won. Obama won in large part because, tactically speaking, his team pitched a better game in the primary: They outmaneuvered the Clinton campaign in some fine points of caucus strategy; they tapped into a groundswell of small-dollar fund-raising online; and they scored some big early endorsements from established Democrats on Capitol Hill who made the upstarts' candidacy more plausible. All that was enough to give him the nomination.

It's hard to argue that the candidate was the problem. The truth is that Hillary was a strong candidate who ran a strong campaign in 2008, one that, were it not for the presence of another strong candidate running another strong campaign, could easily have propelled her to the White House. And to the extent that her campaign was not perfect (no campaign ever is), there is no particular reason to view those shortcomings as an indictment of Hillary's own political skills.

The story of Hillary Clinton, presidential candidate, is not the story of a politician whose ambition wrote checks that her talent couldn't cash, resulting in a hubristic downfall on the big stage. It's the story of a politician who came in a very close second in one of the most thrilling primary races of all time, learned from her loss, and is ready to run an even stronger race the second time around.

⌒

The right's attempt to cast Hillary as a bad politician is but one example of how Republican strategists focus on three different audiences in their effort to derail Hillary's candidacy. Because most voters already have a fixed view of Hillary, a consequence of having been in public life for more than two decades and having always garnered blanket coverage in the press for her every move, together with the fact that there are fewer swing voters in the electorate overall, Republicans know that one focus must be on turning out their own base. In other words, they need to feed red meat to voters who are already against Hillary—so that they keep up the fight, feel their efforts are working, and ultimately turn out to vent their hostility at the voting booth. (The strategy runs the real risk of overreaching and alienating those genuinely on the fence, but the Republicans seem determined to run it anyway.)

Of course the conservative base needs no prompt to hate Hillary, as she's been the target of a deeply held personal enmity for years that goes far beyond ordinary partisanship (though the fact that she is the most formidable Democrat on the scene, the most admired woman in the country, married to an exceedingly popular ex-president, and leading every Republican in every poll adds a sense of urgency). Despite the conflicting negative stereotypes conservatives propagate (Hillary the dyed-in-the-wool Big Government liberal, or Hillary the ambitious power seeker in it for nothing but herself), what's underneath their animosity can be traced to the simple fact that Hillary is a strong and accomplished woman rising in what in many ways is still a man's world, so much so that she is poised to break the last glass ceiling. Her role as a trailblazer in every step of her career—from working woman to full political partner to senator to secretary of state and now front-running Presidential candidate—upends the traditionalists' view of the way the world should be, as does the fact that both she and her husband represent American meritocracy at its best. Then, too, conservatives, particularly those still fighting the culture wars of the prior decades, fear the liberal social and culture changes they have long thought Hillary represented since she burst on the national scene as an inadvertent warrior in those wars years ago.

The second audience consists of panicky Democrats who—while they support Hillary's policies, admire her record for the most part, and long for the history that would be made with her election and the progress that would be preserved and extended under her leadership—

are prone to the self-defeating angst that, as we saw in the first half of this book, often gets in the way of winning. As a committed Democrat now myself, I think I've observed the party long enough from the inside to say that there's nothing worse than a "worried Democrat"— particularly one who leaks those worries anonymously to the press. For this species, the sky is always falling.

By attempting to foment worries about the viability of Hillary's candidacy—rational and irrational, substantive and silly—the right hopes to undermine the Democratic unity that is part of her formidable political standing. The right's strategy is to split the party enough to create an opening for a primary challenge to Hillary so that she would presumably be a weakened general election candidate. In this, a natural audience for the right is a faction of Democrats who have never felt the Clintons were liberal enough to suit their tastes: They don't like their pragmatic approach to problem solving at the expense of fixed ideology, and see their efforts to create a truly big tent in the party by including moderate interests as impure. Failing that, the right seeks to suppress the Democratic vote by spreading doubt and dampening enthusiasm for Hillary's candidacy.

And they aren't hiding what they're up to. Thus it was that throughout the spring of 2015, Matt Drudge endlessly hyped Martin O'Malley's potential challenge to Hillary. In a column called MATT DRUDGE REALLY LIKES MARTIN O'MALLEY, Chris Cillizza of the *Washington Post* observed, "Drudge has become an out-and-out advocate for O'Malley." And in an editorial entitled QUID PRO CLINTON, the *Wall Street Journal* wrote, "The operating Clinton assumption is that the 'progressives'... will fall meekly into line as they always have. Maybe they will, though the 2016 election risks of doing so are rising with each disclosure of Clinton sleaze."

Republican operative Ed Rogers came right out and said it in a *Washington Post* column: "Doesn't the drip, drip, drip of damaging revelations deflate her supporters? Maybe the hope is that voters will become numb to it. But I don't see how Clinton's supporters can be both numb and enthusiastic at the same time. Enthusiasm drives out turnout. Numbness has got to suppress it."

For evidence that the strategy was working one needed to look no further then the op-ed page of the *Washington Post*, where anxious "liberal" columnist Richard Cohen opined, "I have grave doubts about Hillary Clinton's viability," citing her lack of a "resounding message" and even "her marriage to Bill" as flaws.

In reaching the first two audiences, the right aims to enlist the press as a third. The press corps has always been obsessed with anything and everything Clinton. They're covered them the way the British tabloids cover the royals. As we've already seen, there is no shortage of column inches or website pixels for Hillary news, because Hillary news sells— and as we shall see, there is no limit to how inflammatory, unsubstantiated, self-contradictory or downright false the right-wing bait can be while still being uncritically reported on by otherwise credible outlets as legitimate. The press knows, moreover, that an intramural Democratic fight would boost ratings and click-throughs.

Aside from obvious commercial benefits, what explains the media's fixation on all things Clinton, a fixation that routinely is so negative?

Let's remember that those who run the big, influential media outlets constitute a power center in their own right. Research shows that the elite media's ideology skews a bit to the left socially, a bit to the right economically. By party affiliation, they're probably mostly Democrats. More important, though, they see themselves as keepers of a kind of established pecking order in Washington and in certain elite sectors in New York. They set the rules; they set the parameters of the debate.

In the beginning, the Clintons—a young, dynamic Democratic couple from Arkansas of all places—were seen as interlopers by certain elitists of the Washington village. To them, the Clintons were white trash who didn't belong. And they were treated as such by the likes of Sally Quinn and David Broder of the *Washington Post*, who routinely wrote about the first couple with condescension and disdain. It was as if they would have been more comfortable—which is to say more powerful—as the keepers of order under a nice, moderate Republican president, say George H. W. Bush or Bob Dole. When the Clintons beat those entrenched Republicans and upended the order, the displaced establishment seethed. (As columnist Peggy Noonan put it, Hillary was nothing but a "highly credentialed rube.")

A second group of journalists and pundits appointed themselves as keepers of personal ethics and morality. They tend to caricature the Clintons as gamers and hypocrites, always falling short of their lofty ideals. These were the holier-than-thou people who back in the 1990s claimed Bill Clinton's private affair was the public's business even though the vast majority of the country disagreed, and who faulted Hillary as a "false feminist" for staying with her husband in the aftermath (as if it was a feminist principle to abandon your family in a time of personal difficulties).

Today, their political voyeurism—even by a new crop of younger pundits—is focused on the long-running narrative that the Clintons are personally greedy. "You don't have to be a political strategist to lament that the Clintonian approach to ethics seems always to err in favor of taking the check," according to Ruth Marcus of the *Washington Post*. Marcus used the Yiddish word *chazer* to describe Hillary. "It means 'pig,'" she explained, "but has a specific connotation of piggishness and gluttony. This is a chronic affliction of the Clintons." So, the Clintons are barnyard animals.

A third group is the guilty liberals—people who understand that real greed, corruption, and hypocrisy are institutionalized in today's GOP but go harder on the Clintons regardless. Having been battered by the right for decades with allegations of "liberal bias," they lean over so far in the other direction so as never to be seen as "soft" on or "in the tank" for the Clintons.

Ever since Bob Woodward and Carl Bernstein became famous for their reporting on Watergate, a fourth group are suckers for Republican payback schemes to scandalize Democrats. And during the 1990s, when the right-wing adopted a strategy of scandalizing the Clintons as the only means of defeating them, this is how the press corps got pulled in. By now you know the litany: Whitewater, Travelgate, Filegate, Vincent Foster's suicide, Hillary's Rose Law Firm billing records, the Clinton body count, Hillary's cattle futures trades, Pardongate, et cetera. All were subject to various and sundry official investigations, countless column inches and cable TV segments, and deranged "reports" from the fringe right wing—all amounting to nothing in the end.

Clearly, these four groups overlap with one another. They all know that the Clintons were innocent as charged and saw them withstand it all—a resilience that only produces a palpable and perverse sense of frustration that somehow they are getting away with something, and compounds the frantic effort, which is accelerated today in the ever more competitive news cycle, to "get" the Clintons. This syndrome is a product of an unholy alliance between their political enemies and much of the press corps—all of which serves to rile up the conservative base as nervous Democrats look on.

⌒

Over the remaining chapters in this book, as we look at how conservatives plan to solve their Hillary problem (and, make no mistake—their bluster aside, they know she presents a huge problem), we'll continue to see how conservatives play to these three audiences—the Republican base, the worried Democrats, and the political press corps.

Some of their tactics have been part of the Republican playbook for years, proving powerful against even the strongest Democratic candidates. Indeed, one of the most effective involves turning their opponent's greatest strength into a weakness, especially a weakness of character.

Karl Rove built his reputation on running this play to perfection. In 2004, the war hero John Kerry was turned into a liar, a coward, and a traitor. In the 2000 South Carolina Republican primary, Bush allies spread rumors suggesting that John McCain's time as a prisoner of the Viet Cong at the infamous "Hanoi Hilton" had rendered him mentally incapable of being president.

A decade later, Rove was still running the same play. Recall the ads run by his American Crossroads and other conservative groups attacking Democrats of "cutting Medicare." In truth, of course, it was the *Republican* plan that would have eliminated traditional Medicare; Democrats, in the Affordable Care Act, had put the program on sounder footing. Recognizing their vulnerability among seniors, Republicans figured out how to flip the advantage, turning what should have been a Democratic strength into a weakness once again—and scaring flat-footed Democrats away from taking on an issue that should have worked to their benefit.

Thus, in 2016, whatever Republicans fear most about Hillary, they will inevitably try to turn it against her.

In chapter 7, we'll take on the first of five central myths about Hillary—that she was a do-nothing secretary of state. We'll see how the right has tried to rewrite Hillary's record. Fearful that her service as America's top diplomat will give her unique credibility to talk about foreign policy, while avoiding the age-old canard that Democrats are weak on defense, conservatives have tried to argue that her time in Foggy Bottom was devoid of accomplishments, a stream of self-promoting, sightseeing travel punctuated by a fecklessness that, in their contorted analysis, caused international crises years after she left office.

A critical part of the attack on Hillary's State Department legacy is the right's calculated misrepresentation of the events that took place at the American compound in Benghazi, Libya, on September 11, 2012—a terrorist attack in which four Americans lost their lives. Chapter 8 explores how conservatives have shamelessly politicized that tragedy, hunting fruitlessly for scandal in the ashes and, when none could be found, manufacturing a myth that Hillary was somehow implicated in the attack and its aftermath—all so that they could harass her with endless partisan investigations designed to inflame her opponents, dismay her supporters, and entice the press.

In chapter 9, we'll debunk the myth that Hillary is a shady money-grubber by turning to the Clintons' history of philanthropy that has saved and improved millions of lives. We'll expose the right's attempts to muddy the Clinton Foundation's path-breaking charitable work on behalf of the neediest people around the world with the outrageously false suggestion that it illustrates not the Clintons' outsized generosity, but rather their corruption.

And in chapter 10, we'll look at how, unable to compete with Hillary's message for shared prosperity, Republicans are choosing instead to attack the messenger, using distorted personal caricatures and papering over her actual record in an attempt to undermine another one of Hillary's strengths: her credibility on the most important issue of the election, the economy, by propagating the myth that Hillary is out of touch with the middle class.

Of course, such tactics would be used against any Democrat. But the special dynamic that surrounds the Clintons—the passionate loathing from the right, the tendency toward panic on the left, and, most of all, the long history of antipathy from the putatively neutral press corps—offers special opportunities for the scandal launderers to ply their trade.

In chapter 11, we'll examine a case study of how a small nugget of information about Hillary's e-mail habits can be misrepresented, inflated, and echoed until, for a brief moment, it looks like the magic bullet that will finally stop Hillary or, at least, scandalize the issue enough so that the myth that she's devious and secretive takes hold.

Finally, in chapter 12, we'll see how the myth of Hillary as man-eater has evolved and endured over the years, examining how the blatant sexism that culminated in despicable attacks against Hillary in 2008 is likely to appear in more subtle forms in 2016.

As we'll see again and again throughout, the case against Hillary is often rich with irony.

When it comes to her political prowess, are we supposed to think that Hillary is a cross between Nixon and Machiavelli, a paranoid manipulator who squashes dissent and hides from the press—or that she is really a hapless bumbler who can't run a campaign, maintain message discipline, or control her own allies?

And when it comes to analyzing the political landscape ahead of 2016, are we to conclude that Hillary is overexposed, that after a quarter century the nation is suffering from "Clinton fatigue"—or that she will suffer from "hiding" from the press, not spending *enough* time in the public eye? Is Hillary's inevitable rise to the Democratic nomination a curse—or is it a mirage? And will America reject her because they've had enough of political dynasties—or are people ready for a third President Bush in a generation?

When it comes to her tenure as secretary of state, are we to see Hillary as just a figurehead who rarely engaged in any actual diplomacy—or are we to hold her personally responsible for every major world crisis that has occurred since she took office (not to mention the deaths of four Americans in Benghazi)? And when it comes to her economic agenda, is she a closet socialist—or a crony capitalist in disguise?

Even when it comes to the ugly sexism that continues to dance around the edges of their critique of Hillary, conservatives can't keep their story straight: Is she a castrating bitch who crushes the testicles of anyone in her path—or is she only able to run for president because of her husband's accomplishments? When she displays emotion, is that an example of Hillary cynically using her gender for political gain—or is it an example of why her gender is a political liability?

The truth is that, for Hillary's haters, it doesn't matter. It never has. Ever since I was doing the Clinton haters' dirty work, they've ultimately never been fueled by logic, moved by policy debates, or influenced by facts; it's always been personal, and that's what's made it durable.

Indeed, in a strange inversion of their own personal obsession with

Hillary, by the time she declared her candidacy in April 2015, the right seemed to have settled on the line of attack that it was Hillary for whom everything was personal. It was all about her.

Going forward, then, we can expect to see little debate about Hillary's views on issues—convenient for Republicans trying to avoid those issues—because Hillary is said to have no actual beliefs. As right-wing *Wall Street Journal* columnist Bret Stephens put it: "In other words, she's singing a Song of Herself. She will say, do, and be pretty much anything to get elected."

The Republicans aim to make the 2016 race all about "character"—in a tired and ugly replay of the 1990s. But in this, the last battle of the Clinton Wars, Hillary's haters are more desperate than ever before—and nothing will diminish their drive to deny her the White House.

They'll impugn her political skills all the while portraying Hillary as more political than the average politician—more cautious, more calculated, more conniving, more ambitious, in it only for herself. And they'll take what would be considered typical behavior by any other politician and sensationalize it.

The Republicans will be shooting blanks. Hillary Clinton is already the most vetted candidate for the presidency in modern American history. The question is, if they shoot enough of them, what effect will it have? The more they attack Hillary personally, the more they expose their bankruptcy of ideas.

Yet conservatives are banking on the notion of Clinton fatigue to serve their partisan interests. The idea is that through repetition of "scandal" after "scandal," they can turn off enough undecideds and depress the Democratic base enough to win the election. "There's Hillary fatigue already out there," Reince Priebus, the RNC chairman, crowed in June 2014. "It's setting in."

But the idea of Clinton fatigue is just more Republican wishful thinking: Clinton fatigue is itself a myth, albeit one that much of the media buys into.

As early as her first run for the Senate back in 1999, it was a consensus among journalists that Clinton fatigue could hurt Hillary, though it clearly didn't. "The Mayor [Giuliani] may also be helped by the so-called Clinton fatigue factor. A lot of voters have had their fill of Bill and Hillary and would like to move on. For those voters, almost any other candidate will do," a *New York Times* columnist reported in June 1999. That same year, CNN reported, "From bimbo eruptions to draft dodging to pot smoking to Whitewater to the Lincoln Bedroom to Monica Lewinsky, Clinton's personal life has drained the country.... Americans have long since tired of that soap opera. The message is, enough already, and it's showing up politically in the form of Clinton fatigue."

In the 2000 presidential race, advisors to Al Gore appeared to embrace the theory that President Clinton was a net negative, prevailing on Gore to sideline him from the campaign trail. As the *New York Times* reported the conventional wisdom about Clinton at the time, "The glaring Clinton failure is the character issue, including the extramarital activities that led to his impeachment. Pollsters say that 'Clinton fatigue,' a weariness with the scandals, has been sapping energy from the Gore candidacy.'"

Well, we all know how that worked out. Analysts concluded after Election Day that had Clinton been out campaigning for Gore in any number of states, he clearly would have pulled his vice president over the finish line. Buying into "Clinton fatigue" was a dumb idea then, and it's an even dumber idea now—despite what the Republicans and the media tell you to think.

In fact, a number of political observers have suggested that Clinton fatigue is a real phenomena—but that it afflicts the press corps itself, not the public. NBC's Chuck Todd, for example, explained: "I think there is much less Clinton fatigue in the Democratic Party than there is in the press corps, which, by the way, is going to be a separate challenge for her."

Indeed, as events unfolded in 2014, Todd's analysis was borne out, as "Clinton fatigue" was cited as a real thing by reporters and commentators—left, right, and center.

- *Slate*: "The issue lurking behind Clinton drama is really one of Clinton fatigue."
- *New York Times* columnist Frank Bruni wrote of people who "suffer bone-wearying Clinton fatigue."
- Fox News' Neil Cavuto: "Do we have a case here of potentially Clinton fatigue?"
- MSNBC contributor Donny Deutsch: "I like Hillary, I just think there's such a fatigue there."

Yet through it all, for over a decade, there's never been any evidence that the country is tired of the Clintons, who remain the most popular and respected political leaders of their generation. And as that last battle of the Clinton Wars approached, Hillary emerged as more viable than ever.

Hillary may start this race in an enviable position. But she will have to fight uphill to keep it that way. The "Clinton rules"—defined by *New York Times* columnist Paul Krugman as "the way pundits and some news organizations treat any action or statement by the Clintons, no matter how innocuous, as proof of evil intent"—are in effect.

Even when allegations of scandal are totally without merit, Hillary will be considered guilty until proven innocent—and even when the allegations are proven false, she will be considered responsible for creating the appearance of impropriety. Even when she engages in unprecedented transparency, Hillary will always be suspected of hiding something. And even when the attacks against her would have crossed every line imaginable were she any other politician, the right will never face consequences for taking their campaign of personal destruction one step further.

Or will they? That is the challenge for Hillary: to win a fight in which her opponent will have the Koch brothers' treasure, the scandal launderers' expertise, and an army of foaming haters in his corner; a fight in which some of her own supporters may fall prey to relentless right-wing propaganda and in which the referees in the press corps not only won't enforce the rules against low blows, they'll administer them; a fight in which punches were flying long before the bell even rang.

## Chapter Seven

# Showdown at Foggy Bottom

Not so long ago, Democrats and Republicans agreed: Hillary Clinton was an outstanding secretary of state. Tapped by Barack Obama to serve as America's top diplomat—a move that inspired comparisons to Lincoln's famous "Team of Rivals"—she got to work restoring America's standing in the world that had been greatly set back during the bellicose, tone-deaf presidency of George W. Bush.

"Hillary consumed herself with the question of how to reverse the damage Bush had done to America's reputation," authors Jonathan Allen and Aime Parnes wrote in their book *HRC*. She did this, they reported, by infusing "the theory of 'smart power' into America's foreign policy. The term, coined by Clinton administration Pentagon official Joseph Nye, is shorthand for an approach to influencing other countries that combines traditional 'hard power' such as military force and economic sanctions with the 'soft power' of inducing foreign nations to change their behavior by offering carrots such as political or economic assistance."

When Hillary left office, the world viewed the United States far more favorably than it did just before she took office. From Germany and France, to Mexico, Argentina, and Japan, U.S. favorability ratings increased by 20 points or more.

She also won praise from Republicans for her efforts. In May 2012, Republican senator Lindsey Graham of South Carolina described Hillary Clinton as "one of the most effective secretary of states, greatest ambassadors for the American people that I have known in my lifetime." Three months later, he heaped more acclaim upon her in the *New York Times*: "She is extremely well respected throughout the world, handles herself in a very classy way, and has a work ethic second to none."

John McCain called Hillary "an international star" who has done "a really tremendous job." Senator Orrin Hatch, the Utah Republican, said, "I think she's done a good job," adding, "I have high respect for her." Even former Vice President Dick Cheney called her "one of the more competent members of the current administration," which, for him, counts as fulsome praise.

Then Hillary left the State Department, having added an impressive four-year stint as America's top diplomat to her already strong qualifications for the presidency. And with President Obama reelected and conservatives turning their attention to 2016, all that approbation suddenly disappeared down the memory hole.

In December 2013, *Politico Magazine* offered conservative pundit and former Jesse Helms aide Danielle Pletka (along with other right-wingers) the opportunity to bash Hillary as "enormously ineffective." Fox News pundit Doug Schoen, who has apparently inherited Alan Colmes's old job as the Democratic strategist whose job it is to lose arguments to conservatives, wrote, "She can point to no significant accomplishments as secretary of state."

Suddenly, the talking point was in the air: Hillary hadn't really *done* anything in Foggy Bottom. Yes, she had broken Madeleine Albright's record for most nations visited, traveling to 112 different countries and covering nearly a million miles in pursuit of diplomatic progress. But in conservatives' eyes, this wasn't evidence of Hillary's work ethic, but rather proof that she was more interested in ceremony than getting anything done.

As *Slate*'s David Weigel chronicled, "the old conventional wisdom" about Hillary's excellent work at the State Department "makes for dull copy"—and, sure enough, the mainstream press was ready to play along with the new attack. Weigel clipped an excerpt from right-wing radio host Hugh Hewitt's show in which *New York Times* magazine writer Mark Leibovich was, more or less, bullied into agreeing that Hillary had no accomplishments:

HEWITT: How would you describe Hillary Clinton's achievements as Secretary of State?

LEIBOVICH: Geez. Look, I think, I don't cover the State Department. Look, you have that look on your face like you expect me to duck this question.

HEWITT: No, I expect you not to be able to say anything, because she didn't do anything.

LEIBOVICH: I actually didn't, I don't, here's the deal. I have not written any stories on Hillary Clinton since 2008. How about, what's like the graceful way to duck a question?

HEWITT: Not even duck, just as if we're playing Jeopardy!

LEIBOVICH: Yeah, I honestly don't know.

HEWITT: Nobody can come up with anything, Mark.

LEIBOVICH: Yeah, let's see. What did she do? I mean, she traveled a lot. That's the thing. They're always like, well, she logged eight zillion miles. It's like, since when did that become like diplomacy by odometer?

At Correct the Record, we quickly realized what was happening—Republicans were trying to invert the truth to destroy their opponent's advantage, and the political media, never terribly well versed in the intricacies of foreign policy, was an easy mark.

This is how false narratives are born—how Al Gore becomes a serial liar and an elitist, how John Kerry turns from a war hero into a coward and traitor, how Mark Pryor becomes an enemy of Medicare instead of the one person in the Arkansas Senate race who wanted Medicare to continue to exist. These baldly false assertions need to be contested whenever they're made—loudly, consistently, and even repetitively.

So we developed a long list of Hillary's accomplishments as secretary of state, the highlights of which are summarized here so that you can have it handy, too:

- Hillary helped impose the toughest sanctions in Iran's history by securing support from intractable members of the global community after several months of "grueling diplomacy" according to the *Washington Post*. As the *Wall Street Journal*'s conservative editorial board grudgingly admitted, "Mrs. Clinton surely pulled out every stop to get Russia and particularly China...on board." As Hillary herself put it, "I spent four years sharpening a choice for Iran's leaders: address the international community's legitimate concerns about their nuclear program or face ever-escalating pressure and isolation. With support from Congress and our allies, our diplomacy yielded the toughest international sanctions ever imposed." Hillary's leadership on the sanctions issue was widely credited with bringing about the landmark agreement with Iran that thwarts its nuclear capabilities for a decade.

- Hillary played an integral role in the New START treaty with Russia, successfully pushing the missile reduction agreement through a divided Senate and entering the treaty into force at a Munich meeting with her Russian counterpart. She personally lobbied fifty U.S. senators to pass it, including key Republicans. The result was fewer nuclear missile launchers—and thus a safer world. And while Hillary made progress with Russia, she refused to defend Russia's policies when they clashed with our own.

- She successfully negotiated a cease-fire to end eight days of hostilities between Israelis and Palestinians in Gaza—"right," as *Politico* reported, "at the moment hope seemed dead for a rapid end to the violence." Hillary traveled to the region to negotiate with Israelis and Palestinians, bringing in Egypt as the sponsor of the cease-fire agreement, and quelling the tide of violence.

- Alongside the other members of the president's national security team, Hillary helped bring an end to the war in Iraq and laid the foundation for an end to the war in Afghanistan, organizing NATO allies to stand up for a postwithdrawal support plan. Discussing the end of the two wars that had lasted since the first term of the Bush administration, President Obama credited "the great work that Hillary did and her team did and the State Department did."

- She spearheaded the administration's "pivot to Asia" strategy, which Martin Indyk of the Brookings Institution called "Obama's most lasting strategic achievement," noting that Hillary "laid the groundwork, built the relationships, and developed the complex architecture of the new strategy—and she turned up at that pivotal moment in Vietnam in July 2010 to declare the U.S. commitment to the region." When it came to China's influence in Asia, Defense Secretary Robert Gates said, "Secretary Clinton was very much in the lead." Hillary also broke new ground in opening up the country of Burma, which had not been visited by a secretary of state in half a century.

- Hillary built a coalition to topple Libyan dictator Muammar Qadhafi and bring an end to the massacres taking place there, using what the *Washington Post* described as "her mixture of political pragmatism and tenacity to referee spats among NATO partners, secure crucial backing from Arab countries, and tutor rebels on the fine points of message management." According to *Newsweek* columnist Michael Tomasky, "Whatever Libya's future holds, Muammar Gaddafi's gone, and Benghazi—well before it became a fake Fox News 'controversy'—it's the place where thousands of lives were almost certainly saved. Clinton led the way in making it happen." GOP Senators Marco Rubio, Roy Blunt, Mark Kirk, John McCain, and Lindsey Graham all lauded Libya's liberation.

- Hillary focused on economic engagement, reaching three new free trade agreements (Colombia, Panama, and South Korea), as well as fifteen new Open Skies agreements, including with Japan, Brazil, Saudi Arabia, and Israel. According to *Bloomberg Businessweek*, "Clinton has argued that commercial diplomacy and the promotion of trade, long the neglected stepchildren of the foreign policy establishment, are central to U.S. strategic interests.... Her work as a spokeswoman for American business is a less visible part of her legacy. Yet it may be the most durable."

- Thanks to Hillary's focus on economic statecraft, U.S. exports increased by a third—exports to China alone increased by half in just two years. As *Bloomberg* reported, she created a "business-promotion machine." Her victories included a $21 billion deal with Boeing that will bring one hundred thousand jobs to Americans, $100 million for an Ohio startup's electric vehicles, a $5 million Swiss contract for a Virginia flight company, a $668 million contract for Palo Alto firms to build a national broadband network in Australia, a deal between General Electric and Vietnam worth $80 million, and more.

- Hillary led the charge as the State Department adapted to emerging issues such as cybersecurity, creating the Center for Strategic Counterterrorism Communications to fight terrorists online, fulfilling her pledge "to integrate all the tools of American power to combat terror threats." She also helped create the Bureau of Energy Resources to protect energy infrastructure and help move the world to cleaner energy.

- Hillary was the first secretary of state to prioritize women's rights around the world; as *Newsweek* reported, it is in the area of "hardships faced by women and girls across the world that her impact has been most profound." She created a critical new position within the State Department: ambassador-at-large for global women's issues. And she "implemented concrete objectives and actions to marshal U.S. expertise and capacity to address and prevent gender-based violence" across the globe. Truly, this was visionary leadership.

- And, of course, as a member of the national security cabinet, Hillary lent key support to the raid that killed Osama bin Laden. As *Newsweek* reported, Defense Secretary Gates recommended an air strike with no forces on the ground. CIA Director Leon Panetta supported a raid by Special Forces on the ground, and so did Secretary of State Hillary Clinton, who argued Obama "had to take the risk."

Armed with the facts, Hillary's supporters were able to get the word out, often using our list of accomplishments when facing off on the cable airwaves. We helped place dozens of op-eds focusing on specific aspects of her record at State. Slowly but surely, the truth got its boots on: Hillary's singular accomplishment, earning back respect for the United States abroad in the wake of George W. Bush's brazen and tragically inept policies, had broken through.

All our work was done in anticipation of June 2014, when Hillary herself would have an opportunity to tell her own story with the release of her book *Hard Choices*: part personal memoir, part policy prescription, and part retrospective on the decisions she'd had to make in Foggy Bottom. Now voters would hear from Hillary herself that she has what it takes to defend and advance America's interests and values abroad on the complex and ever-changing international stage.

⌒

For everyone in Washington, the book's release was an exciting moment in a presidential precampaign that had been slow to develop. Insiders (or their assistants) rushed to bookstores to flip through the index, wondering if their names were mentioned. Political reporters scoured the text, looking for juicy details, entertaining anecdotes, or declarations of future ambition. (Catching a likely presidential candidate admitting that he or she is, in fact, going to run is a favorite pastime of the Washington press corps.)

But partisans on both sides had the release date circled on their calendars, because the book's release and reception—and Hillary's long-awaited appearances as part of her book tour—would be a chance for both sides to define Hillary's legacy as secretary of state.

For the Republican outfit America Rising, the release of *Hard Choices* was an opportunity to push their alternate reality of Hillary's tenure at the State Department.

Their characterization of Secretary Clinton wasn't always coherent—was she a passive and feckless bystander to history, or a bumbler who committed unforced errors? Was she tied at the hip with President Obama's most controversial decisions, or painfully out of step with her own administration? But coherence didn't matter. The task for America Rising was simply to ruin Hillary's victory lap, framing what she clearly believed to be a platform for a potential presidential run as damaging or even disqualifying.

America Rising didn't wait for their copy of *Hard Choices* to arrive from Amazon before trying to tear it apart. At 8:30 p.m. on the Sunday night before the book's release, they leaked an e-book they had prepared in advance, pointedly titled *Failed Choices*. This was an attempt to rebut in advance ("pre-but," in the parlance of political operatives) Hillary's account of her time in Foggy Bottom, a tenure that an America Rising official declared to be "without a signature accomplishment and instead defined by her significant and tangible failures."

Priced at $2.16, *Failed Choices* wasn't intended to turn America Rising into the hottest new conservative publishing house. In fact, the American people weren't the audience at all (although, no doubt, it would have made a great gift for the Fox-watching conservative uncle in your life). This was an attempt to frame the initial coverage of the book's release, which would also serve as a sort of soft launch to coverage of Hillary's still-theoretical presidential campaign. Book reviewers would explore whether *Hard Choices* was a good read, but it was the political reporters who would write about it as, effectively, a campaign document whom America Rising was hoping to sway.

It was no surprise to see America Rising try to pre-but Hillary's book, a tactic we frequently used ourselves. Nor were we surprised by the content of their screed; for weeks, we had been keeping a careful eye on Republican pundits and politicians, patiently cataloguing the false attacks, putting together responses, and preparing for the battle that her book would spark.

Three weeks before *Hard Choices* was released, we sent reporters a lengthy memo laying out two dozen Republican attacks on Hillary's State Department experience, along with the facts about each. And within two hours of *Failed Choices* leaking online that Sunday night in June, we had blasted a point-by-point debunking of their predictably false claims to reporters, progressive allies, and our growing online audiences—a surprise "pre-bunk" of their "pre-buttal" that succeeded in stealing Rising's thunder.

&#x223F;

The number one claim, of course, was the one we had been fighting for months.

As *Failed Choices* puts it, "No one would dispute Clinton's familiarity with landing strips in foreign capitals or the star status with which she was received at many of those outposts, but what remains unclear is what policy benefits Americans gained from all her travels."

By now, of course, this claim was deeply ingrained in the conservative mind-set. Even John McCain no longer seemed to think Hillary had done a "tremendous job," taking to MSNBC to sniff, "She visited more countries than any other secretary of state. But what concrete policy, or decision or whatever it is, was she responsible for?...And I think she would have trouble answering that."

And speaking at a conservative summit in Iowa, fringe Republican presidential hopeful Carly Fiorina complained, "Flying is not an accomplishment. It is an activity."

America Rising quotes an account by the writer Andrew Sullivan as evidence that even Hillary's allies (which he was not) can't explain

what, exactly, she has gotten done—not just in Foggy Bottom, but in
her entire career:

> I was having dinner with a real Clinton fan the other night, and
> I actually stumped him (and he's not easily stumped). What have
> been Hillary Clinton's major, signature accomplishments in her
> long career in public life? What did she achieve in her eight years
> as First Lady exactly? What stamp did she put on national policy
> in her time as Senator from New York? What were her defining
> and signature achievements as secretary-of-state?

This echoed the right's argument that not only had Hillary failed
to accomplish anything as Secretary of State, she hadn't accomplished
anything, ever. Newt Gingrich declared that she was just "famous for
being famous." Fox News' Keith Ablow wondered what qualifications
Hillary could possibly be bringing to the job of president, "other," of
course, "than being the wife of the president."

The reality is that Hillary Clinton has always been a workhorse, not
a show horse. As First Lady, Hillary had eschewed the traditional "host-
ess" role (much to the dismay of conservatives who cast her as ambitious, controlling, and just about every other euphemism to indicate
their disapproval when faced with a smart, powerful woman) in favor
of taking the lead on health-care policy, helping to create the Children's
Health Insurance Program, and laying the foundation for the eventual
victory on universal health care. And as senator, working effectively in a
chamber that for most of her tenure was controlled by the Republicans,
she frequently reached across the aisle to achieve tangible victories on
behalf of veterans and 9/11 first responders. (We'll cover her economic
policy achievements at greater length in a future chapter.)

The image of Hillary jetting around the world for photo ops—the
accusation that she was nothing more than a frequent-flyer diplomat—
never rang true, and it fell apart entirely in the face of the actual record
of accomplishment we detailed.

Ironically, this attack is also undermined by the right's opposite assertion—that in between what America Rising smugly demeans as "building relationships by meeting people"—Hillary was responsible for creating every major international crisis our country currently faces.

Conservatives want to point to whatever story happens to lead the international section of the newspaper, and if it's a story about instability abroad, say it was all Hillary Clinton's fault.

A perfect example of this blame game was the escalating situation in Ukraine, which presented a dilemma for American policy makers— and offered an opportunity for conservatives to blame Hillary, then out of office for a year, for allowing the crisis to occur, when in fact Hillary had predicted it.

The crux of the Republicans' argument blames Vladimir Putin's aggression on the so-called reset—an early Obama administration attempt to rebuild a productive relationship between the United States and Russia. As secretary of state, Hillary had been at the forefront of the policy, working with her counterpart, Russian foreign minister Sergei Lavrov, to reestablish stronger ties in the wake of Russia's 2008 invasion of Georgia. She famously offered Lavrov a red plastic Reset button as a token of American hopes for renewed cooperation. (The button made a bit of a translation error, using the Russian word for *overcharged* where *reset* should have been.)

With Putin out of presidential office and the more moderate Dmitri Medvedev in his place, the Obama administration clearly felt that progress was possible. And while Republicans have forgotten it, the record shows that progress was indeed made in the early days of the reset. The New START treaty marked an enormous step forward in the cause of nuclear disarmament, an agreement to reduce American and Russian nuclear arsenals to their lowest levels in a half century. Russia agreed to allow American military planes to transport so-called lethal materials over Russian airspace, a major advance in securing Russian cooperation for American antiterror efforts in Afghanistan. And thanks in large part to Hillary's diplomatic efforts, Russia was convinced to come on board with sanctions against Iran, the toughest in history, which led to a temporary halt in the Iranian nuclear program.

All of this was progress that made the world a safer place. None of it would have been possible without the "reset." And none of it implied, as conservatives have argued, that Hillary and the Obama administration were taking Vladimir Putin lightly. As early as 2008, Hillary herself had warned publicly that Putin was not to be trusted, pointing to his past as a KGB agent. "By definition," she said, "he doesn't have a soul." And even before she arrived in Foggy Bottom, she had been clear that she viewed relations with Russia as a balancing act, one that required us to find areas of mutual interest without taking our eye off the ball and compromising our position. That, indeed, is how all complicated diplomacy works.

When Putin restored himself to the Russian presidency in 2012, the situation changed, as Hillary would later explain in an interview with CNN's Fareed Zakaria. "I knew that he would be more difficult to deal with," she said, adding, "I think that what may have happened is that both the United States and Europe were really hoping for the best from Putin as a returned president. And I think we've been quickly, unfortunately, disabused of those hopes." By late 2012, she was warning that Russia was attempting to re-Sovietize Eastern Europe.

And while Hillary had left office as secretary of state long before the Russian incursion into Ukraine, she continued to publicly voice skepticism about Putin's intentions and concern about his increasing belligerence in the leadup to the crisis. In February 2014, she warned in a speech, "I believe, and this is just my opinion, if there is an opportunity for him to consolidate the position of Russia in eastern Ukraine, he will look seriously at doing that."

As the tragic news from Eastern Europe began to dominate the headlines, Republicans didn't hesitate to politicize the situation. "At best," claims *Failed Choices*, the reset "could be described as a hopelessly naïve attempt at diplomacy with Vladimir Putin. At worst, it was a deadly miscalculation that only empowered him to support some of the world's worst leaders and regimes, trample on the rights of Russians, and weaken American prestige."

Suddenly, the conservative media was ablaze with the latest talking points about the reset. Conservative pundit S. E. Cupp warned that if Hillary "thinks she's going to get off the hook for it, she's sadly mistaken," adding in an appearance on CNN, "This is going to haunt her for the next two years." *Fox and Friends* hosted, I imagine, more foreign policy talk than ever before, blasting a chyron about the FAILED RUSSIAN RESET and making sure to note underneath, "Clinton one of the architects of that policy."

Meanwhile, under the headline HILLARY CLINTON'S UKRAINE—AND 2016—PROBLEM, *Politico* noted ominously that Hillary would be "tethered" to her time as secretary of state.

Republican politicians followed suit. "This whole 'reset policy' with Hillary Clinton," mused Mitt Romney on Fox News in August 2014, "I think is one of the most embarrassing incidents in American foreign policy." Romney couldn't help but offer some advice to his former staffers at America Rising: "That picture of her with the foreign minister of Russia, smiling ear to ear with that red reset button, I presume that's going to be an ad."

All the while, we were working to remind reporters and voters alike that not only had the reset occurred long before Putin's return to power and the Russian invasion of Ukraine, but that it had been a success, leading to tangible advances in U.S.-Russia relations. We circulated an op-ed to this effect from retired U.S. Army general Hugh Shelton, a former Special Forces soldier who served as chairman of the Joint Chiefs of Staff as part of a thirty-eight-year military career.

"Our nation's approach to Russia," Shelton explained, "should mirror that of Secretary Clinton's: clear-eyed and aware of what we are dealing with while working simultaneously to advance America's interests."

Indeed, while Republicans were eager to blame Hillary for events that occurred after she had left office, it is hard to argue that the progress made while she was secretary of state wasn't worth making—and difficult for anyone with any understanding of diplomacy and any integrity when it comes to judging its results to conclude that the reset was in any way responsible for Putin's behavior years later.

In fact, in a poll taken shortly after Putin's invasion of Ukraine, two-thirds of Americans approved of Hillary's time as secretary of state.

⌒

Meanwhile, America Rising was cynically trying to drive a wedge between Hillary and the left by reminding them of her Iraq War vote—which was politically costly for her during the 2008 primary—and terrifying them with the prospect of a return to Bush-era foreign policy. The right wanted nothing more than to encourage a vigorous primary challenger on Hillary's left, hoping that she might end up wounded in her own party, or at least pegged as moving too far left for the general.

Rand Paul talked up his libertarian streak by imagining Democrats choosing him over Hillary because, in his words, "we're worried that Hillary Clinton will get us involved in another Middle Eastern war, because she's so gung-ho."

It worked on some: Ralph Nader, last seen helping to hand George W. Bush the 2000 election, popped his head up to argue that Hillary "thinks Obama is too weak, he doesn't kill enough people overseas. So she's a menace to the United States of America."

Even Jon Stewart described her as "competent" and "very bright" but "a little hawkish for me."

But is Hillary really an unreconstructed hawk? Here's how she described her approach in an August 2014 interview with the *Atlantic*:

> Most Americans think of engagement and go immediately to military engagement. That's why I use the phrase "smart power." I did it deliberately because I thought we had to have another way of talking about American engagement, other than unilateralism and the so-called boots on the ground.

And we don't just have to go by Hillary's words—we have four years of actions to examine. On the thorny issues of war and peace, Hillary's tenure at the State Department not only demonstrates what her "smart power" theory looks like in practice, it inoculates her from Republican attempts to shoehorn her into their caricature of Democrats as weak on foreign policy.

A fair reading of Hillary's record paints her neither as a hawk nor a dove, but rather both a forceful and a measured leader who holds two advantages on foreign policy unrelated to simplistic ideological labels: She's actually done the job well, and no Republican will ever be able to credibly talk down to her on international issues.

And what of that Iraq War vote? Today, many remember it simply as a vote in favor of the disaster that was the Bush administration's pursuit of Saddam Hussein—what MSNBC host Steve Kornacki called "a major step in the march to war in Iraq."

But the Democrats who cast that vote—the majority of Senate Democrats—did so with the hope and belief that it would actually help to slow that march. President Bush had already declared that he could go to war without Congress's assent—just as his father had a decade earlier. Democrats wanted him to go instead to the United Nations to build an international coalition, and Bush suggested that he would be able to do so if he could show that Congress was standing behind him.

The *New York Times* reported at the time that Hillary "said she had concluded that bipartisan support would make the president's success at the United Nations 'more likely and, therefore, war less likely.'"

If you believed the president, a yes vote was a vote to strengthen the last diplomatic tool in his arsenal—and a no vote was a vote to strip him of that tool.

Hillary has described her yes vote as a "mistake." But the mistake was simply that she, like many other Democratic senators who couldn't imagine that a president would actually lie us into war, gave George W. Bush the benefit of the doubt.

Conservatives are, of course, free to continue reminding progressives that Hillary once placed too much trust in the last Republican president, and brother of their likely nominee—who repeatedly flubbed the question of whether he would have supported W.'s war in Iraq and resurrected a number of neocon cheerleaders for that war into his own foreign policy kitchen cabinet.

∼

America Rising's *Failed Choices* was intended to ruin Hillary's book tour, but their effort failed.

While the right never laid a glove on Hillary's book, credible reviewers widely saw it as making a clear and convincing case for how Hillary's leadership skills would serve her well as president.

In the *Washington Post*, Dan Balz wrote, "Through nearly 600 pages, she comes across less a visionary and more a practical-minded problem solver."

His colleague, David Ignatius, agreed: "The book should reinforce the case of those who believe Clinton is well prepared to be president."

"For voters who worry about a complex world," wrote CBS News's John Dickerson, "Clinton will be the candidate most equipped to show voters that they will not be taking a risk by putting the world in her hands."

Readers saw in *Hard Choices* a future commander in chief who will be admired by our friends, feared by our adversaries—and respected by both.

True, there would be more battles to win if Hillary's leadership was to remain her greatest strength. But the first round had gone to the truth.

∼

Having failed to turn the release of *Hard Choices* into an opportunity to undermine Hillary's record of accomplishment in office, Republicans resorted to trying to frame the book's reception among the public as underwhelming. Going from attacking Hillary's tenure at State to launching petty arguments about how many copies the book sold or how many people showed up for a signing was a major step down.

And it's not like this argument held much more water either: *Hard Choices* was one of the best-selling political memoirs of the decade, spending three weeks at number one on the *New York Times* best-seller list and far outpacing similar books authored by other 2016 contenders like Marco Rubio and Scott Walker (whose anemic sales we had researched, and released, anticipating this line of attack). Meanwhile, people lined up for more than seventeen hours for Hillary's first signing, and large crowds turned out for her appearances everywhere from San Francisco to Edmonton.

Hillary also hit an array of media outlets on the book tour—everything from NPR to Fox News. In all, Hillary sat in the hot seat for almost four hours of television interviews, commenting on everything from trouble spots for U.S. policy makers in every part of the globe to economic challenges facing the nation. But it was only two words in one interview—with ABC's Diane Sawyer—that got all the media attention.

Michael Kinsley once said that a gaffe is when a politician gets caught saying what he really thinks. In this sense, Hillary did trip herself up when she told Sawyer that her family was "dead broke" on leaving the White House. As we'll explore at length in chapter ten, the statement was accurate—the Clintons faced a mountain of legal debt from defending themselves against partisan GOP investigations in the '90s—but it provided an opening the Republicans couldn't manufacture on their own.

The Republican message machine kicked into high gear, twisting Hillary's remark into a Mitt Romney–like gaffe, improbably claiming that she was somehow out of touch with a public she had served for more than thirty years. That the right was able to so easily coax the media into trampling on Hillary's otherwise successful book launch by making "dead broke" into a defining controversy foretold the tough fights ahead.

## Chapter Eight

# How Benghazi Became #Benghazi

One of Hillary's goals in *Hard Choices* was to put the Benghazi pseudoscandal to bed. She wrote about the tragedy with candor and insight and emotion. Hillary made clear that as secretary of state, she took responsibility; she took action focused on how to prevent future attacks; and she was transparent with the public throughout the ensuing investigations of the attacks. For reasonable readers, that was the end of the story.

But *Hard Choice*'s passages on Benghazi only inflamed her critics, for they were given nothing new to work with. Thus the right's shameless, macabre efforts to politicize the deaths of four Americans in the attack on our military compound in Benghazi will persist into the 2016 election and perhaps beyond.

The truth about Benghazi is that there's plenty for Americans to mourn, some lessons for policy makers to learn, but absolutely nothing for Hillary Clinton to be ashamed of. And yet it remains a powerful campaign issue for Republicans. A solid 58 percent majority of voters are dissatisfied with the way Hillary handled the Benghazi issue. In order to understand how that happened—how the Republicans managed to create something out of nothing—it's worth going back to the beginning and telling the whole true story, not just of the attack, but of the right-wing smear campaign that grew from its ashes.

⟿

Before Benghazi became #Benghazi—a symbol for racially tinged conservative suspicions that a man named Barack Hussein Obama somehow had to be a terrorist sympathizer; a stimulus package for dishonest right-wing journalists and politicians craving attention and financial support from the easily misled Republican base; and a phony scandal that Republicans desperately hope will keep Hillary Clinton out of the White House—it was simply a heartbreaking tragedy.

On September 11, 2012, the eleventh anniversary of the terrorist attacks on New York and Washington, seven Americans were working at a small American compound in Benghazi, Libya: J. Christopher Stevens (a well-regarded diplomat who was serving as our ambassador to Libya), Sean Smith (the compound's thirty-four-year-old chief information officer), and five security personnel charged with protecting them. The larger American presence in the city was at a facility about a mile away known as the annex, which hosted a CIA operation and other American officials.

At around 9:30 p.m. local time (3:30 p.m. in Washington, DC), the smaller compound in Benghazi came under attack. As gunfire rang out, Stevens and Smith were quickly moved to a safe room. But the attackers poured cans of gasoline around the compound, setting two buildings ablaze—including the sanctuary in which Stevens and Smith were huddled. Five American security personnel didn't stand a chance against waves of hostile fighters, and they were unable to extract the two men before the inferno of smoke and fire claimed their lives.

Sean Smith died on-site. Chris Stevens was eventually taken to a hospital by Libyans who knew and respected him, but he could not be resuscitated.

After 11:00 p.m., the fighting receded, and a security team from the CIA annex was able to evacuate the small compound, bringing the survivors back to the annex. Meanwhile, a security team was scrambled from the Libyan capital of Tripoli, chartering an aircraft as soon as they could in the middle of the night and arriving at the annex around 5:00 a.m. with the intention of evacuating the Americans. But within minutes of their arrival, the hostile forces turned their attention to the annex in a brief but furious attack. Three mortar rounds hit the roof of the building within a ninety-second span. Tyrone S. Woods, a member of the team who evacuated the small compound, and Glen Doherty, a member of the rescue team just arrived from Tripoli, were killed.

Twelve hours after the first attack began, the evacuation was complete. Some thirty surviving Americans had safely escaped from Benghazi—bringing with them the bodies of those who had perished.

That's what happened in Benghazi. And if the right had never spun up the attack into a fake scandal, that's exactly how we might remember it today: as a tragedy in which four patriots who had taken on difficult and dangerous assignments in service to their country lost their lives.

In addition to their sacrifice, we might remember the enormous courage displayed by the small group of operatives who somehow managed to save the lives of the five security personnel who had faced overwhelming fire at the compound, recover Sean Smith's body in the midst of incredible chaos, and safely evacuate dozens of people from the annex.

And, yes, we might try to learn from the tragedy, asking important questions about whether our security protocols were sufficient to protect American diplomats in hot zones like Libya, and whether steps needed to be taken to help prevent something like this from happening again.

Perhaps such a clear-eyed assessment would never have been possible in a political environment in which the GOP turns even minor controversies—let alone complex and emotionally fraught episodes like the Benghazi attack—into partisan food fights. But what happened in the aftermath of that fateful night—the process by which tragedy was turned into scandal—was remarkable, even by modern American standards.

Today, Benghazi remains, in the eyes of the right, one of Hillary Clinton's most damaging political liabilities—despite the absence of any evidence, from ten independent reviews and congressional inquiries, including those led by Republicans, that she did anything wrong before, during, or after the attack.

It's a seemingly perfect attack against Hillary, because it ties together a series of conservative tropes about her: that she's secretive and imperious, cold and uncaring, obsessed with her political standing, and calculating in everything she does. It offers the right wing the opportunity to reinforce decades-old stereotypes of liberals as limp on defense, weak in fighting terrorist enemies, always eager to cut and run. Republicans get the chance to launch fishing expeditions—backed by the power of Congress—that remain unaccountable to the public and wholly political in their intent. Conservative media can speculate wildly about What She's Covering Up. And it offers countless opportunities for the mainstream media to get drawn into the scandal launderers' game.

Benghazi was a tragedy. But "#Benghazi," as conservatives tweeted over and over again in an attempt to keep the story alive, is a hoax: a series of false accusations, ridiculous conspiracy theories, and unsupported innuendoes, a partisan attack unmoored from facts.

But it's no stretch to say that for conservatives, the facts of what happened that night are practically irrelevant, because the politicization of the Benghazi tragedy began well before those facts were even clear.

And it's only a little bit of a stretch to suggest that it all started because Mitt Romney screwed up his nominating convention.

⌒

You remember that convention: Clint Eastwood yelling at an empty chair, Chris Christie's speech that was mostly about Chris Christie (and not about his party's nominee), the program that ran long and pushed Romney's star turn out of the prime hour for live news coverage. But aside from the series of embarrassing missteps on the part of Romney's team, the candidate himself made a serious mistake in crafting his acceptance speech: On the biggest stage of the campaign, with a general electorate audience tuning in to hear his case, Mitt Romney didn't say one word about the American troops who were still fighting and dying in Afghanistan.

The media roundly criticized this glaring omission, and voters may have taken note, as well: Romney's single-point lead in the ABC News/*Washington Post* poll had turned to a six-point deficit by the time the Democratic convention ended a few weeks later.

September 11 offered Romney a chance to fix his error as he spoke before the National Guard Association convention in Reno. He and President Obama had agreed to hold off on any negative campaigning during the anniversary of the 9/11 attacks; Romney would declare in his remarks that it was not "a time and a place" for criticizing the president. But he could still offer effusive praise for American troops, outline his foreign policy agenda, and suggest ways to improve veterans' health care—in short, he could clean up the mess he'd made by ignoring all these topics in his convention speech.

Word of an attack on the Benghazi compound reached the Romney campaign as the candidate flew from Reno, where his speech had been well received, to Florida, where he planned to campaign the next day. The initial information was muddled and contradictory. The attack had begun at night, and it wasn't even clear then it was over.

It had been a tumultuous day across the Middle East. Outside the embassy in Cairo, some three thousand protestors had rallied to condemn an American-made YouTube video that mocked the Prophet Muhammad. Could the day's biggest news from Cairo be related to the breaking news from Libya? Nobody knew.

Tellingly, the Romney campaign decided to shoot first and ask questions later. Forget about the 9/11 political truce; the time and place to hit the president was right now. Indeed, just a couple of hours after

Romney assured the crowd in Reno that he wouldn't attack the president on September 11, his campaign issued a press release. Not satisfied with simply expressing sorrow over the loss of American life or resolve that the attackers should be brought to justice, Romney attempted a bank shot to turn the attack into a political football right away, excoriating the administration for a statement made by Embassy Cairo in the wake of the protests there that echoed condemnations of the YouTube video:

> I'm outraged by the attacks on American diplomatic missions in Libya and Egypt and by the death of an American consulate worker in Benghazi. It's disgraceful that the Obama administration's first response was not to condemn attacks on our diplomatic missions, but to sympathize with those who waged the attacks.

The campaign first attempted to embargo the release until after midnight to avoid breaking the 9/11 truce, but that would have meant missing the late news and the deadlines at many newspapers, so at 10:24 p.m. Eastern time, the Romney release went live. That statement still rings out as shockingly disingenuous today for three reasons.

The first, of course, was that Romney was accusing a sitting president of sympathizing with terrorists on the eleventh anniversary of the most infamous terrorist attack in American history.

The second was that Obama himself, along with Secretary Clinton, shared the view that our embassy in Cairo's statement had been too conciliatory; in fact, even before Romney's release hit reporters' in-boxes, the White House and the State Department had repudiated it. "Let me be clear," said Secretary Clinton in her statement, released *before* Romney's. "There is never any justification for violent acts of this kind." The White House concurred, adding: "The statement by Embassy Cairo was not cleared by Washington and does not reflect the views of the United States government."

The third would end up being perhaps the most ironic: Like the Obama administration and many other observers, Romney's team was speculating that there might well be a link between the protests over the video in Cairo and the attack in Benghazi; when this was later found not to be the case, Republicans would savage the Obama administration for suggesting such a connection in the early days after the tragedy.

But that wouldn't come to light for some time. As America woke up to the disastrous news from Libya on the morning of September 12, commentators were sharing their shock and even outrage that the Romney campaign had rushed to violate the 9/11 truce, attacking the administration for a statement it had already disavowed in order to make the outrageous claim that President Obama, always under conservative suspicion for being "un-American," sympathized with terrorists.

Given such a backlash, a less desperate candidate might have retreated. But Romney, setting an example that the GOP would follow for months and years to come, felt he had no choice but to exploit the dead Americans for partisan gain. He called a press conference the next day and repeated his attack, even the part that had been proven wrong: "I also believe the administration was wrong to stand by a statement sympathizing with those who had breached our embassy in Egypt, instead of condemning their actions," he said, ignoring the reality that the administration had not stood by that statement in any way whatsoever.

⌒

With just two months to go before the election and President Obama ahead in the polls, Romney and the Republicans knew that Benghazi might be their last chance to rally. They looked for anything that could turn the tragedy into an example of President Obama's weakness, incompetency, corruption—anything that would stick.

The first story they told was that the administration was falsely attempting to cast the attack as something other than terrorism in order to minimize the terrorist threat and vindicate Obama's "soft on terror" approach to the world so that it wouldn't come back to bite him in November.

They focused on Ambassador to the United Nations Susan Rice's appearances on five Sunday shows on September 16. Using talking points put together and signed off on by the intelligence community for congressional staff, Rice described the government's preliminary assessment that the attacks were inspired by the protests—while making it very clear that the assessment was ongoing and the conclusion could change.

"We'll wait to see exactly what the investigation finally confirms," she told Jake Tapper of ABC News, "but that's the best information we have at present."

In the following days and weeks, facts emerged that complicated this early assessment. The Benghazi attack hadn't been spontaneous violence that emerged organically from the protests that rocked the Middle East that day, but rather a planned and premeditated assault on Americans.

The right grabbed on to this one thread with both hands and hoped to yank hard enough to unravel the entire Obama administration, which stood accused by conservatives of lying about the attack's origins to cover up a weak antiterror policy.

Turning this into a scandal required conservatives to accuse the president of putting partisan politics ahead of national security (which probably came relatively easy for them). It required them to believe that the president who ordered the raid that killed Osama bin Laden was afraid to talk about terrorism during a campaign. And, of course, it required them to forget not only that Rice had cautioned that her assessment was preliminary, but that the Romney campaign had made *the exact same preliminary assessment* in its press release.

But that didn't stop conservatives from trying, as they took a page from the Bush-Cheney playbook to demagogue the issue and frighten

Americans on the eve of an election. "It looks and smells and probably is a cover-up," said Fox News host Eric Bolling, adding that the "White House is covering up for what is going to end up being a terrorist attack on American soil."

Rice's statements on those Sunday shows—and the provenance of the talking points she was speaking from—became the subject of plenty of congressional grandstanding during the investigations that would ensue. Ultimately, they gave Republican senators an excuse to block her nomination to succeed Hillary Clinton as secretary of state. But they didn't end up factoring into the November election, because just a few weeks later, Mitt Romney took an even bigger swing at President Obama—and whiffed completely.

The talking point that Obama was so averse to confronting the threat of terrorism that he wouldn't even utter the word was a staple of the conservative talk shows for years. It all began when the president spoke in Cairo in 2009, calling for a new era of relations between the West and the Islamic world, a speech that was widely praised just about everywhere but on Fox News. Fox managing editor Bill Sammon had noticed something, e-mailing his staff to say: "My cursory check of Obama's 6,000-word speech to the Muslim world did not turn up the words 'terror,' 'terrorist,' or 'terrorism.'" The president had, in fact, spent much time discussing the fight against "violent extremists who pose a grave threat to our security," but he hadn't said the T-word, so Fox News ran with the story, airing Sammon's argument multiple times over the next twenty-four hours.

So the idea that Obama was playing politics by covering up terrorism in Benghazi fit a preexisting conservative meme, one that Romney himself fell prey to onstage at the presidential debate on October 16.

Asked about what happened in the Benghazi tragedy, Obama discussed his administration's response, outlined newly implemented increased security measures designed to protect diplomats, and defended Hillary Clinton's performance as secretary of state. Then, he took on a claim Romney had just made about the president's "apology tour" (a popular conservative falsehood suggesting that Obama had apologized to America's adversaries, when in fact he never had) and his "strategy of leading from behind."

"The day after the attack, Governor," the president said, "I stood in the Rose Garden and I told the American people and the world that we are going to find out exactly what happened. That this was an act of terror and I also said that we're going to hunt down those who committed this crime."

Rather than engage on the substance of the administration's diplomatic security policies or counterterrorism record, Romney decided to take a cue from the conservative hive mind and attack the president on his rhetoric: "I think it's interesting the president just said something which—which is that on the day after the attack he went into the Rose Garden and said that this was an act of terror."

"That's what I said," the president replied.

Romney continued: "You said in the Rose Garden the day after the attack, it was an act of terror. It was not a spontaneous demonstration, is that what you're saying?" Clearly, he thought he was moments away from a spectacular gotcha moment. And he was—just not the one he was expecting.

Obama, of course, knew what Romney was doing. "Please proceed, Governor," he said.

Romney wheeled around to face the audience like a prosecutor eyeing up a jury. "I want to make sure we get that for the record, because it took the president fourteen days before he called the attack in Benghazi an act of terror."

"Get the transcript," said Obama. But someone already had.

"He did in fact, sir." It was Candy Crowley, the CNN moderator. "So let me—let me call it an act of terror..."

Obama decided to ice the cake, raising his voice to ask, "Can you say that a little louder, Candy?"

Crowley repeated: "He did call it an act of terror."

By rushing to attack the president on 9/11, Romney had done enormous damage to his credibility. And by relying on the conservative echo chamber for his talking points during the debate, without taking the simple step of verifying that what they were saying was true, he stepped in it once again on a big stage at a critical moment.

While Romney and his allies were busy trying—and spectacularly failing—to score political points off dead Americans, the Obama administration was taking steps that showed just how seriously it took the terrorist attacks. Using a procedure established under a 1986 antiterrorism law, Secretary Clinton commissioned an Accountability Review Board (ARB), cochaired by Ambassador Thomas Pickering, who had served five Republican and Democratic presidents as a diplomat and State Department official, and Admiral Mike Mullen, chairman of the Joint Chiefs of Staff under both President Bush and President Obama, and filled out with several other well-respected officials. ARBs had been commissioned after other attacks on State Department facilities, including the 1983 attacks on the Marine barracks in Beirut in the Reagan era and the 2004 attack on an American consulate in Saudi Arabia during George W. Bush's tenure—neither of which were polticized by the Democratic Party in the way Benghazi would be by the Republicans.

Under Hillary's direction, the State Department took the rare step of releasing the results of the ARB to the public—an act of transparency that earned her no credit from critics. The Benghazi ARB interviewed more than one hundred parties at all levels of government, and ended up delivering a stark verdict, finding that "systemic failures and leadership and management deficiencies at senior levels within two bureaus of the State Deparment...resulted in a Special Mission security posture that was inadequate for Benghazi and grossly inadequate to deal with the attack that took place."

Further, the ARB found that "certain senior State Department officials within two bureaus demonstrated a lack of proactive leadership and management ability in their responses to security concerns posed by Special Mission Benghazi, given the deteriorating threat environment and the lack of reliable host government protection."

The ARB's report won modest praise from conservative senators (John McCain, Lindsey Graham, and Kelly Ayotte wrote in a *Washington Times* article that it "sheds important light on some of the failings within the State Department"), and it got results: Four State Department staffers were placed on administrative leave, and the Obama administration was offered twenty-nine recommendations for policy changes that could help improve security at State Department facilities overseas, which it immediately set about implementing. By January, as Hillary left office, sixty-four action items had already been created, and most of them had already been taken or were in the process of being carried out.

But Republicans persisted in producing episode after episode of Scandal Theater. The right-wing media grasped at straws, looking for any new angle, and Fox News hosts stood by, ready to fill the broadcast day with innuendo. Mainstream journalists tried to sift through the details in order to evaluate the partisan claims, thereby giving them oxygen. And, most of all, Republican politicians eager for the face time, adulation, and fund-raising bumps demanded hearing after hearing, hoping to keep asking questions until they heard an answer they thought they could pounce on.

At the front of that line were two House Republicans. Darrell Issa of California, one of the wealthiest members of Congress, had been in the House for a decade after getting rich from his car alarm company. Now, as chairman of the Committee on Oversight and Government Reform, he was the House's king of pseudoscandal, holding the same position that Representative Dan Burton of Indiana had during the Clinton years, when Burton shot a bullet into a watermelon while trying to validate conspiracy theories about Vincent Foster's suicide. Issa's colleague, a telegenic Utahan Tea Partier named Jason Chaffetz, led the committee's Subcommittee on National Security. With their subpoena power, the two were in a position to hold hearings on any subject they wanted—and they wanted to talk about Benghazi.

Anyone who believed that Issa and Chaffetz were planning to improve on the ARB's investigation must not have been paying attention during the 1990s, when Republican congressional investigators used the powers of their office not to find facts, but to harass and embarrass the Clintons.

Indeed, the Republican investigations quickly revealed themselves to be nothing more than witch hunts. As Democratic minority staff on the House committee complained, "The Chairman and his staff failed to consult with Democratic Members prior to issuing public letters with unverified allegations, concealed witnesses and refused to make one hearing witness available to Democratic staff, withheld documents obtained by the Committee during the investigation, and effectively excluded Democratic Committee Members from joining a poorly-planned congressional delegation to Libya."

It was, as Oversight Committee ranking member Elijah Cummings of Maryland put it, "investigation by press release." Chaffetz in particular was on his way to right-wing stardom, becoming a frequent guest on Fox News, which covered the proceedings almost nonstop. (At one hearing, Issa's remarks were carried live, but when it was Cummings's turn to speak, the network cut away to an interview with John Bolton, the former Bush U.N. ambassador.)

Leaks were fed regularly to rouse the conservative base and titillate the press corps. In their fervor, Republicans repeatedly revealed classified information that put American lives in danger. Issa didn't care, telling State Department officials, "Anything below 'Secret' is in fact just a name on a piece of paper."

And at the end of the day, Issa and Chaffetz found nothing. In fact, ten congressional committees would investigate Benghazi and find nothing. There would be more than fifty senior-level staff briefings, fourteen public hearings, multiple independent reviews, dozens of interviews, countless "accidental" disclosures, thousands of man-hours, and millions of taxpayer dollars, and not one piece of evidence to suggest wrongdoing by the Obama administration, or that anyone had attempted to cover up the facts or mislead the public. Nothing.

At times, their attempts were downright laughable. For example: During one hearing, Defense Secretary Leon Panetta and Joint Chiefs of Staff Chairman Martin Dempsey testified that, following an initial meeting with the president, neither had spoken directly to him again on the night of September 11.

The right-wing media stoked faux outrage. Michael Barone of the *Washington Examiner* wrote, "Obama apparently wasn't curious about what was happening in Benghazi. He wasn't too concerned either the next morning, when after the first murder of a U.S. ambassador in 33 years, he jetted off on a four-hour ride to a campaign event in Las Vegas. I don't think you have to be a Republican partisan to consider that unseemly"—but it helps.

Fox's Monica Crowley made sure to loop Hillary into the accusation when she said that "the two leaders of the U.S. government were unaccounted for that night. We have no narrative of where they were or what they were doing."

In fact, as Panetta and Dempsey had testified at that same hearing, the president had instructed them to respond immediately and deploy all available forces—and, as Dempsey testified, "his staff was engaged with the National Military Command Center...pretty constantly through the period, which is the way it would normally work."

The misinformation spread to false reports of Hillary's role. Laura Ingraham asked Republican representative Peter King during an interview on her radio show, "We know that the secretary of state had not [had] a single conversation with the commander in chief. Not one during this attack. Not one conversation? That seems bizarre to me. I mean that's just one point, but that's a pretty darn good question. Why?"

"Absolutely," King responded. "It's an excellent question, and to me it's one that, it's unfortunate that it even has to be asked. I mean, you'd think they would have been on the phone or in contact continually."

"My God," exclaimed Ingraham.

Actually, as Hillary had testified months earlier, she spent the afternoon and evening at the State Department—coordinating with military, intelligence, and national security officials; working to get cooperation from Libyan officials; receiving situation updates; and participating in secure videoconferences. And, to answer Ingraham's question, in addition to working closely with his top staff, Hillary did in fact speak with Obama that evening,

⌒

Even the fondest hopes of the Republican base (and the slickest promises from scammy online fund-raising pitches) couldn't turn Benghazi into an impeachable scandal—but with Hillary out of office and clearly lined up to be a formidable presidential candidate in 2016, she became a more inviting target for the Benghazi truthers.

The would-be scandal became an endless pseudoscandal. "Privately," as *Politico* reporter Mike Allen told Charlie Rose in 2013, "Republicans say that Benghazi probably wouldn't be an issue if it weren't for Hillary Clinton."

Meanwhile, as most Democrats saw it, Obama had been reelected, the Accountability Review Board had done its work, and the barrage of congressional investigations was seen as an annoying but ultimately harmless sideshow.

But I was worried, because I saw Republicans gearing up to run another one of their time-tested favorite plays. After all, none of this was new. None of it ever is. I kept thinking about Whitewater.

Much like Benghazi, the point of Whitewater wasn't that the Clintons had done anything wrong (in fact, none of the Whitewater allegations against them ever withstood even the slightest scrutiny). The point, at least for conservatives, was that there was so much to investigate—so many pointed questions to ask, so many innuendos to spread, so many leaks to give to friendly reporters willing to put unsubstantiated allegations into print under the guise of revealing what was being looked into.

And the longer the Whitewater investigations dragged on, the more Republicans could claim to investigate, simply by accusing the Clintons of obstructing the inquiry that kept finding nothing. The old saying is that the cover-up is worse than the crime. But if you're an unscrupulous right-wing operative, you don't even need to prove that a crime was ever committed to make it seem like there's a cover-up. If a Democrat can't prove a false negative, the game can go on forever.

Thus, it's no wonder that the first attempt to make Hillary the issue was the one I watched from afar while on vacation: accusing her of faking her concussion to get out of facing the music by testifying before Congress. Couldn't she prove she hadn't faked it?

When, a few weeks later, Hillary recovered and testified, conservatives promptly accused her of faking her emotions at the loss of four Americans, relying on another Hillary stereotype, that of a coldhearted shrew whose emotions were never authentic.

"For me," she told the Senate Foreign Relations Committee, tearing up as she spoke, "this is not just a matter of policy, it's personal. I stood next to President Obama as the Marines carried those flag-draped caskets off the plane at Andrews. I put my arms around the mothers and fathers, the sisters and brothers, the sons and daughters, and the wives left alone to raise their children."

It was hard to watch that moment and square it with the right's caricature of Hillary as uninterested in anything but her own political future. But they tried anyway, accusing her of putting on a show. Laura Ingraham tweeted a quote that Hillary was "lip-synching crying about Benghazi victims." Rush Limbaugh called it "part of the script." Sean Hannity claimed that her feelings were "staged, probably at the direction of" James Carville. And Republicans in office agreed: Senator Ron Johnson of Wisconsin echoed to *BuzzFeed*, "I think she just decided before she was going to describe emotionally the four dead

Americans, the heroes, and use that as her trump card to get out of the questions."

You can decide for yourself whether Hillary Clinton—who clearly and repeatedly took responsibility as secretary of state, who fully and publicly answered questions under oath again and again, who authorized an independent investigation and immediately began implementing its recommendations so as to avoid future attacks—was only pretending to care about what happened in Benghazi, or whether Republican operatives bent on portraying Hillary as cold and uncaring were always going to paint whatever she said about the attack as, well, cold and uncaring.

Either way, the focus on Hillary was no accident. Even as they have pretended to be interested only in the truth, Republicans haven't been able to help themselves from revealing their true purpose in focusing on her role in the tragedy.

Appearing on *Fox News Sunday*, RNC chair Reince Priebus made it clear: "If she's even thinking about running for president, I think she has been disqualified because of her actions here." Rand Paul called Benghazi "her main Achilles' heel." Benghazi remains a key fundraising tool for the anti-Hillary SuperPACs, including America Rising (whose e-book *Failed Choices* featured a chapter on Benghazi), Stop Hillary PAC (which gathered more than 120,000 signatures on a listbuilding petition demanding that Hillary testify before yet another Republican committee), and even a new group called The Benghazi Truth PAC.

But what, exactly, are they claiming? Here are three of the most notable falsehoods:

## The "critical cables"

An April 2013 report by five Republican House chairmen (led by Darrell Issa) mentioned Hillary Clinton's name thirty times and Barack Obama's only eleven. Its very first bullet made it clear that Hillary was now the target of the investigation, and revealed their first substantive claim:

> Reductions of security levels prior to the attacks in Benghazi were approved at the highest levels of the State Department, up to and including Secretary Clinton. This fact contradicts her testimony before the House Foreign Affairs Committee on January 23, 2013.

Not only were Republicans accusing Hillary of personally leaving the Benghazi compound vulnerable, they were claiming she perjured herself when she testified that concerns about inadequate security "did not come to [her] attention or above the assistant secretary level where the ARB...placed responsibility."

As proof, the Republican report cited two documents described as "critical cables." One was sent on March 28, 2012, from then ambassador Gene Cretz "to Secretary Clinton" asking for more security resources in Libya. The second was an April 19, 2012, response "bearing Secretary Clinton's signature" acknowledging and denying the request.

Issa ran to Fox News to boast, "She said she did not participate in this, and yet only a few months before the attack, she outright denied security in her signature in a cable, April 2012." Host Brian Kilmeade helpfully explained that the cable "sharply contradicts her sworn testimony." "Damning," said *Townhall*. A "bombshell," raved *Fox Nation*. HILLARY LIED, AND FOUR DIED IN BENGHAZI, read a headline in an *Investor's Business Daily* editorial.

Rand Paul trumpeted that, in light of the "critical cables," "Mrs. Clinton should never hold high office again." Karl Rove's SuperPAC ran a ninety-second web ad that ignored Barack Obama and focused on Hillary as the main Benghazi villain.

But the entire "critical cables" attack was based on a basic misunderstanding of how the State Department works. As fact-checker and longtime State Department reporter Glenn Kessler wrote in his *Washington Post* column, "Cables are in effect group e-mails, which are stored in a database and made available to people with the proper security clearances." Moreover, "every single cable from Washington gets the secretary's name at the bottom, even if the secretary happens to be on the other side of the world at the time."

As secretary of state, Hillary "signed" hundreds of thousands of cables during her tenure—which doesn't mean she wrote, or even read, them all, a practice that dates back through previous administrations. The entire attack, Kessler found, "relies on an absurd understanding of the word 'signature.'"

## *Americans "left behind" / the stand-down order*

In May 2013, Fox News host Eric Bolling talked about the motto of the U.S. armed forces: "Leave no one behind. Leave no one under fire wanting or wondering if America was going to come back and help them. That's what Barack Obama, Hillary Clinton, and the administration did on September eleventh of 2012. They left four Americans to die because they said 'Stand down, don't go help,' and that is a problem."

This was a shocking claim, even by Fox News standards, but it neatly captures the desperate tone of conservatives struggling to find a smoking gun. *FrontPage Mag* spelled it out: "The Obama administration undoubtedly understood that its decision to leave defenseless Americans, including our ambassador, to needlessly die at the hands of al-Qaeda-linked jihadists would not go over well for a commander-in-chief in the throes of a presidential election and a secretary of state angling for the Oval Office in 2016."

On *Townhall*, Katie Pavlich wrote, "The men in Libya were left to die as military forces were told to stand down." And on Fox News, KT McFarland, who had run against Hillary for the Senate in 2006, attempted to square the circle: "I've got a guess that it's something that was a political decision. And not only a political decision not to give them the kind of security they wanted, but it was probably a political decision not to rescue them."

Nobody has ever explained why Obama or Hillary would have thought leaving Americans to die in a terrorist attack was good politics. But the facts make the question irrelevant: No one was "left behind" in Benghazi. The survivors and the bodies of the deceased were evacuated within twelve hours of the attack.

The more serious charge, then, is that additional armed forces, prepared to respond to the attack and thus, perhaps, thwart it before it could claim lives, had been mysteriously ordered to stand down.

Here's where this claim began: In a private interview prior to his public testimony, diplomat Gregory Hicks told House staffers that an additional team of CIA and military personnel and contractors had been preparing to board a plane in Tripoli when its commander, Lieutenant Colonel S. E. Gibson, "got a phone call from SOCAFRICA which said, 'you can't go now, you don't have the authority to go now.' And so they missed the flight.... They were told not to board the flight, so they missed it."

Republicans quickly leaked partial excerpts of the private interview, and it became the basis for a dramatic moment in Hicks's public testimony when Jason Chaffetz asked him how the team "react[ed] to being told to stand down." Chaffetz used the term again on Fox: "We had people that were getting killed, we had people who are willing to risk their lives to go save them, and somebody told them to stand down." Issa doubled down on the attack in a press release: "Who gave the order for special operations forces to stand down, preventing them from helping their compatriots under attack?"

If this rhetoric makes you think of Jack Nicholson imploding on the witness stand in *A Few Good Men*, that's no accident. It was an inflammatory charge, infused with mystery, encouraging people to imagine Obama (or, even better, Hillary) inexcusably denying life-saving assistance to Americans under fire. Republicans clearly expected the trail to lead straight to the upper reaches of the administration. "To a lot of people's understanding," Fox host Steve Doocy told his audience, providing the "Who's there?" to Issa's "Knock, knock" press release, "the only people who could say stand down would be the president of the United States and the secretary of defense."

Hicks, of course, never used the term "stand down" or referred to an order from the White House. But the existence of such an order was treated by conservatives as established fact, and Fox aired the accusation at least eighty-five times in the following weeks.

Conservatives never got their *A Few Good Men* moment, however, because no stand-down order had ever been given. As chairman of the Joint Chiefs of Staff General Martin Dempsey would explain, the team had actually been "told that the individuals in Benghazi were on their way back and that they would be better used at the Tripoli Airport—because one of them was a medic—that they would be better used to receive the casualties coming back from Benghazi and that if they had gone, they would have simply passed each other in the air."

Lieutenant Colonel Gibson confirmed that he had not received a stand-down order, and his commanding officer corroborated his testimony.

The truth is, even if Gibson's team had boarded the plane, it would not have left the tarmac—let alone arrived in Benghazi—until nearly an hour after the second attack occurred. They would have been too late to save any lives, and, indeed, lives may have been jeopardized because survivors might have landed in Tripoli only to find that the medic had gone to the scene from which they had just been evacuated.

Of course, Fox News never corrected the record. Rather than wrestle with the fact that they had, effectively, falsely accused the U.S. military of falling short in its duty to protect Americans—thus slandering the men and women who keep us safe—conservatives continued to insist that the phantom order had been given.

## The "whistleblowers"

As claim after claim fizzled in the face of the facts, conservatives kept hoping that something would emerge to cast blame on Hillary Clinton.

In mid-April 2013, CBS News's Sharyl Attkisson rode to their rescue with a report claiming that "multiple new whistleblowers [were] privately speaking" to congressional investigators. Her report pointed to letters, leaked by Issa's committee, asking the CIA, the Department of Defense, and the State Department to help obtain security clearances for attorneys so that whistleblowers at that agency could lawyer up—in the event, as Issa cleverly suggests, "the agency subsequently retaliates against them for cooperating with the committee's investigation."

New witnesses being intimidated and retaliated against by Hillary and her top aides to suppress damning information? It was just the sort of thuggish behavior that the right would expect of the vaunted "Clinton machine." The story lit up the Washington sky. After all, this was CBS News, not Fox. Indeed, days after Attkisson broke the story Issa had leaked to her—with the scandal freshly laundered and ready for pickup—Issa promptly announced a hearing to "examine evidence that the Obama administration officials have attempted to suppress information."

But Attkisson proved to be an untrustworthy source—belying her network's reputation as a credible and serious outlet, but surprising few who were familiar with her record.

Previously, Attkisson had received notoriety for reporting that cast doubt on the safety of vaccines, and acclaim from the right for her investigations into the Bureau of Alcohol, Tobacco, and Firearms' so-called Fast and Furious operation—another popular conservative conspiracy theory falsely alleging that the Obama administration allowed guns to be trafficked across the U.S. border with Mexico. She even received an award at a Conservative Political Action Committee conference for her intrepid reporting.

After leaving her job at CBS, Attkisson joined the right-wing Heritage Foundation, and she wrote a book about her experiences in the news business. Darrell Issa was the guest of honor at the book party. As part of the launch, she claimed, bizarrely, that the government had attempted to hack her personal computer, releasing a video illustrating what she claimed was an unnamed government agency using keystroke logging software to track her movements. On the video, you see a Microsoft Word document with text rapidly disappearing from the screen, what Attkisson calls "my computer file…wiping at hyperspeed before my eyes."

WATCH SOMEONE IN THE GOVERNMENT TAKE OVER SHARYL ATTKISSON'S COMPUTER, screamed *Townhall*. On Fox, Howard Kurtz called it "highly sophisticated hacking," "chilling stuff."

This was too rich. At Media Matters, we called a computer security expert, who looked at Attkisson's video and quickly figured out what it showed: Her backspace key was stuck.

So, in retrospect, it's not surprising that it was Attkisson who reported the next big break in the Benghazi case.

The whistleblower story helped create the sense that the investigation was still unfolding, long after multiple investigations had run out of gas. Even if Republicans were never able to produce damning evidence of Hillary's complicity, by keeping the issue alive they could continue asking questions—if nothing else to distract her and give her opponents a chance to suggest that the country was still owed answers. "Here's the ugly truth" is a pretty fun thing to say at a press conference; "we still don't know the truth" is almost as good.

So it's no wonder that the week after Attkisson's report, Issa announced that his panel would "examine evidence that Obama administration officials have attempted to suppress information about errors and reckless misjudgments."

And in short order, a familiar face appeared on the scene: Victoria Toensing, an attorney who, along with her law partner and husband, Joseph diGenova, had been key players in the scheme to bring down the Clintons back in the 1990s. I have no doubt that had I not left my old world, I might have been one of the reporters eagerly playing stenographer as Toensing whispered in my ear.

This time, I had to watch from the sidelines as she made the rounds on Fox News and right-wing radio. "I'm not talking generally, I'm talking specifically about Benghazi—that people have been threatened. And not just the State Department. People have been threatened at the CIA," Toensing claimed.

"It's frightening, and they're doing some very despicable threats to people. Not 'We're going to kill you,' or not 'We're going to prosecute you tomorrow,' but they're taking career people and making them well aware that their careers will be over."

It became such a big story that Fox's Ed Henry even demanded to President Obama's face that he help "people in your own State Department saying they've been blocked from coming forward."

Toensing's client was Gregory Hicks (the diplomat who was treated as the source of the "stand down" talking point, even though he'd never said those words). As the deputy chief of mission for the Libya delegation, and someone who had spoken to Ambassador Chris Stevens during the attack and reported to Secretary Clinton that night, Hicks was credible. But when he testified, Hicks didn't say what conservatives were expecting to hear.

One Congressman asked him whether he had been interviewed by the State Department ARB. Hicks had, more than once. Hicks had also spoken to the FBI as part of its investigation.

Okay, so maybe he hadn't been kept quiet—surely he had been punished for speaking out? After all, Toensing had claimed that Hicks had been "demoted."

Actually, not so much, he explained. Hicks had returned to a government job in Washington for personal reasons. "My family really didn't want me to go back. We'd endured a year of separation when I was in Afghanistan in 2006 and 2007. That was the overriding factor. So I voluntarily curtailed—I accepted an offer of what's called a no-fault curtailment. That means that there's—there would be no criticism of my departure of post, no negative repercussions." As was later revealed, Hicks even kept his salary and rank in his new job.

So much for that claim. But conservatives pounced on something else Hicks said before the committee: that the State Department had ordered him "not to allow" himself and his colleagues "to be personally interviewed" by Representative Chaffetz during his fact-finding mission to Libya. *Breitbart News* ran a new story headlined: WHISTLEBLOWER: HILLARY'S STATE DEPT. TOLD ME NOT TO TALK TO CONGRESS.

Not quite. As the *New York Times* later reported, "Mr. Hicks had been free to talk to Mr. Chaffetz, but that department policy required a department lawyer to be present during interviews for any Congressional investigation."

The GOP's "star witness," as Dana Milbank would later write in the *Washington Post*, "was of little use to Republicans in their efforts to connect the lapses in the Benghazi response to Clinton or to the Obama White House."

∾

That fall, another CBS reporter, Lara Logan, had a scintillating report about a previously unheard-from whistleblower: a security contractor using the pseudonym "Morgan Jones" who claimed to be an "eyewitness" to the attack. "Jones's" story was dramatic—he claimed that he had scaled a wall of the Benghazi compound, personally struck a terrorist in the face with his rifle butt, and later went to the hospital, where he saw Ambassador Stevens's body.

This looked like big news: Someone who was there the night of the attack was willing to talk about what he'd seen (the five security personnel who'd been in the safe room with Stevens and Smith had declined to step into the public eye, testifying privately to the FBI and the State Department ARB). And "Jones" charged that not only was the compound inadequately protected, but, even more devastating, that the late Sean Smith had shared similar concerns. Lindsey Graham announced that he would block confirmation of every single Obama nominee until "Morgan Jones" and other government witnesses got to testify before Congress. Benghazi was about to break open once again.

"Morgan Jones" was actually named Dylan Davies, and his story started to crumble almost immediately. Davies, it quickly emerged, had a book coming out two days later—a book published by Threshold, which you may remember is a conservative imprint of Simon & Schuster, which in turn is owned by CBS (Logan never disclosed this during her report). From monitoring Fox, Media Matters picked up that the network had been using Davies as a source but broke contact after he asked for money, thus establishing that Davies didn't even meet the standards of Fox.

But CBS pressed on with its report on Davies's claims—claims that, it turned out, were totally refuted by Davies's own prior accounts. In the incident report he wrote three days after the attack and submitted to his employer, Davies wrote that he never got near the compound—in fact, he spent most of the evening at home. He had not seen Ambassador Stevens's body. He wasn't an eyewitness at all. And not only had he revealed this to his employer before changing his story to write the book and get on TV, he had told the FBI the same: He wasn't there and hadn't seen a thing. CBS had swallowed a lie whole and regurgitated it onto the air.

For several days, Media Matters ran a campaign exposing the *60 Minutes* report's flaws and calling for the network to retract the story. Within two weeks, the story had been taken down, Logan had been placed on administrative leave, and Davies's book had been recalled from stores.

Still, when CBS acknowledged their mistake, they did so in a brief, ninety-second correction that failed to explain how, exactly, a story made up out of whole cloth had made it onto CBS's air, leading us to demand that CBS open a full investigation into what had gone wrong (including the possibility that Logan had been consulting with Lindsey Graham while working on the story).

Despite the best efforts of the conservative media—and the assistance of some in the mainstream press—the right is still looking in vain for its Benghazi whistleblower.

On the Friday before Thanksgiving 2014, the Republican-led House Intelligence Committee released a report summing up two years of work. The *New York Times* reported: "A report released late Friday about the fatal 2012 attacks in Benghazi, Libya, left Republicans in the same position they have been in for two years: with little evidence to support their most damning critiques of how the Obama administration, and then-Secretary of State Hillary Rodham Clinton, responded to the attacks."

After all this, the Benghazi witch hunts have produced nothing. No stand-down order. No blocked rescues. No muzzled whistleblowers. No attempt to mislead the public. Without a smoking gun, Republicans have spent the last two years—and will likely spend the next two—blowing smoke.

So why do they persist? The answer is that while conservatives would be thrilled to find some previously undiscovered evidence to blame Hillary Clinton for the Benghazi attack, they don't need it for their strategy to work. The right, no doubt, has polled the issue, so they know that voters have heard enough about Benghazi to believe that there is blame to be assessed somewhere in the government. They know they've succeeded in sowing the suspicion that there is some further truth not yet told.

They also know that, as long as they continue to talk about Benghazi as some kind of unsolved mystery, the media will continue to hype the "ongoing investigation" into "what really happened that night."

In Media Matters' exhaustive e-book debunking of the right's various lies, *The Benghazi Hoax*, we described Benghazi as a MacGuffin, the late director Alfred Hitchcock's term for "an obscure plot driver whose real significance derives from the way that it motivates the characters." So if we want to know what Benghazi really means, we should look at how it has motivated the characters in our story in the lead-up to Hillary's 2016 campaign.

Benghazi spurred President Obama and Hillary Clinton to review and enhance protections for Americans who serve abroad—Americans like Chris Stevens, Sean Smith, Tyrone Woods, and Glen Doherty. It offered new material for Republicans and conservative media to paint Obama as weak on terror and to undermine Hillary's reputation as a strong secretary of state while burnishing the image of her as a self-serving liar. It provided future opportunities for the blowhards on Capitol Hill, where it was widely thought that the head of the Benghazi inquiry, Trey Gowdy, was angling for a federal judgeship in the next GOP administration. It seduced mainstream journalists too willing to buy right-wing spin in search of something tantalizing to report.

And it was the foundational element of a media dynamic in which everything the Clintons say or do is scandalized—even their path-breaking global philanthropy.

## Chapter Nine

# No Good Deed Goes Unpunished

Full disclosure: I'm a donor to the Clinton Foundation. And, at the level I've given—a few thousand dollars over the years—I'd be considered a substantial donor, since 90 percent of Foundation supporters contribute $100 or less annually.

If that fact surprises you, it should, for the incredibly broad donor base the Foundation attracts to its path-breaking global philanthropy is one of those telling details the press never bothers to tell.

Indeed, of all the controversies that have swirled around the Clintons for years now, it's their work on behalf of the world's neediest that has been most seriously distorted through both partisan sniping and journalistic malpractice.

⌒

The real story of the Clinton Foundation starts back in 2000, when Bill Clinton's two decades of public service through elected office ended, and he found another way to serve, chartering the William J. Clinton Foundation in 2001. After eight years in the White House, and with a long list of domestic and international accomplishments under his belt, he was well regarded, still relatively young, and, as always, committed to using his talents for the greater good.

As Hillary went to work for the people of New York in the United States Senate, the former president traveled the world, meeting with leaders from every walk of life and drawing inspiration for the Clinton Foundation's work.

A meeting with the prime minister of St. Kitts–Nevis at the 2002 International AIDS Conference—and the urging of Nelson Mandela—led to an initiative to combat the global rise of HIV/AIDS, which would eventually become a program called the Clinton Health Access Initiative, focused on improving access to care and treatment around the world. It was a commendable mission for a former president—lowering the prices of life-saving medications—and it became just the first of many such philanthropic initiatives.

The former president's 2005 heart-bypass surgery inspired a partnership with the American Heart Association to address the childhood obesity epidemic. Clinton's own concern about global warming was at the heart of the Clinton Climate Initiative. And having devoted special attention to Haiti throughout his presidency, it's no surprise that his Foundation rushed to the rescue after that nation experienced a horrific earthquake in 2010.

In September 2005, the Clinton Foundation held its first Clinton Global Initiative—an annual meeting of world leaders, CEOs, philanthropists, and other prominent individuals at which each is encouraged not just to talk about pressing issues, but to commit to meaningful action. "Over the course of 10 Annual Meetings, members of the CGI community have made more than 3,200 commitments, which have improved the lives of over 430 million people in more than 180 countries," according to the Clinton Foundation.

Today, the Foundation—renamed the Bill, Hillary & Chelsea Clinton Foundation in order to recognize that philanthropy is a family venture for the Clintons—is focused on a variety of important programs. These include:

- Because of the Foundation's work, more than 27,000 American schools are providing more than 16 million students with healthy meals in an effort to fight obesity.
- The Foundation has made lifesaving antiretroviral drugs more affordable and accessible for more than 9 million people—many of them babies born with the infection—fighting HIV/AIDS through the Clinton Health Access Initiative.
- The incomes of more than 85,000 farmers in places like Malawi, Rwanda, and Tanzania have been raised through training programs and improving market access.
- More than 33,500 tons of greenhouse gas emissions have been reduced annually in the United States—part of a carbon offset of 200,000 tons of $CO_2$ globally through the Clinton Climate Initiatives' Trees of Hope program.
- The Clinton Foundation helped lower the cost of malaria drugs by 80 to 90 percent in nine countries.
- Job One is connecting young people with employment opportunities through commitments by U.S. private sector businesses.
- Too Small to Fail focuses on improving the health and well-being of children in their first five years of life.
- And No Ceilings encourages and empowers women and girls to participate fully and equally in their communities.

Over the years, political leaders from across the spectrum have heaped praise on the Clinton Foundation for making the world a better place. John McCain raved about "the good work you have done to relieve suffering across the earth, and to spread hope." Mitt Romney described the Foundation's "astounding impact" at a CGI Annual Meeting, telling the audience, "One of the best things that can happen to any cause, to any people, is to have Bill Clinton as its advocate." Former First Lady Laura Bush, Fox News founder Rupert Murdoch, New Jersey governor Chris Christie, and former secretary of state Colin Powell have all appeared at Foundation events. Even Christopher Ruddy, CEO of

*NewsMax* and a card-carrying anti-Clintonite from back in the day, pledged a seven-figure donation, saying, "This work is innovative in its scope and in its purpose. I have always found it nonpartisan."

In fact, the Foundation is a 501(c)(3) not-for-profit organization, which means that it is "absolutely prohibited from directly or indirectly participating in, or intervening in, any political campaign on behalf of (or in opposition to) any candidate for elective public office."

But Hillary Clinton is running for president. And all that praise from conservatives who understood and supported the Foundation's mission? It's disappeared down the memory hole.

Now a universally praised philanthropic organization, its noble work on behalf of the world's neediest, supported by leaders and donors of both parties, has suddenly morphed into a crass political adjunct of Hillary Clinton's presidential campaign.

⌒

While it may seem difficult to complain too much about an organization that takes from the rich and gives to the poor, raising over $100 billion through CGI and direct foundation grants to combat social ills in more than 180 countries, the Clintons' partisan opponents and some in the press roll their eyes at the Clinton Foundation's work. They misportray it as an extension of their political reach—a way to keep their network of advisors together, maintain ties with wealthy donors, and continue to accumulate favors.

In the eyes of critics, all those lives saved and changed were merely happy accidents; the Clinton Foundation is a front. And while it may state that its mission is "to bring people together to take on the biggest challenges of the twenty-first century," Clinton antagonists claim that its real purpose is—as the real purpose of everything Bill and Hillary have ever done has been—to enrich and empower the Clintons.

"The Clinton Foundation is not and never has been a charity," as the *Wall Street Journal* editorial page charged. "Bill and Hillary created it in 2001 as a vehicle to assist their continuing political ambitions, in particular Mrs. Clinton's run for the White House. Any good the foundation does is incidental to its bigger role as a fund-raising network and a jobs program for Clinton political operatives."

Kimberley Strassel, a columnist for the paper, renown for its trumpeting of the empty "Clinton Scandals" in the 1990s, wrote, "What's clear by now is that this family enterprise was set up as a global shakedown operation, designed to finance and nurture the Clintons' continued political ambitions. It's a Hillary super PAC that throws in the occasional good deed."

It may be news to Rupert Murdoch, who owns the *Journal* and has contributed to the Foundation through his News Corporation, that he was actually funding Hillary's presidential bid, but no matter.

The idea of "Clinton, Inc.," a vast and secretive empire devoted to the promotion of Bill and Hillary's selfish interests, incorporates several of the narratives conservatives hold dear. And, as we'll see, it is "Conservatives, Inc." (Koch, et al.) funding this phony story line.

They depict Bill Clinton, at his core, as a huckster, the charming Slick Willie who always manages to get away with whatever he wants, skating by with a wink and a rakish grin. They malign the Clinton Foundation as just his own personal slush fund, enabling him to jet around the world, hobnobbing with celebrities, backslapping with cronies.

And with Hillary's political ambitions taking center stage, the old caricatures of her have seeped into her enemies' attack on the family's philanthropy. The right-wing smears the Foundation as a favor bank to support her political career, digging for some kind of quid pro quo that can prove some less than altruistic intent—never finding the "quid" or the "quo."

For years after Hillary left the Obama cabinet and joined the Foundation, scores of right-wing researchers had been fishing for an angle on the Foundation—and in early 2015, it looked like they had found one.

⌒

Before Hillary Clinton became secretary of state in 2009, the Clinton Foundation entered into an agreement with the Obama administration designed to eliminate potential conflicts of interest that could arise when Hillary was making policy decisions that could affect donors to the Foundation. As had been public record for years, the Clinton Foundation, a global philanthropy, relied in part on donations from abroad, including from foreign governments. The agreement allowed governments that had previously donated to the charity to continue giving and set up a review process for new contributor countries.

A February 2015 article in the *Wall Street Journal* reported the breaking news that when Hillary left Foggy Bottom in 2013, the self-imposed agreement had been lifted. Ignoring the fact that the agreement was specifically focused on preventing conflicts of interest while she was in office—conflicts that were obviously no longer in play with Hillary a private citizen again—the *Journal* claimed that its sunset raised "ethical questions."

The game was afoot.

The *Washington Post*'s resident neocon Jennifer Rubin burst into flames as soon as the "extraordinary report" was published, declaring that Hillary's "egregious judgment and untrammeled greed raise real questions about her priorities and ethics." Rubin did her best to raise the stakes of the story, referring to former Virginia Republican governor Bob McDonnell, who was convicted on corruption charges after making calls to aid a donor. (There's always a motive of payback for actual Republican scandals in the GOP-generated pseudoscandals). Rubin asked, "What would be the remedy if, once in office, Hillary Clinton extended her office not only to make calls but also to approve policy and financial arrangements worth billions back to these countries? How will the American people ever be satisfied we are getting her undivided loyalty?"

Rubin was sure to specify that even if "she were now to give all the money back," Hillary still would be suspect. "Republicans should and will, I predict, pummel her with this," she wrote, warning, "If the [mainstream media] is not entirely in her pocket, they will as well."

Meanwhile, on Fox News, reporter John Roberts wondered if

"governments that contributed to the Clinton Foundation [might] have a special in at the White House." The *Washington Free Beacon* speculated that "these donations could be viewed as another way in to Clinton's potential campaign."

How did the *Wall Street Journal* dig up this devastating information? By looking at the Clinton Foundation's website. That was their "Deep Throat." That's right: The only reason the scandalmongering right wing, acting in concert with the mainstream press, was able to mount repeated attacks on the Clinton Foundation was the Foundation's own commitment to transparency. Unlike most charities, the Clinton Foundation discloses all of its contributors' names publicly and refuses to take anonymous contributions, even though such donations are permissible under law and welcomed by many other such groups. In fact, as the *Washington Post* reported, "In posting its donor data, the foundation goes beyond legal requirements, and experts say its transparency level exceeds that of most philanthropies."

The *Wall Street Journal* spent nine months digging through all that publicly available data, looking for some kind of impropriety, some kind of conflict of interest, only to report, "There is no evidence of that with the Clinton Foundation."

While Rubin and others trumpeted the fact that the Clinton Foundation had accepted donations to fund global programs to empower women from repressive governments like Saudi Arabia, the United Arab Emirates, and Qatar (which, as Rubin ominously warned, was "a prominent backer of Hamas"), no one produced any evidence to suggest that, as secretary of state, Hillary had gone easy on these countries—indeed, she aggressively contested their policies, including delivering a "scalding critique of Arab leaders" during a visit to Qatar.

The *Wall Street Journal* never found any evidence of a quid pro quo, because there was none—nothing to suggest that any government ever got anything in exchange for contributing to the Clinton Foundation's work.

The only thing they found was that, once Hillary Clinton was no longer secretary of state, the agreement that the Foundation had voluntarily entered into *while* she was secretary of state was no longer in effect.

Still, the *National Journal*'s Ron Fournier, a Clinton pseudoscandal obsessive, called the Foundation's acceptance of foreign donations—or, as he termed them, "financial favors"—"stupid and sleazy." So much for objective journalism. The *Washington Post* declared that her family's philanthropy now posed a "unique political challenge" for Hillary, and that it "has already become a cause of concern among Democrats." And *Vox*, eager to stoke Democrat panic over the burgeoning "scandal," pointed out that despite the fact that nothing illegal or unethical had occurred, "having a husband who runs a non-profit foundation that's soaking up foreign cash does not help her win."

By the way, nobody bothered to speculate that Jeb Bush might run into the same problems—even though he had a *father* who ran a non-profit foundation that soaked up foreign cash. Like many presidential libraries and initiatives, the George H. W. Bush Presidential Library received seven-figure donations from Kuwait, Saudi Arabia, Oman, the United Arab Emirates, and other countries.

Indeed, drawing on the relationships a president builds during his time in office is a common and accepted way to build support for his postpresidential contributions to society.

It's also, frankly, a way to make personal income, a time-honored tradition going back in recent times to Gerald R. Ford, Ronald Reagan (who got $2 million for one speech in Japan back in 1989), George H. W. Bush, and continuing through Bill Clinton. But Clinton's speeches appear to be the only ones the media finds newsworthy. On June 8, 2015, *Politico Playbook*—the widely read insider news report—ran the following item:

"On talk circuit George W. Bush makes millions but few waves," by Michael Kruse—*Politico*

True to form, the piece, which noted that some of W.'s speaking fees came from foreign sources, landed with a dull thud inside the Beltway.

But the rules are different for the Clintons: *Business Insider* reported that "an aide for one of the likely 2016 GOP candidates" e-mailed a quote hoping to pump up the *Journal* story and concluding, "Only the Clintons..."

⌒

A follow-up story in the *Washington Post* gave the right another bite at the apple.

In 2010, as the Clinton Foundation rushed to aid Haiti in the wake of the devastating earthquake, an unsolicited and unexpected donation of $500,000 arrived from the government of Algeria. It was quickly distributed as direct aid to help the people of Haiti and disclosed publicly on the Clinton Foundation website—but, as the Foundation acknowledged, it should have gone through an ethics review at State first.

If conservatives could prove that the government of Algeria had somehow exacted a concession from the secretary of state in exchange for half a million dollars in earthquake relief aid, then this omission might indeed signal a real scandal, albeit a surprisingly low-budget one.

But the record shows that, as secretary of state, Hillary aggressively challenged the government of Algeria. As the *Washington Post* reported in its initial story:

A 2010 State Department report on human rights in Algeria noted that "principal human rights problems included restrictions on freedom of assembly and association" and cited reports of arbitrary killings, widespread corruption and a lack of transparency. Additionally, the report, issued in early 2011, discussed restrictions on labor and women's rights.

Hillary continued her criticism after leaving office, writing in *Hard Choices* that the nation had a "poor human rights record."

Then in March, the *New York Times* attempted to further the "scandal," pointing to the Foundation's "acceptance of millions of dollars in donations from Middle Eastern countries known for violence against women and for denying them many basic freedoms," suggesting that this was at odds with Hillary's long career as a champion for women and girls, and warning ominously, "This was not how she intended to reintroduce herself to American voters."

Again, though, a look at Hillary's actual record shows that donations to the Clinton Foundation never stopped her from aggressively pursuing the cause of women's rights, even when that meant directly criticizing governments that had given to the charity. For example, the Clinton Foundation accepted a donation from the government of Saudi Arabia—but Hillary was a strong supporter of women who were protesting against that nation's ban on female drivers. And the *Times* itself had previously recorded her being the first U.S. secretary of state to issue a "scalding critique of Arab leaders" for repressing women during a trip to Qatar.

Still, the *Times* article drew the absurd conclusion that these donations made Hillary "vulnerable on the subject" of gender, offering a variety of Republicans space to recite their talking points in addition to regurgitating them in the reporter's voice.

These stories in early spring were just a prelude of the onslaught to come. Though the stories proved nothing, they did signal to the right wing that the mainstream press was becoming invested in the story line that the Foundation was a shady enterprise. And that they'd chase any lead to prove it.

It was the perfect setup. And that's when a Republican operative named Peter Schweizer stepped up to take a center-stage role in a carefully coordinated assault on the Clinton Foundation's work.

Reporters on the Clinton beat had been buzzing for weeks about a new book by Schweizer called *Clinton Cash*. Its thesis—that Hillary, as secretary of state, made favorable government decisions for donors to the Clinton Foundation—was one that many of these same reporters, egged on by the Republicans, had pursued for months. They were eager to see if Schweizer had the goods that so far had eluded them.

News of the book first broke in a *New York Times* piece that hyped its charges and praised the author for "meticulous" research. The *Times* went on to trumpet the "focused reporting" of *Clinton Cash* as "the most anticipated and feared book of a presidential cycle still in its infancy," and that it would prove to be both "problematic" and "unsettling" for the Clintons. The article provided only a small clue about Schweizer's ideological leanings, noting that he had worked for both George W. Bush and Sarah Palin.

The *Times* mentioned in passing that Schweizer ran an outfit called the Government Accountability Intitiative, but failed to tell readers this was a right-wing opposition research shop behind his book, bankrolled by a foundation associated with the main donor to Ted Cruz's presidential SuperPAC and by a donor fund the Koch brothers use as a pass-through to hide their giving. Schweizer had also appeared as a featured speaker at Koch-sponsored political conferences and worked for archconservative North Carolina senator Jesse Helms.

Nor did the *Times* explore the author's long and seriously flawed journalistic record. A seven-thousand-word report on the author's background by Media Matters—all sourced to public information—found he had a long history of issuing retractions and corrections, including a false allegation that a sitting Democratic senator had committed insider trading. The *Washington Post* had called a claim by Schweizer's organization—that President Obama skipped more than half of his presidential daily briefings on intelligence matters—"bogus."

In essence, Schweizer was charging that Hillary Clinton, who spent every waking moment of her tenure as secretary of state protecting U.S. security interests—and winning bipartisan praise for her efforts—had secretly sold our security down the river in exchange for some grants to the Clinton Foundation. The grants, of course, were going not to line the Clintons' own pockets but to do things like fight the AIDS epidemic and bring relief to victims of natural disasters. If that scheme sounds far-fetched to you, apparently the editors of the *New York Times* thought otherwise.

Everything about *Clinton Cash* looked like a Republican oppo hit sandwiched between hard covers by HarperCollins, Rupert Murdoch's publishing house. It was no surprise that Murdoch's Fox News had struck an exclusive deal with the author for TV promotion. But when the *Times*, in its initial report on the book, disclosed it also had an exclusive deal with Schweizer, journalistic eyebrows were raised, including within the *Times*.

The effect of the *Times*' dark deal with Schweizer, working alongside Fox News to market *Clinton Cash*, was obvious. First there was the substantial commercial benefit that news coverage of a book in the *Times* brings an author. Sources in the publishing world buzzed that such banner treatment for a book from the *Times* was worth more than a million dollars in free publicity, all accruing to the benefit of a journalistically discredited GOP hit man, whose work was already being bankrolled by right-wing billionaires, including money from a shadowy fund the Koch brothers use to hide their giving.

But such a deal also confers the *Times* imprimatur. "The book has credibility *because* the *New York Times* cut a deal with the author," wrote *Esquire*'s Charles Pierce. The *Times* thought it was promoting *Clinton Cash*. But all it was doing was conferring its prized journalistic credibility on Koch Cash.

And why did the *Times* do it? "I will make the Toby Ziegler bet with Carolyn Ryan [the *Times* bureau chief] that her newspaper linked up with this character because her newspaper has had a hard-on for the Clintons from the time it botched the original Whitewater story right up until last Sunday, when its star political columnist [Maureen Dowd] went off her meds again."

There it was, the old Whitewater vendetta surfacing again. But on the hypercompetitive Clinton beat, there was also always a commercial angle at work, one that in this case benefitted not only Schweizer but probably the *Times* as well. In a later interview with the paper's public editor, Margaret Sullivan, about the impact of the *Times* political coverage, Ryan seemed to reveal that she was editing *Times* stories with an eye to creating online buzz. She "mentioned that commenters from Matt Drudge to Dylan Byers of *Politico* to Andrew Kaczynski of *BuzzFeed* have praised the coverage or aspects of it," Sullivan wrote. Ryan was publishing Drudge-bait.

If Ryan saw nothing amiss in the *Times'* active collaboration with anti-Clinton operatives, the deal gave the paper a black eye in journalism circles and with its readers, not to mention the consternation within the *Times* itself, where many in the newsroom considered it a terrible lapse in judgment. In addition to questions about the editorial decision to give the book prominent exposure—and thus legitimacy—many *Times* readers wanted to know more about the terms of the Schweizer deal itself.

Yet a newspaper that routinely demands a high degree of transparency from public officials appeared loath to meet those standards when it came to valid questions about its own conduct. What were the terms of the deal? Was money involved? Why did the *Times,* with its tremendous resources, need material from Schweizer's book to pursue Clinton story lines? How was the arrangement "exclusive" if Fox also had an "exclusive" on the book? Who negotiated the deal?

On these and other questions, the *Times* was initially mum. In a quote to *Politico,* Ryan stonewalled, spinning the deal in one terse sentence as routine practice when it clearly wasn't.

Ultimately, the *Times* public editor endeavored to get some answers for readers. Sullivan concluded that no money had changed hands—though she noted there would certainly be considerable financial benefit accruing to the author from exposure in the *Times*—and that the deal contained no unusual restrictions on how the *Times* would use or treat the material. However, Sullivan concluded, "The *Times* should have been much more clear with readers about the nature of this arrangement." And despite Sullivan's best efforts, the exact terms of the deal remained secret.

By now you may be wondering why the *New York Times* is figuring so prominently in a book about "the right-wing plot to derail Hillary."

And you'd be right to wonder. Isn't the *New York Times* the nation's newspaper of record? Wasn't it once the home of giants of journalism like James Reston and Tom Wicker and Anthony Lewis? Isn't its motto "Without Fear or Favor"? Didn't you grow up believing what you read in the *Times*? Doesn't it still publish thousands of column inches of quality reporting each year? And by the way, doesn't the *Times* follow a liberal editorial line?

To all of those questions, of course, the answer is yes. And that's precisely the point.

Conservative politicos may appear on Fox News and right-wing talk radio to throw red meat to the conservative base of the GOP, but when they want to package something as real news, leak it to the press, and get it into the bloodstream of mainstream conversation to mislead the public at large, they turn not to Fox but to the *New York Times*.

How did this happen?

For at least twenty years now—back to the time I was doing it myself—clever Republican operatives have known that they can do maximum political damage to their Democratic and progressive opponents only by manipulating the elite media, which sets the news agenda for most of the country. Speaking to the converted through Fox News and talk radio serves as an important rallying point, but only when story lines spill over, say from Fox to CNN, is the full political effect of the operation achieved.

And in pursuing this strategy of infecting the media at large with their viruses of misinformation, the right correctly sees the *New York Times* as the chief host body. If information is the coin of the realm in Washington, the *Times* is the number one target to exploit. After all, even in a time of radical changes in the way people consume their news, the *Times* can still affect a news cycle like no other media outlet in the country.

Its liberal reputation makes it all that much more valuable as a counterintuitive megaphone for conservative propaganda. And in modern campaigns—with their emphasis on turning out base voters, as true swing voters have become a rare breed—coopting the *Times* is an ingenious linchpin in the GOP strategy to foster doubt and dissension among Democrats about their own candidates—Hillary especially.

After all, who would believe the "liberal" *New York Times* was in cahoots with GOP spinmeisters?

Unfortunately, at various times since the Clintons first came on the national political scene in 1992, that demonstrably has been the case.

Consider the 1990s.

Remember Jeff Gerth, the former *New York Times* reporter who is perhaps best known for breaking the Whitewater story, which suggested the Clintons gave improper favors to their investment partner in the land deal? Published at the height of the 1992 presidential campaign, his error-strewn report, instigated by the Clinton's GOP political foes in Arkansas, showed no wrongdoing by the Clintons—if the *Times* thought it finally could match the *Washington Post* with its very own Watergate, the story was a big flop.

A later analysis of the original Gerth story by CNN correspondent John Camp identified nineteen errors of fact in it. But its false insinuations of impropriety implanted in the paper an institutional anti-Clinton bias that continues to afflict the newsroom today.

Analyzing the Whitewater affair, Tom Fiedler, the executive editor of the *Miami Herald*, later wrote: "The first reporter to fall for the [Whitewater] tale was the *New York Times*' Jeff Gerth, an investigative reporter. He produced an almost incomprehensible report on the Clintons' Whitewater land investments in early 1992. But incomprehensible or not, the fact that it appeared in so prestigious a paper as the *New York Times* insinuated that something must have been wrong."

In the years that followed, the Gerth story and his many others that reiterated his false assertions eventually spawned the highly politicized $70 million federal investigation of the Clintons led by Starr. Official Washington was engulfed in a miasma of scandal for years, and a number of *Times* men (and women) would stay stubbornly attached to a skewed view of the Clintons as charlatans, if not criminals, despite all evidence to the contrary.

Two years after his botched Whitewater piece, Gerth was back with a *Times* report alleging that during Bill Clinton's tenure as governor of Arkansas, Tyson Foods Inc. "benefitted from a variety of state actions, including $9 million in government loans, the placement of company executives on important state boards and favorable decisions on environmental issues." The lengthy article suggested that Tyson might have been the beneficiary of these purported state actions because a top lawyer for the company had advised Hillary Clinton on lucrative investments.

A month later, the *Times* posted a belated correction, asserting that the article "misstated benefits that the Tyson Foods company received from the state of Arkansas," and noting that "Tyson did not receive $9 million in loans from the state."

In an *American Journalism Review* article on Gerth's late 1990s reporting on Wen Ho Lee, a Los Alamos National Laboratory scientist accused of stealing U.S. nuclear secrets and passing them to China, journalist Lucinda Fleeson reported, "The major points outlined in the *Times*' first blockbuster story were found to have little resemblance to what eventually became clear was the truth…By late summer 1999, many of its key points had been knocked down. But by then too much erroneous and speculative information was in play, and the story of the country's secrets stolen from Los Alamos had become fuel for another assault on President Clinton by Capitol Hill Republicans." Once again, Gerth was a hit-and-run offender.

During Hillary Clinton's 2008 presidential run, Gerth was back with a nasty book about her, written with his *Times* colleague Don Van Natta, entitled *Her Way*. The news in the book consisted of persistent claims and insinuations of criminal or unethical conduct on Hillary Clinton's part by former investigators who had worked for the failed Starr Whitewater inquiry and who had been unable to prove any of it despite spending years and tens of millions trying to do so. Character assassination between hard covers, the book was excerpted in the *New York Times Magazine*, dutifully presented as objective reporting. *Her Way* was really "His Way"—perhaps Gerth's way to get back at Hillary when his earlier Whitewater reporting had failed.

During Clinton's presidency and beyond, until his retirement from the paper in 2005, William Safire, who had been appointed a *Times* op-ed columnist after serving as a PR flak and speechwriter for Richard Nixon, enjoyed enormous influence in the *Times* Washington bureau, setting the tone for much of its Clinton coverage, and mentoring and protecting favored reporters like Gerth. Safire sat on the Pulitzer jury that awarded Gerth a prize in 1999 for a story that suggested Bernard Schwartz, the CEO of Loral Space and Communications, and a campaign contributor to the Clinton-Gore campaign, had gained a U.S. waiver for a commercial satellite launched by the Chinese in exchange for his donations. Safire promoted Gerth's hot exposé in his column as "the sellout of American security," and pushed it for the Pulitzer. There was only one thing wrong with Gerth's Loral story. Just like his Whitewater and Wen Ho Lee reporting, it was significantly flawed. The federal investigation a year after Gerth was awarded his Safire-inspired Pulitzer Prize concluded that there was "not a scintilla of evidence—or information—that the president was corruptly influenced by Bernard Schwartz" and that the matter "did not merit any investigation."

Early in Safire's tenure, the *Times* had been warned by one of its most revered former reporters, David Halberstam, that Safire would indelibly tarnish the paper's reputation if he were kept on. In a letter to publisher Arthur Ochs Sulzberger, who'd hired Safire, Halberstam wrote, "Safire...is a paid manipulator. He is not a man of ideas or politics but rather a man of tricks...It's a lousy column and it's a dishonest one. So close it. Or you end up just as shabby as Safire."

Halberstam's letter was nothing if not prescient. Writing for *Salon* in March 2000, Joe Conason recounted the numerous false accusations Safire leveled against the Clintons over the years, including Safire's January 1996 headline-making column that called Hillary Clinton a "congenital liar." Conason wrote:

Again and again over the past several years, Safire has charged the Clintons and their associates with such offenses as fraud, conspiracy, perjury, witness tampering and obstruction of justice. Using the jargon of Watergate to emphasize their culpability, he has written about the so-called Clinton scandals as if even the most minimal professional scruples and cautions did not apply to him—let alone the standards of fairness that are held sacred at the newspaper of record and in all reputable news organizations ... But a newspaper as uniquely powerful as the *New York Times* carries unique responsibilities. When one of its most prominent writers recklessly damages the reputations of people who turn out to be innocent of the offenses he has alleged, a reckoning is in order.

The reckoning never came (at least while Safire was alive).

If Safire represented one type of Clinton crazy at the paper, the vengeful Nixonian out for payback, Howell Raines, a liberal Southerner, represented another. First as editorial page editor and then as executive editor of the paper, Raines was one of the Clintons' most vocal journalistic opponents during the entire Clinton presidency. Unlike Safire, Raines was not grinding a political axe, but rather one based in class difference and personal style.

Early on in his presidency, the *Times* editorial page, then edited by Raines, "published a contemptuous, unsigned piece mocking the Clintons' decision to vacation on Martha's Vineyard. The put-down column came complete with condescending references—'Lake of the Ozarks,' and 'Li'l Abner'—to Clinton's modest upbringing. To Raines, Clinton was little more than white trash," Eric Boehlert wrote for Media Matters.

Referring to Gerth, Safire, Raines, and the rest of the anti-Clinton muckraking crew at the *Times* in the 1990s, Boehlert summed up, "They were among the reporters, editors and columnists who were genuinely obsessed, in a weirdly personal way, with bringing down the Democratic president, acting as conveyor belts for the GOP and its vast army of Clinton-hating minions who were eager to peddle trash under the guise of news. For years, the *Times* was more than happy to oblige and to set the Beltway's anti-Clinton tenor."

Now, we have the troubling figure of Carolyn Ryan. She is installed at the helm of the *Times* Washington bureau and is said to have her eye on getting the paper's top job one day—but is regarded by a number of her colleagues as a bantamweight in comparison with the many esteemed editors who have held the prestigious and powerful position over the years. Ryan has astonished colleagues in the bureau by wrongly claiming credit for the good work of others in a crass effort to impress the paper's owners, they say.

Rather than following her well-regarded predecessors' example, Ryan's ticket to the top seems predicated on following in the footsteps of William Safire and Jeff Gerth, whose lamentable records did nothing but bring disrepute on the newspaper. Another story on the Clinton Foundation, commissioned on Ryan's watch, long before the Schweizer deal was inked, set the tone.

The August 2013 front-page hit on the Clinton Foundation falsely described typical and lawful accounting and revenue-booking protocols for nonprofits as financial irregularities. In fact, there were no such irregularities, as Foundation officials tried to explain to the paper prior to publication—all to no avail. The paper, suggesting mismanagement, reported that the Foundation ran in the red three years.

The right wing squealed with delight that the *Times* had been enlisted in its anti-Clinton crusade. Rush Limbaugh applauded the paper's "injurious" work on the former first family.

In a long open letter, posted on the Foundation's website after the *Times* story appeared, President Clinton explained how nonprofit accounting works: "For any foundation with a substantial number of multi-year commitments, the 990s [tax forms] will often indicate that we have more or less money than is actually in our accounts." For example, Clinton cited the fact that in 2005 and 2006, as a result of multiyear commitments, the Foundation recorded a more than $100 million surplus, "though we collected nowhere near that. In later years, as the money came in to cover our budgets, we were required to report the spending but not the cash inflow." Clinton also reported that in two years, 2007 and 2008, when the Clinton Foundation, like many charities, was hit by the economic showdown, it dipped into cash reserves to cover vital programs, like HIV/AIDS and malaria. This was a management decision, not mismanagement. In another year, 2012, the *Times* just got it wrong, as the Foundation actually ran a surplus.

One of the two reporters on the story later told someone in the Foundation's orbit that the story got facts wrong, but despite Clinton's public statement pointing this out, the paper arrogantly refused to run a correction. Rather than deal honestly with the situation, the paper ran a short news article, under the headline BILL CLINTON DEFENDS FAMILY'S CHARITY, and never mentioned that the 2012 deficit allegation was false, leaving intact the false impression of lingering financial problems.

Editors, of course, are paid to make news judgments, but they should do so with the kind of impartiality that Ryan, according to some of her colleagues in the paper, seems incapable of, at least when it comes to the Clintons. Experienced journalists in the *Times* Washington bureau, I've been told, are appalled at Ryan's unprofessionalism on the Clinton beat.

"She has a hard-on for Hillary," said one source in the *Times*. "She wants that coonskin nailed to the wall."

It was Ryan who made the case for assigning a full-time beat reporter to cover Hillary back in 2013, when Hillary was a private citizen and two years before she would make a decision to declare her candidacy for president. Most media outlets followed suit, producing a flood of excessive and at times trivial coverage. In defending the decision to public editor Sullivan, Ryan justified it by asserting "there is a certain amount of opacity and stagecraft" surrounding the Clintons—implying, wrongly, that they purposely mislead the public—without citing any evidence for such a palpably biased assertion.

That was Ryan's mindset about the Clintons. She rendered a harsh judgment about the Clinton family, describing it as "dysfunctional" in a January 2014 appearance on NBC's *Meet the Press*. And in an interview on the same program in July 2015, Ryan, who is one of the most important *news* editors in the country, used the occasion to opine that

Hillary lacked "authenticity" and is unable to deliver an "uncalculated" message, points lifted right from the Republican playbook. So much for professionalism and impartiality.

⌒

For all the advance hoopla, and the controversy over the *Times* involvement, *Clinton Cash* didn't deliver. Schweizer tried in vain to find a correlation between foreign donations to the Clinton Foundation and actions taken by the State Department but there were none. He relied on faulty, conspiracy-laden time lines to imply, but never clearly allege, wrongdoing. On its website, in fact, the publisher of *Clinton Cash* stated clearly that the book "does not allege illegal or unethical behavior." And in interviews, the author himself claimed, lamely, that he was just "asking questions," that he had turned the book over to real journalists so they could further his investigation, and that if only he had subpoena power or access to Hillary's e-mails, he would have nailed his target.

Many news outlets reviewing the book panned it.

- ABC News: The author offers "no proof."
- *Time*: The book is based on "little evidence."
- Yahoo News: "No smoking gun."
- *Politico*: "No evidence."

Yet the *Times* dug in, keying off Schweizer to revive an old story suggesting that a Clinton Foundation donor had won Hillary's approval of the sale of a uranium company to Russia. But the chronology was off. The donor, Frank Giustra, had sold his interest in the company in 2007, two years before Hillary became secretary of state. Further, there was no evidence that Hillary Clinton was personally involved in the decision— or that she could have even made it. Deals that are deemed important to national security are made by the Committee on Foreign Investment in the United States. The Committee is comprised of multiple federal agencies, and the deal's approval required at least nine federal officials and agencies, as well as independent agencies entirely outside of the State Department's purview. According to Jose Fernandez, the former assistant secretary who was the State Department's principal representative on the committee at the time, "Mrs. Clinton never intervened with me on any CFIUS matter."

The *Times* reported that donations from an executive of the company that was sold to Russia, Uranium One, had not been disclosed by the Clinton Foundation, as required by the agreement reached between the Foundation and the Obama administration when Hillary took office. But that was wrong, too. The executive donated to the Clinton Giustra Enterprise Partnership, a Canadian philanthropy separate from the Clinton Foundation. The partnership's donations to the Clinton Foundation were properly disclosed. It was the Canadian partnership that doesn't disclose its donors, because it's prohibited from doing so by Canadian law governing nonprofits.

The *Times* uranium story—which plugged the Schweizer book—was published on the front page on April 24. The next week, Fox News was set to air a one-hour special, *The Tangled Clinton Web*, also promoting Schweizer's book and highlighting the uranium issue. Featured on the Fox special was none other than the *Times* reporter Jo Becker, who had written the *Times* piece. When Fox released a promotional clip of its special to the press, the clip featured Becker—allowing Fox to exploit its alliance with the *Times* to enhance its own credibility. According to *Times* guidelines, reporters are to avoid appearing on TV forums "that emphasize punditry and reckless opinion-mongering." Fox certainly fits that bill, but maybe *Times* reporters get a special dispensation when pushing false stories trashing the Clintons.

The *Times* also touted the charge that Hillary had pushed for the U.S.-Colombia Free Trade Pact to benefit Foundation donors. Again, not only was the chronology off, but the truth was the opposite of what was alleged. Hillary publicly opposed the trade deal after the contributions to the Clinton Foundation from donors favoring the deal came in. The donations were made in 2006 and 2007, and Hillary was vocal about her opposition to the trade deal while she was running for president in 2007 and 2008. Hillary's position changed in favor of the pact only after she joined the Obama administration, after new labor restrictions were added to the deal, and after the agreement became a priority for the Obama administration. David Axelrod, a White House advisor when Obama sought to pass the trade deal, called the idea that this was done to reward Clinton Foundation donors "nuts."

So, no quid pro quos. No failure to properly disclose donations. What we were left with was 100 percent innuendo—the definition of a political smear. Yet the press continued to report on "questions raised," on "appearances," on "how things looked." And to Hillary's critics, the answer was obvious: Things looked bad. Pressed for any sort of evidence for the allegations being made in an interview on *Morning Joe*, former Bush aide Nicolle Wallace finally conceded that there was none, but deemed the Clinton dealings "shady" nonetheless.

Through it all, the *Times*, Schweizer's partner, continued to protect *Clinton Cash* even as many other news organizations—organizations that didn't have "exclusive" deals with the author—were finding and reporting on his many errors. But not the *Times*, which stuck by Schweizer as if he was one of their own reporters, and once again never corrected the record on any of it.

In what could be interpreted as a jab at his own newspaper's shabby performance, *New York Times* columnist Paul Krugman summed it up this way:

If you are old enough to remember the 1990s, you remember the endless parade of alleged scandals, Whitewater above all— all of them fomented by right-wing operatives, all eagerly hyped by mainstream news outlets, none of which actually turned out to involve wrongdoing. The usual rules didn't seem to apply; instead it was Clinton rules, under which innuendo and guilt by association were considered perfectly OK, in which the initial suggestion of lawbreaking received front-page headlines and the subsequent discovery that there was nothing there was buried in the back pages if it was reported at all.

Some of the same phenomenon resurfaced during the 2008 primary.

So, is this time different? First indications are not encouraging; it's already apparent that the author of the anti-Clinton book that's driving the latest stuff is a real piece of work.

Again, maybe there's something there. But given the history here, we'd all be well advised to follow our own Clinton rules, and be highly suspicious of any reports of supposed scandals unless there's hard proof rather than mere innuendo.

Oh, and the news media should probably be aware that this isn't 1994: there's a much more effective progressive infrastructure now, much more scrutiny of reporting, and the kinds of malpractice that went unsanctioned 20 years ago can land you in big trouble now.

The aggressive progressive pushback that Krugman cited—from the Clinton campaign itself and outside groups like Media Matters—made a difference. Schweizer's right-wing ties became part of the story, and his journalistic credibility was questioned pretty much everywhere he went to flack the book.

But in the new media environment, the days of killing off a hit job disguised as a book like this were over. The book's intended audience reacted as if on cue. The right-wing base went out and bought the book in droves—giving new meaning to "Clinton cash"—and the Fox News Channel showered it with more than $100 million in free publicity. A pandering Mitt Romney accused Hillary of having been "bribed." And the *Wall Street Journal* editorial page called for a criminal investigation.

The mainstream press, hardly chastened by the experience, was teed up for more. One *New York Times* writer stated flatly that going forward, in the absence of a strong primary challenge, the press would function as Hillary's opposition. At least the *Times* got that right.

And the worried Democrats were, well, worried. Asked about the impact of a stinging column on what he called the "disastrous" post-Clinton presidency, liberal writer Jonathan Chait speculated that it might "open up more space for a primary challenge."

⌒

The false attacks on the Clinton Foundation were in a sense attacks on the notion of philanthropy itself. For what contemporary effort better fit the conventional modern definition of philanthropy as a "private initiative, for public good, focusing on quality of life"? In any fair view, the Clintons, especially the former president, deserved to join the pantheon of history's most esteemed philanthropic actors.

Instead, their honorable motives were routinely besmirched, their good works defiled, by a partisan right-wing campaign of distortion, abetted by the news media. The Republicans aimed to turn the Clinton Foundation into 2016's version of Mitt Romney's Bain Capital—an Achilles heel portrayed by Democrats as a rapacious, job-killing, corporate-greed machine. Of course, the only difference was that they were complete opposites. In this truth-twisting analogy, Hillary Clinton, a public servant for nearly three decades, now would be recast as an aloof and uncaring member of America's corporate elite.

## Chapter Ten

# The Romney-ization of Hillary Clinton

In September 2014, the *Washington Free Beacon* broke a story the editors hyped as big news:

> Previously unpublished correspondence between Hillary Clinton and the late left-wing organizer Saul Alinsky reveals new details about her relationship with the controversial Chicago activist and shed[s] light on her early ideological development.
>
> Clinton met with Alinsky several times in 1968 while writing a Wellesley college thesis about his theory of community organizing.
>
> Clinton's relationship with Alinsky, and her support for his philosophy, continued for several years after she entered Yale law school in 1969, two letters obtained by the *Washington Free Beacon* show.

Alinsky, of course, is a popular bogeyman for conservatives, who have used him as an avatar for everything they loathe and fear about populist grassroots politics. Throughout Barack Obama's presidency, the right has looked for connections between Obama and

Alinsky—two community organizers and, to conservatives, two terri-fying socialists. So, to the right, that Hillary Clinton had a connection to Alinsky was proof of her radical sympathies.

But the story fell flat, even in the outer sphere of right-wing social media networks. So don't expect to hear much about Saul Alinsky as conservatives focus their attacks on Hillary. As we explored in chapter 6, the political terrain is shifting beneath Republicans' feet, causing even their own standard-bearers to feign interest in issues like economic inequality; hurling accusations of "socialism" doesn't work anymore. Indeed, economic ideas that might previously have been denounced as socialistic are meeting with growing acceptance.

Thus, the right's early efforts to spoil Hillary's coming-out party as a presidential candidate focused not on attacking her as being too liberal, but rather on portraying her emphasis on growing economic equality as simply a pose. They're trying to cast her as an inauthentic messenger for progressive economic policies, nothing more than another crony capi-talist, out of touch with middle-class families and devoid of credibility when it comes to improving people's lives.

Indeed conservatives don't really want to turn Hillary Clinton into Saul Alinsky, after all. They want to turn her into Mitt Romney.

Romney's economic policies, of course, offered little to the middle class. But their details didn't really matter; Democrats succeeded in painting him as *personally* lacking empathy for ordinary people. Their best ally in that cause was named Mitt Romney: there was the time he said, "Corporations are people, my friend," the time he tried to identify with NASCAR fans by pointing out that he had friends who *owned* teams, the time he mused about how much he likes to fire people, the time he was caught on tape attacking 47 percent of the American people as takers living off the government.

By the time Democrats ran ads featuring laid-off workers—victims of purges by Romney's firm—everyone knew that Mitt Romney was out of touch with the middle class; they had heard the evidence in his own words. And by the time voters zeroed in on the choice between

Obama and Romney, it didn't matter what Romney's actual policy proposals were. He could have come out in favor of actual, literal socialism; nobody would have believed him.

Especially when they're struggling as the middle class has in the wake of the Bush recession, voters are looking for someone they can identify with, someone who has been through some of the same things they have, someone they trust to really understand what's going on in their lives. And when they looked at Romney, they saw a guy who had a car elevator in his house.

In the same vein, conservatives figure they won't have to wrestle with Hillary Clinton's strong middle-class economic message if they can disqualify her as a messenger.

And, as always, the media is more than willing to help. In particular, a story about the Clintons' personal finances is catnip to a political press that, beginning with the Whitewater tale twenty years before, loves to chase stories of how the Clintons are supposedly always grasping for money. Whether they were a young couple getting cut in on a sketchy Arkansas land deal or plutocratic power brokers bestriding the world stage, the same phony story line persisted.

～

When Hillary Clinton left the State Department, she accepted a variety of speaking engagements, some of which paid an honorarium or were donated to the Clinton Foundation in exchange for her time. Many more she did for free in support of other worthy causes.

It's not uncommon for elected officials to embark on paid speaking careers after their time in office, of course. For example, the *New York Times* reported that Jeb Bush "appears to have generated millions" from "more than 100" paid speeches to corporate groups since 2007, part of an "unapologetic determination to expand his wealth," which Bush justified by explaining "that his finances had suffered during his time in government."

And while Hillary's speaking fee was sizable, it was in no way out of

line with the sums charged by other public figures. Her predecessor as
secretary of state, Condoleezza Rice, charges as much as $150,000 to
speak. Another former secretary of state, Colin Powell, has charged up
to $200,000. And Rudy Giuliani (whose Cabinet experience extends
to his failed suggestion that felon Bernie Kerik be allowed to run the
Department of Homeland Security) once pocketed $270,000 for a sin-
gle speech to a private equity firm.

But, as always, the rules are different for Hillary. And under those
Clinton rules, Hillary's fee—"said to be upwards of $200,000 per
speech"—was quickly described by the *Washington Post* as a "potentially serious political problem." The Clintons, per the *Post*, "are established members of the 1 percent, leading lives far removed from the
millions of middle-class voters who swing elections."

In just two months, the *Post*'s Chris Cillizza dedicated more than a
dozen blog posts to obsessing over Hillary's wealth, continually giving
Hillary's opponents space to say what Cillizza was more than willing to
conclude himself: "The Clintons are not 'average' people."

"You have a money problem," insisted *Post* columnist Ruth Marcus.
It's a "liability," warned an 1,800-word front-page news article. The
*Washington Post* was your around-the-clock source for right-wing talk-
ing points about how Hillary was out of touch.

And did Americans care? Not a whit. An NBC News/*Wall Street
Journal*/Annenberg poll, taken in the midst of the "controversy," found
that 55 percent of Americans believed that Hillary relates to and
understands average Americans. "It's doubtful that the public holds the
Clintons' wealth against them," *Post* columnist Dan Balz concluded.
But it wasn't for lack of effort on his newspaper's part.

The *Post* wasn't alone. Reporters hammered on Hillary's wealth,
insisting that there must be something untoward afoot and never
mentioning the millions the Clintons had donated to charity as they
became wealthy. "Ex-presidents make money like this, not candidates
before they run," scolded Chuck Todd on *Morning Joe*, leaving out the
buckraking of Jeb Bush and Rudy Giuliani as well as the fact that most

precampaign candidates (and arguably even a few ex-presidents) are less accomplished and in demand than Hillary.

In July 2014, the story broke that Hillary would speak at an October fund-raiser at the University of Nevada, Las Vegas (UNLV), with special attention paid to her $225,000 fee. But the controversy surrounding the event ignored that the fee was to be donated to the Clinton Foundation, not to Hillary herself; not to mention that months before the event, Hillary's anticipated presence had helped sell out the best tables, raising more than $350,000—just the third time in history the annual event would generate net profit.

Then the focus turned to a speech at the University at Buffalo. Again, as with *all* of Hillary's university speaking fees, this one would also go to the Clinton Foundation to continue the Clintons' charitable endeavors. But Jennifer Rubin, the conservative press release distribution engine posing as a *Washington Post* columnist, suggested that perhaps Hillary benefited by receiving a tax deduction—false, since the payment never touched Hillary's account and went directly to the charity. Rubin wrongly also assumed that the speaking fee was paid from university funds—false, since these honoraria were paid for by private donors.

Then some intrepid Republican researcher dug up a copy of Hillary's speaking contract, which specified arrangements for flights and hotel rooms, press policies, and other ephemera like staging and backstage accommodations. The *Wall Street Journal's* James Taranto was scandalized: "And along with the hummus and crudité[s], they demanded 'coffee, tea, room temp sparkling and still water, diet ginger ale…and sliced fruit.'" Hummus! The very nerve!

"It reminds us of Van Halen," Taranto persisted, referring to the hard rock band known the world over for demanding to be provided with a bowl of M&Ms in every dressing room on their tours—with all the brown M&Ms removed. (Actually the band did it in order to make sure producers were paying attention to the contract rider—if a producer missed the M&M clause, perhaps he also missed an important safety check. Hillary's outrageous request for water, on the other hand, was probably just a matter of hydration.

"We don't have kings and queens in America, or at least we shouldn't," sniffed Jon Ralston, dean of the Nevada press corps, as the controversy about Hillary's UNLV speech raged pointlessly on. "But when I see the red carpet UNLV is rolling out for Hillary Clinton in two months I start to wonder."

It was a target-rich environment for the GOP oppo gang at America Rising, which snapped a photo of Hillary entering a tony New York department store. "If Hillary is going to run for President," snarked its spokesman, "she might be advised to take a lengthy sabbatical from her $200k per pop speaking tour and private shopping sprees at Bergdor's to try and reconnect with what's happening back here on Earth."

⌒

What, exactly, are we really talking about here? What had Hillary done—heck, with the exception of Rubin's blind thrusts, what had she even been *accused* of doing—that would merit this kind of singularly vicious treatment? Hadn't other public figures accepted similar speaking fees? Weren't many of Hillary's going to charity? Don't many accomplished people receive invitations to give paid speeches? Doesn't everybody like hummus?

The answer, as always: Hillary is held to a double standard. And never was that more clear than when, according to her critics, she had what was spun as a Mitt Romney moment while speaking to Diane Sawyer:

SAWYER: You've made five million making speeches? The president's made more than a hundred million dollars?

CLINTON: Well, you have no reason to remember, but we came out of the White House not only dead broke but in debt. We had no money when we got there, and we struggled to piece together the resources for mortgages for houses, for Chelsea's education. You know, it was not easy. Bill has worked really hard and it's been amazing to me. He's worked very hard. First of all, we had to pay off all our debts. You know, you had to make double the money because of, obviously, taxes, and then pay off the debts and get us houses and take care of family members.

The words "dead broke" set off sirens inside the war rooms of every right-wing group in Washington. "This is outrageous," tweeted Reince Priebus. "How out of touch is Hillary Clinton when 'dead broke' = mansions & massive speaking fees?"

But the truth is, the Clintons were worth between $350,000 and $1 million when they moved into the White House—as close to middle-class as any modern presidential family has ever been. And thanks to the right's years-long campaign of partisan investigations, they would leave the White House in worse financial shape. When Hillary ran for the Senate in 2000 (a job that, at the time, paid a healthy but not exorbitant $141,300 a year), she had to file a financial disclosure form showing her with assets between $781,000 and $1.8 million—and legal debts as high as $10.6 million.

They really did have to pay off those debts (it took four years). They really did need to find a place to live (here, they leaned on family friend Terry McAuliffe, who put up his own money to personally secure the mortgage that made it possible). They really did have a college-age daughter. And they really did pitch in to help less fortunate members of their family.

Were the Clintons one paycheck away from the poorhouse? No. But Diane Sawyer asked a question about why Hillary and Bill Clinton had chosen to accept paid speaking gigs, and Hillary answered, honestly, that they had made alleviating financial pressure a family priority.

Conservatives, of course, painted this as a moment when Hillary revealed how out of touch she is with everyday Americans—and the media had little trouble accepting the right's framing of the story. But "dead broke" was really a moment of personal candor. After all the media yammering about how Hillary needed to be less cautious and practiced, here she was, saying something unrehearsed and revealing, and that same media reported it as a huge misstep.

Hillary couldn't win. If the media had bothered to look beyond how the remark fit into conservatives' strategy to discredit Hillary, they might have found that it shed some light on the real story of her life.

Unlike Mitt Romney—or, for that matter, Jeb Bush—Hillary Rodham was not born into power and privilege.

"My grandfather," she told a sold-out crowd at an EMILY's List event in March 2015, "was a factory worker—started at the age of 11, worked until he was 65, and got to retire. His son, my father, went to college, was a small businessman who worked really hard and made a good life for us. My mother had a terrible, abusive childhood, had to leave at the age of 14 to go work in order to support herself, having been abandoned by both her parents and her paternal grandparents, never got to go to college—but had a spark of resilience that kept her going and gave her the capacity to create a family filled with love and support."

Hillary was raised middle class in Park Ridge, Illinois, where she attended public school. She worked her entire life, from the age of thirteen on, in a variety of jobs that included supervising a park near her house and, memorably, cleaning salmon in Alaska.

After law school, she eschewed far more lucrative options and chose a path of public service, working for the Children's Defense Fund. She was the first director of the University of Arkansas, Fayetteville's legal aid clinic. When she and Bill Clinton got married in 1975, the wedding took place in their living room.

In time, as Bill built his public career, she would build a successful legal practice to help support the family, but she never lost her focus on children and families, leading a task force as Arkansas' First Lady to reform the state's school system and, when Bill was elected president, championing the cause of children's health care.

"We know how blessed we are," she told the *Guardian* in June 2014. "We were neither of us raised with these kinds of opportunities, and we worked really hard for them....All one has to do is look at my record going back to my time in college and law school to know not only where my heart is, but where my efforts have been."

Anyone who knows the Clintons—or has followed their trajectory—knows that for them making money has always taken a backseat to serving others. At every opportunity, they chose to devote their time and energy to improving their community, their country, and their world, repeatedly opting to serve the public rather than cash out. For anyone else, a story like theirs would be part of a stump speech, proof that they not only understand what it was like to grow up middle class—they'd lived it—in Bill's case, rising from what was truly desperate poverty.

And it's that admirable and powerful personal story the Republicans seek to erase, even if it means demonizing hard work, merit, and personal achievement—quintessential American values the Republicans usually try to claim as their own—but that the Clintons in fact embody.

~

In part, the Hillary-as-Mitt strategy is an exercise in inoculation and projection on the part of conservatives contemplating their own presidential field. The early front-runner (and, in my opinion, still the most formidable Republican nominee) is Jeb Bush, whose own ability to relate to voters is a giant question mark.

Bush can be condescending and arrogant, with an air of entitlement, which doesn't come as a surprise given that he is the son and brother of a president who was quickly tapped as the establishment favorite despite not having held office in a decade. Indeed, he carries with him all the baggage his brother brought to the race in 2000: He made his fortune off his family's name, and his accomplishments would have been impossible had he not been born a Bush. The last Bush on the car lot, he is the definition of a dynastic candidate.

Moreover, unlike George W., Jeb lacks a story of personal redemption that could give him more of a human touch. He's great in a room of wealthy donors, but conservatives can't help but have noticed that he lacks the charisma to shine in smaller interactions with ordinary people. Reporters took note that when a crew of his supporters showed up to showcase their enthusiasm at the 2015 Conservative Political Action Conference CPAC, a major stop on the Republican cattle call circuit, they weren't dressed like real grassroots activists—more than one compared the scene to the "Brooks Brothers riot" from 2000.

Questionable political instincts, an inability to relate to everyday Americans, a life of privilege, the personality of an aloof plutocrat: That's the false image Republicans would like us to see when we look at Hillary, but it is also what they must actually see when they take a clear-eyed look at Jeb Bush.

◦⟋

Meanwhile, the "Romney-ization" attack is also designed to reach the left—it's part of an ongoing GOP effort to drive a wedge between Hillary and her progressive base.

In the early spring of 2015, American Crossroads—Karl Rove's SuperPAC—released a thirty-second Web ad that neatly squared the circle between the insinuations of shady dealings with foreign governments covered in the last chapter and the attack on Hillary's populist bona fides.

The audio is a speech by Senator Elizabeth Warren:

Powerful interests have tried to capture Washington and rig the system in their favor. The power of well-funded special interests tilts our democracy away from the people and toward the powerful. Action is required to defend our great democracy against those who would see it perverted into one more rigged game where the rich and the powerful always win.

On screen is grainy footage of Hillary posing with foreign leaders, and a series of chyrons. THE CLINTONS' FOUNDATION TOOK MIL-

LIONS FROM FOREIGN GOVERNMENTS, one warns, taking the *Wall Street Journal*'s inflammatory headline and putting it to its proper use as a scare quote in an attack ad. We see the names of suspicious-sounding countries like the United Arab Emirates, Saudi Arabia, and Qatar (a prominent backer of Hamas, the chyron notes) before seeing a couple of critical comments from Democratic county chairs.

The ad ends with a question: "Powerful foreign governments are ready for Hillary. Are we?"

It's a seemingly perfect ad because, in addition to scaremongering about the Clinton Foundation's ties to foreign governments, it not so subtly reminds the media of one of its favorite hobbyhorses—the implied conflict between Hillary and Warren.

Appearing at a rally for Massachusetts gubernatorial candidate Martha Coakley in October 2014, with Warren at her side, Hillary told the crowd, "Don't let anybody tell you that it's corporations and businesses that create jobs. You know that old theory, trickle-down economics. That has been tried, that has failed. It has failed rather spectacularly."

To conservatives, this sounded a lot like when President Obama told a Roanoke, Virginia, crowd that, "If you were successful, somebody along the line gave you some help. There was a great teacher somewhere in your life. Somebody helped to create this unbelievable American system that we have that allowed you to thrive. Somebody invested in roads and bridges. If you've got a business—you didn't build that. Somebody else made that happen."

The president's point was that wealthy Americans owed a lot to investments made in the public good: schools, infrastructure, and so on. But conservatives couldn't resist clipping "you didn't build that" out of context and framing it as an attack on entrepreneurs.

Similarly, Hillary was making a fairly routine argument against conservative economic policy, but "don't let anybody tell you that cor-porations and businesses create jobs" was irresistible bait for the right. Within a week, Jeb Bush was waving that quote in front of a conservative audience in Colorado, reveling in the audience's jeering of Hillary's supposed disregard of the private sector.

Ripping quotes out of context was nothing new for Republicans, but the story had a deeper meaning for the media. "Hillary Clinton's gaffe about jobs," Howard Kurtz opined for Fox News, "is resonating for several reasons—not least because the media have decided she's no Elizabeth Warren. The media narrative du jour is that Hillary is out of step with the populist mood of the Democratic Party—as embodied by the Wall Street–bashing Massachusetts senator who many pundits are still hoping will challenge her. So they are guaranteed to pounce on any mistake that feeds Hillary's image as an establishment figure who is struggling to be more like Liz."

"Clinton's clumsy language reveals a politician woefully out of sync with her party's progressive populist base," wrote Luke Brinker for *Salon*. "Her awkward attempt to relate to the Elizabeth Warren wing of the Democratic Party calls to mind Mitt Romney's cringe-inducing efforts to woo GOP conservatives during his last presidential bid."

Once again, here is the manufactured image of Hillary as painfully out of touch with the voters she is trying to reach. And Republicans are happy to help this false narrative along, even if it means, in effect, attacking Hillary from the left. A month before, the RNC had put out a video featuring Hillary introducing Goldman Sachs CEO Lloyd Blankfein onstage at the Clinton Global Initiative's annual meeting.

Such a video is unlikely to move Republican voters; it's more likely intended to sow doubt and undermine Hillary's support on the left. Some Democrats, such as MSNBC's Krystal Ball, have piled on, complaining that Hillary "seemingly can't get enough of hobnobbing with economic elites and cultivating donors."

Adam Green, cofounder of the Progressive Change Campaign Committee, which frequently hectors Democrats from the left, told the *Boston Globe*, "There are a lot of unchecked boxes with Hillary Clinton when it comes to economic populism and corporate accountability. There are definitely red flags."

*Harper's* commissioned liberal writer Doug Henwood for an essay titled "Stop Hillary" in which he twisted the facts to argue that Hillary was a corporatist wolf in progressive sheep's clothing.

And then there are those like the leaders of the online activist group MoveOn who rather cynically see the opportunity to build their e-mail lists and make some money by backing "a more progressive alternative." MoveOn joined forces with a PAC that was trying to draft Elizabeth Warren for president, despite the fact that she said emphatically she wasn't interested and even signed a letter with her fellow women senators urging Hillary to run.

It was all part of a misinformed campaign by some on the left, unwittingly serving the interests of the right and enabled at every turn by a press corps that always favors conflict as a good story, to gin up a primary challenge to Hillary.

Even some progressives who don't necessarily oppose Hillary are eager to see her have a tough primary. Zephyr Teachout, a progressive icon who had just finished an unsuccessful attempt to defeat New York's Democratic governor Andrew Cuomo in a primary, made the case on MSNBC: "Please, we need people to run against Hillary Clinton because if she's not debating anyone on education policy or on tax policy then we all lose. Not only does she need a challenger from the left, we should have five people—ten people—running for president. If we don't have a Democratic Party challenger, that is a democratic tragedy."

Katrina vanden Heuvel, editor of the *Nation*, made a similar argument, couched as concern for Hillary's own candidacy. She told *Politico*: "Even the most ardent Hillary fans should understand that sometimes not only her party and the country—but the candidacy—would be better served if she has competition."

～

But is there really a rationale for a challenge from Hillary's left? In a previous chapter, we looked at the phony claim that Hillary would be an unacceptably hawkish president. What are we to make of the claim that she would be a sellout to Wall Street?

This claim, too, is bogus. In her first campaign for the presidency, Hillary sounded many of the same notes that have endeared Elizabeth Warren to the progressive left, beginning with advocating fiercely for Warren's idea for a Financial Product Safety Commission (which was passed into law in 2010 and now exists as the Consumer Financial Protection Bureau).

In addition, Hillary's aggressive plan to hold Wall Street accountable included proposing that financial institutions involved with derivatives be subject to minimum capital requirements, that shareholders get a vote on executive compensation, that the so-called carried interest loophole be closed, and that the Securities and Exchange Commission crack down on short selling.

One columnist estimated that Hillary "might bring the toughest regulatory scrutiny of any president in a generation."

The truth is that Hillary has been on the side of the middle class long before the "Warren wing" of the Democratic Party existed. In the Senate, she repeatedly introduced legislation to make sure that the federal minimum wage would increase whenever congressional salaries did, and cosponsored bills to increase the minimum wage five different times, a commitment that dates back to her support of minimum wage increases when she was First Lady.

Hillary also worked across the aisle to help out-of-work Americans by extending unemployment benefits. She twice introduced the Paycheck Fairness Act to prevent employer retaliation against workers who claim wage discrimination, and cosponsored the Lilly Ledbetter Fair Pay Act, which expanded workers' rights to take pay discrimination cases to court.

She supported progressive tax policies and opposed the Bush tax cuts that were tilted toward the top. She worked to expand access to early childhood education for children in low-income families. She introduced bills to expand the Children's Health Insurance Program (CHIP) she helped create as First Lady.

Indeed, while Hillary's attempt to spearhead the passage of universal health-care legislation during the first Clinton administration—an unusually substantive role for a First Lady—may have fallen short, it not only resulted in the development of CHIP but also helped lay the groundwork for the passage of the Affordable Care Act fifteen years later. In a fair telling of the story, Hillary would be remembered not for the initial failure in 1994, but for the progress she helped make toward the ultimate goal achieved in 2010.

Meanwhile, her commitment to economic justice dates all the way back to her time as a private citizen, when she joined the Children's Defense Fund straight out of law school rather than seek a more lucrative job with a big law firm.

If conservatives—or liberals for that matter—are hoping to drive a wedge between Hillary and the Democratic base, they're going to have to use something other than her actual positions to do it.

And if they are hoping to cast Hillary's progressive economic message as fraudulent so they can lay claim to populism in 2016, they're going to have to ignore or negate a personal story that makes Hillary instantly relatable to middle-class voters; a long public record of advocating for income equality; and a platform that is fully in line with the needs of today's working families.

⌒

At that EMILY's List event, Hillary told a story about waiting with her family for her granddaughter, Charlotte, to be born:

> When Bill and I were at the hospital waiting for our granddaughter to make her grand entrance, one of the nurses there said to me, "Thank you for fighting for paid leave." And I looked at her and thought, here she is taking care of other people's babies, and

having to worry about what happens when her child gets sick, and how she makes all of that work.

Her words stayed with me. I remember being a young mother and having all the balancing acts that we all have to do. I remember one morning getting ready to go to court, and my babysitter was sick, and my daughter was sick, and I was calling desperately to find somebody to come.

I finally found a friend who came and stayed, thankfully, but it just made me so sick inside, because I had to leave my daughter. And I rushed home after I finished in court, and Chelsea was fine, sitting there with my friend, and for the first time all day, my heart stopped aching.

That was one day for me—but for so many moms and dads, that ache is with them every day. That's what the nurse was talking about. That's what we have to stand up for.

Hillary Clinton is not Saul Alinsky, though she wrote her college honors paper about him and corresponded with him. She is not Elizabeth Warren, though she supports many of Warren's reforms. And she is certainly not Mitt Romney. She is a woman who grew up middle-class and has always stayed true to those roots. She is a leader who has always stayed focused on issues affecting children and families. And she is the strongest possible messenger for a progressive vision of a fair and secure economy that works for all Americans—a message that Republicans will do anything to stop her from delivering.

## Chapter Eleven

# E-mails: The *Times* Strikes Again

I f you can't win the argument, try to disqualify your opponent. For two decades, that's been a major component of the right's war on Bill and Hillary Clinton. They've never been able to compete with the Clintons' political skills, with their popularity, with their ideas—so they've staked their hopes on scandalmongering.

Over the past few chapters, we've looked at how Republicans are attacking Hillary's candidacy for president, hoping to turn her greatest strengths against her, and how they're trying to destroy her credibility on an issue that will be at the core of her message, an issue on which the right simply can't compete.

In their hearts, however, conservatives know that their best hope for beating Hillary is to drag the campaign down into the mud. It would be nice if they could find a diamond in that dirt, some disqualifying scandal that could turn voters against her overnight or even force her from the race. They've been looking for that scandal for twenty-five years, and the Clintons have survived every attack. The Clintons' resilience, in fact, has become a part of their political appeal in a nation that sees itself as resilient.

But the new scandalmongering strategy no longer relies on actually finding a scandal. A conviction would be great, but conservatives are in the business of collecting indictments; for the scandal launderers, the journey has become the destination.

$\backsim$

For example, take a look at a Bloomberg News story that ran in January 2015. Here's the lead paragraph:

> Hillary Clinton took more than 200 privately chartered flights at taxpayer expense during her eight years in the U.S. Senate, sometimes using the jets of corporations and major campaign donors as she racked up $225,756 in flight costs.

If you stopped reading the story there, you might think that Bloomberg had unearthed something really damaging. That's a lot of money—and at taxpayer expense, too! But if you read on, you learn a few more things, like:

> Clinton, 67, the frontrunner for the Democratic presidential nomination in 2016, reported the travel in official filings with the Senate.

And:

> There is no evidence her Senate trips, which ranged in cost from less than $200 to upwards of $3,000 per flight, ran afoul of Senate rules, which were tightened by a 2007 ethics law.

And:

> The records were provided to Bloomberg News by a Republican operative.

What's really going on here? Hillary did nothing wrong, or even unusual, as the article itself acknowledges:

> The flights fell within congressional rules and were not out of the ordinary for senators at the time.

Indeed, the "story" here is a story about completely routine activity, disclosed in complete accordance with the rules.

True, it's unlikely that we'll hear much more about these flights, but from the right's perspective, that's okay—it contributes to the sense that "scandal surrounds her," as Republican National Committee Chairman Reince Priebus said. And, even better, as the article helpfully notes, the story "could play into the emerging Republican line of attack that Clinton's wealth and years in government office have left her out of touch with the voters she'll court on the campaign trail."

So, whichever Republican operative pitched it to Bloomberg had a good day when this article was published. And the next morning, he or she was right back at it, pitching an infinite number of paper-thin claims to an infinite number of reporters needing to fill an infinite number of column inches and website pixels, each of them desperate for any new nugget of Hillary news, each of them wanting to be the one who breaks the story that finally brings her down.

That's the other piece of the scandal story: As eager as conservatives are to bring Hillary up on charges of impropriety, the political press corps is like the grand jury who will happily indict a ham sandwich. The media shares conservatives' belief that, somewhere out there, there's a disqualifying scandal—and, if not, that the constant din of pseudoscandal is itself a story worth chasing. There is almost nothing you can say about Hillary that the press won't believe long enough to at least report out the story, thus giving it oxygen and the sheen of legitimacy.

And if all else fails, there's always the *Daily Caller*.

It was Monday evening, March 2, 2015, when my inbox exploded.

The *New York Times* had just published a story by Michael Schmidt, and, at first glance, it looked bad:

> HILLARY CLINTON USED PERSONAL EMAIL ACCOUNT AT STATE DEPT., POSSIBLY BREAKING RULES
>
> WASHINGTON—Hillary Rodham Clinton exclusively used a personal email account to conduct government business as secretary of state, State Department officials said, and may have violated federal requirements that officials' correspondence be retained as part of the agency's record.
>
> Mrs. Clinton did not have a government email address during her four-year tenure at the State Department. Her aides took no actions to have her personal emails preserved on department servers at the time, as required by the Federal Records Act.
>
> It was only two months ago, in response to a new State Department effort to comply with federal record-keeping practices, that Mrs. Clinton's advisers reviewed tens of thousands of pages of her personal emails and decided which ones to turn over to the State Department.

The article even included a juicy quote:

> "It is very difficult to conceive of a scenario—short of nuclear winter—where an agency would be justified in allowing its cabinet-level head officer to solely use a private email communications channel for the conduct of government business," said Jason R. Baron, a lawyer at Drinker Biddle & Reath who is a former director of litigation at the National Archives and Records Administration.

The fact that Hillary used a personal e-mail account had been known for a couple of years, ever since Gawker published a story about it back in 2013. But on Twitter, even steadfast Democrats were freaking out. No government e-mail address? Violating federal law?

Those two words in the headline—BREAKING RULES—were ominous. And conservatives were already crowing, not just about the possibility that Hillary might actually be in trouble this time, but about the way the story fit into their caricature of her as calculating and secretive, someone who put her own political well-being above everything else—even, possibly, our national security; was she conducting diplomacy via Gmail?!?!

Schmidt made sure to underscore that GOP talking point with an editorial comment of his own:

The revelation about the private email account echoes longstanding criticisms directed at both the former secretary and her husband, former President Bill Clinton, for a lack of transparency and inclination toward secrecy.

On top of that, Jeb Bush (whose new communications director was Tim Miller, formerly of America Rising) had publicly and with great fanfare published his own e-mail archives online—the contrast was unmistakable, and if you missed it, Schmidt helpfully reminded you of that, too.

Worst of all, while careful readers could tell that Schmidt's story was sourced to the Republican Committee investigating Benghazi, it hadn't made its first appearance on Fox or in the *Washington Free Beacon*, but was more artfully planted in the paper of record. A story in the *New York Times* gets, essentially, an automatic pass into the next day's news cycle—no outlet has the same power to command every reporter and pundit's attention. Republicans could use the paper's credibility for their own ends ("even the liberal *New York Times*"). And Democrats and liberals, for whom the *Times* is viewed as a reliable source of information, could be counted on to be especially shaken by the revelation.

In short, this was a big deal.

Reading the piece on my phone, I had no idea how much of it was true, nor how much of what was true was actually damaging. All I had to go on was a quote in the article from Nick Merrill, Hillary's personal spokesman, asserting that she had complied with the "letter and spirit of the rules."

In fact, I would have had a lot more to go on if the *Times* had published the meat of Merrill's statement. And *Times* readers, as well, would have had a much better understanding of the issues at play.

Merrill had told the *Times* that previous secretaries of state had used personal e-mail accounts when conducting official business. He told the *Times* that when sending work e-mails from her personal account, Hillary e-mailed other officials on their work accounts, so that those e-mails would be retained by the government. And most important, he told the *Times* that use of personal e-mail accounts was permissible under federal rules, so long as work-related e-mails were retained, which Hillary did. In other words, if Merrill was right on his last point, the *Times'* central allegation was based on a wrong interpretation of the relevant statues.

Why did the *Times* edit out such critical information, cutting Merrill's statement down so drastically?

As Schmidt's story was being put to bed, with its false hint of criminality trumpeted in an accusatory headline, *Times* editor Ryan held forth to collegues that the response from the Clinton spokesman had been edited down to just a few stray phrases because she—Carolyn Ryan—believed it was a lie—and that the Clintons just lie.

Over the course of the evening, though, as other outlets tried to chase the *New York Times* report and I huddled with my staff on conference calls, it became clear that the *Times* had a more glaring problem than Hillary probably did. The *Times,* it turned out, not the Clinton spokesman, was the one lying.

First, and most important, the claim that Hillary had violated the law was wholly unsupported by anything Schmidt had reported.

The article referred to "federal requirements that officials' correspondence be retained as part of the agency's record," part of the Federal Records Act. But some quick research showed that the rules the *Times* suggested were broken were not in place when Hillary was secretary of state. The Presidential and Federal Records Act Amendments of 2014, which declared that official messages sent on personal accounts must be copied or forwarded to official accounts for record keeping, did not become law until more than eighteen months after she had left the State Department. The rules that were in effect during Hillary's tenure at State did not require real-time archiving into State's system, only that relevant records be retained and preserved, which Hillary clearly did.

In other words: The rule Schmidt was accusing Hillary of breaking wasn't a rule at all when he suggested she broke it.

Knowing these facts, the story was starting to make a little more sense. That "new State Department effort to comply with federal record-keeping practices" two months earlier had been a response to the new law. The State Department had, as part of an update to its record preservation policies, asked every former secretary of state dating back to Madeleine Albright to provide records (including e-mails) from their time in office. In response, Hillary had sent more than fifty-five thousand pages of e-mails to be archived.

Within hours of the story's publication, it was obvious that its central claim—that Hillary had possibly broken the law—was false. This alone should have been grounds for a retraction, or at least a prominent correction. By Tuesday morning, when the story appeared above the fold on the front page of the *Times* print edition with the subhead LACK OF ARCHIVING MAY BREAK FEDERAL RULES, we discovered more problems with it:

- The initial version that went online reported that Hillary had provided the e-mails to one of the congressional committees engaged in the Benghazi witch hunt. But the story was later updated to make it clear that she voluntarily submitted e-mails sent from her account after the State Department first sought them as part of updating its records to comply with the new regulations. The *Times* never explained how Schmidt got that wrong.

- Far down in the story, Schmidt noted that Hillary's successor, John Kerry, used a government e-mail account. But while Schmidt relayed this fact in an MSNBC interview the next morning, his original story didn't tell readers that Kerry was, in fact, the *first* secretary of state ever to rely primarily on official State Department e-mail.

- Schmidt wrote, "Before the current regulations went into effect, Secretary of State Colin L. Powell . . . used personal email to communicate with American officials and ambassadors and foreign leaders." This let Powell off the hook—but if that was right Hillary should have been in the clear, too: Her use of personal e-mail *also* came "before the current regulations went into effect."

- And that quote from Hillary's spokesman? The *full* quote was missing from the lengthy article. Schmidt was unable to find room for what Hillary's spokesman actually said. Or did he just not want to undermine his jurcy premise? (Only later did I learn the quote was purposely truncated.)

- Finally, the primary source cited to indict Hillary's use of a personal e-mail account, Jason "Nuclear Winter" Baron, flatly told CNN that he did not believe Hillary had violated the law. Did Schmidt not ask him that question? Or did Schmidt just not find the answer useful?

That Tuesday, March 3, it was the pundits' turn to weigh in on the previous evening's story, and the hot takes were flying. "This will feed the idea she's hiding something," said Dana Bash on CNN, comparing the story to Mitt Romney's infamous "47 percent" tape. Her colleague, Brianna Keilar, speculated that the controversy might spark challenges from other Democrats. In the *Washington Post*, Ruth Marcus wrote, "The Clintons' unfortunate tendency to be their own worst enemy is on display again."

Democrats, meanwhile, awoke in full meltdown. Cable news was looking for guests to defend Hillary's use of personal e-mail; at this early stage of the story, with so many questions unanswered and facts unknown, few volunteered.

But I did. Even though I didn't yet have an answer to every question raised in the article, I did have plenty of evidence to show that the *Times* had misfired badly. The central allegation—that Hillary had broken federal rules—was unsupported by the story; no one, including the lead expert quoted in the story, was backing it up. That was ground we could fight on. I also focused on the fact that the story advanced the agenda of partisan sources in the GOP desperately searching for a way to keep the failed Benghazi investigation active.

Adding to my confidence level was my firsthand experience with many other stories just like this one.

I had seen it all before: the weakly supported accusations of wrongdoing, the feeding frenzy from a press corps hoping to write the Clintons' political obituary, the braying on the right and the panic on the left. My instincts told me that if we just gave the story another poke or two, the whole house of cards would collapse.

So, that Tuesday morning, I assembled all the flaws we'd found in Michael Schmidt's story and sent an open letter to the public editor of the *New York Times* asking for a prominent correction. And when those media bookers started calling around, looking for talkers, I told them to sign me up, doing four shows in one day.

Wednesday morning, I appeared on MSNBC's *Morning Joe*. Hosts Joe Scarborough and Mika Brzezinski were convinced that Hillary was done for, and somewhat incredulous that I was defending her so strongly: "The story," I said, "was wrong. It's based on a false premise." ("I'm not sure what planet I'm on right now," Mika marveled when I refused to admit that *some* law must have been broken.)

Bob Woodward, also on the panel, tried to get me to hedge: "Clearly, it was a good story. You may have some technical disagreements, but we get into this issue—were the walls green, is that really illegal and so forth, it's an important story, won't you concede that?"

But it *wasn't* a good story. The central premise had fallen apart. So I held my ground. No hedging.

Instead, I reminded the audience of what was really going on: "Let's not have a situation where the normal journalistic rules apply to everybody but Hillary Clinton. And let's not forget that the real story here is, you've got a dying Benghazi investigation on Capitol Hill...they want a fishing expedition into these e-mails."

I better understood the reluctance of my fellow Democrats to defend Hillary in that moment when the press notices on my appearances came in. Peggy Noonan called me a "weirdo." The *National Review Online* would cite my "unique mélange of clownishness, self-interest, and hypercompetence," suggesting that I was "taking the heat" for the Clintons like a "good and faithful servant." And Fox News, commenting on my wavy gray locks, called me "Captain Crazy Hair."

To Maureen Dowd, I was officially a Hillary "hatchet." And according to the *Wall Street Journal* editorial page, Media Matters was now to be regarded as a "propaganda operation," while American Bridge was Hillary's "attack machine."

The strangest comment, apparently meant to be an antigay slur, came from the *National Review*'s Jonah Goldberg, who fantasized about my taking orders from Hillary after "slinking" out of a "leather onesie."

All of it was an unpleasant reminder that marginalizing Democrats who forcefully defend their own side—rather than seeking a "reasonable" middle ground and hedging the defense—was all part of the game. And so was the political media's continuing overreaction, as the Sunday shows and op-ed columnists got their chance to weigh in on What It All Meant.

"This isn't about the e-mails," said Cook Political Report's Amy Walter on *Meet the Press*, explaining that "it feeds into this narrative that she isn't a change agent."

On ABC's *This Week*, Mark Halperin declared that he no longer considered her the favorite to be elected president because of the e-mail dustup. "Exhale," urged copanelist Donna Brazile, the Democratic veteran. But Halperin was on a roll: "If this is the way she's going to run her operation, if this is the mind-set she's going to have, I don't think she's going to be president."

CNN's John King wrote a piece headlined HILLARY CLINTON'S EMAIL SCANDAL IS EXACTLY WHAT YOU CAN EXPECT FROM HER PRESIDENTIAL CAMPAIGN.

"Secrecy. Shielding documents. Accusations of arrogance and hypocrisy. Debates about the letter and the spirit of the rules," King wrote, adding, "We have seen this movie before."

In other words, it was all the Clintons' fault. "We do seem to have gotten back into the way-back machine," said NPR's Mara Liasson, "and revisited the Clintons' penchant for scandals and controversy." The "Clintons' penchant"?

Yet, even as all this was in the air, my belief, based on facts, that Hillary had done nothing wrong, and that this would prove to be another fake scandal—grew stronger by the day. Mainstream media outlets had spent the week excitedly chasing the whiff of impropriety, only to end up having to walk back their own coverage when the facts came out:

- In response to my open letter, Margaret Sullivan, the public editor of the *New York Times*, defended the Schmidt story in part, but acknowledged that it "should have been much clearer about precisely what regulations might have been violated." While *Times* editor Carolyn Ryan and reporter Michael Schmidt, both name-checked by Sullivan, naturally described the story as "incredibly solid," in Ryan's words, Sullivan concluded:

    "As the *Times* continues to cover Mrs. Clinton into 2016, it will be dealing with dozens of dust-ups like this one. It's going to be a long campaign, and Clinton coverage inevitably will be microscopically examined and fraught with conflicting reaction.

"Attacks on the reporting will come no matter what. But the *Times* can do itself—and its readers—a lot of good by making sure that every story is airtight: solidly sourced, written with particular clarity and impartiality, and edited with a prosecutorial eye."

- The Associated Press alleged that a "homebrew" e-mail server based in Hillary's house was traced "to a mysterious identity, Eric Hoteham." The name Eric Hoteham, it was noted with an air of tantalizing mystery, did not appear in public records! Later, the AP had to acknowledge that "it was not immediately clear exactly where Clinton's home computer server was run." And the mysterious Eric Hoteham? That was just a misspelling of the name of Hillary's aide who had handled the family's IT needs, Eric Hothem.

- The *Washington Post* reported that a State Department review was under way to determine whether Hillary's use of a private e-mail account "violated policies designed to protect sensitive information." Later, the article's headline was changed, and its language updated, to reflect the fact that the investigation was into whether the e-mails could be safely released, not into whether Hillary had violated the rules.

- *Politico* claimed that by using a private e-mail account, Hillary was at odds with a "clear cut" 2005 Foreign Affairs Manual that "warn officials against routine use of personal e-mail accounts for government work." Later, the story was updated to quote a State Department official who explained that the 2005 policy was "limited to records containing...sensitive information," adding, "Reports claiming that by using personal email she is automatically out of step of that FAM are inaccurate."

∽

With the hopes of finding some clear-cut wrongdoing fading quickly, the story became less about whether Hillary had broken the law and more about her alleged penchant for secrecy. We were no longer having a legal or ethical argument, we were now doing exactly what the Republicans wanted—baselessly trashing Hillary's character even as she was calling for unprecedented transparency.

Two days after the story broke, Hillary had tweeted, "I want the public to see my email. I asked State to release them. They said they will review them for release as soon as possible." And a week later, she held a press conference to answer questions from an antagonistic press corps incredulous that she wasn't throwing herself on the mercy of the court.

As we watched her take the stage from our headquarters at American Bridge, we suddenly heard sirens—a literal fire drill was taking place in our office. People headed toward the exits. I stood up from my chair and raised the volume on my TV to drown out the alarms.

In front of a packed room of reporters, Hillary explained that using her personal e-mail account for official business was clearly allowed by the applicable laws and regulations—and that she made a practice of e-mailing government officials on their ".gov" accounts so that business e-mails she sent would be immediately captured and preserved in the State Department's system, which went beyond what the law required. Moreover, Hillary made clear, even if she had used two accounts, she would have decided which e-mails were retained as government records and which ones were personal. Every government employee made the same decisions every day. Thus, the use of one e-mail address was obviously not some nefarious plot to keep certain communications secret, it was just a matter of personal convenience: Hillary had decided to work from one account rather than two so she would not have to carry a second device to keep in regular touch with family and friends.

Looking back, Hillary acknowledged, it would have been better just to have used two phones. But she had a solid answer for every question, and a nine-page document from her office helped to knock down many of the other false claims that had been made since the *Times* story was published. No, she had never sent or received classified material on her personal account—in fact, only once had she ever used it to correspond with any foreign official. No, her server was never hacked. No, no one ever gained access to it.

And, while she had chosen not to hang on to personal messages about Chelsea's wedding plans and her yoga routines, Hillary had turned over for preservation and public examination the e-mail on her account that related to her duties as secretary of state, again going beyond what the law required.

Hillary went into detail about the process used to cull all the messages from her account that were related to official business:

- First, any e-mail with a ".gov" address in any field was deemed official.
- Next, her team searched for the first and last names of more than one hundred different officials—including potential misspellings of their names. Anything that matched went in the official bucket, as well.
- Finally, a number of terms were specifically searched for—including "Benghazi" and "Libya." Anything that matched went into the pile to be turned over.

In all, there were fifty-five thousand pages of such e-mails in the hands of the State Department. But how, the press howled, do we know that every relevant e-mail was turned over, that there weren't more Hillary was hiding?

In reality, as Hillary suggested in her press conference, it was a question that could be asked of literally every government employee. After all, even if Hillary had used a "state.gov" e-mail address, what would have stopped her from sending and receiving other messages on her personal account? What would stop any government employee from keeping messages away from the prying eyes of the public by using a nonofficial account? And even if Hillary (or any government employee) turned over the entire contents of that nonofficial account, what was to say they didn't delete something first?

It was literally a no-win situation. Hillary was being asked to prove a negative. And here, we finally got to the heart of the matter.

Because barely had Hillary finished her press conference when Representative Trey Gowdy (R-South Carolina), the chair of the new House Select Committee on Benghazi, issued a statement demanding that her private e-mail server be turned over in its entirety.

That's right. Under the guise of their long-failed Benghazi witch hunt, Republicans now felt entitled to riffle through every e-mail Hillary Clinton had ever sent or received from her personal e-mail account: notes from Bill, private conversations with friends, the whole lot. Forget the fishing expedition; they wanted to dredge the whole damn lake.

Perhaps, I wrote in a *USA Today* op-ed, they could hire Ken Starr, the man who turned the Whitewater witch hunt into an investigation into the president's private behavior, to snoop into Hillary's private e-mail. No public official would ever be subject to such an outrageous invasion of privacy.

To prove the point, I demanded that Gowdy turn over all of his personal e-mails so the public could see whether there was anything juicy in there. And, while he was at it, why didn't he have his staff turn over their personal e-mails, too?

I bet we could have some fun with their personal, private communications. But I'm quite sure that, if we got to see what Gowdy and the Republicans were *really* thinking, we'd find proof that this "scandal" has been about keeping the Benghazi hoax alive from Day One.

~

Once again, the *New York Times* got taken for a ride by the Clintons' political enemies.

Writing of the *Times* e-mail scoop for Media Matters, Eric Boehlert put it this way: "And that's the pattern we've seen unfold for twenty-plus years at the *Times*... The *Times* uncorks supposedly blockbuster allegations against a Clinton that are based on vague reporting that later turns out to be flimsy, but not before the rest of the Beltway media erupts in a guttural roar (led by sanctimonious *Times* columnists) and not before Republicans launch investigations designed to destroy the Clintons politically."

And after setting all those wheels in motion, sure enough, by the end of that second week, the *Times* was quietly backpedaling. No longer was the paper of record standing by its bombshell alleging that Hillary "may have violated" federal law. Without ever correcting a word of the initial report, the paper was striking a different tone, explaining that the story was really about the confusion caused by new technology:

> Hillary Rodham Clinton's disclosure that she exclusively used a private email address while she was secretary of state and later deleted thousands of messages she deemed "personal" opens a big picture window into how vague federal email guidelines have been for the most senior government leaders.

In its initial report, the *Times* had claimed that Hillary's "aides took no actions to have her personal emails preserved on department servers at the time, as required by the Federal Records Act." Now the paper finally acknowledged that those rules for preserving emails in real time didn't even exist until after she had left Foggy Bottom:

> While many agencies' current practice is to print and file emails deemed worthy of saving, an Obama administration directive in 2012 mandates that agencies must devise a system for retaining and preserving email records electronically by the end of 2016....
>
> Mr. Obama signed legislation late last year requiring government officials who use personal email addresses for official business to bring those records into the government within 20 days. Before that, the National Archives and Records Administration simply required those messages at some point to be provided to the government.

Those passages represented, in effect, a retraction of the initial Schmidt story. But *Times* readers would never know it, unless they had been carefully parsing every word of the paper's coverage all along. In this sneaky way, Schmidt, who was regarded by some colleagues as nothing but a messenger boy for the Republican Benghazi investigators, was able to cover his posterior, and no one was the wiser. The previous week, the *Times* had claimed that Hillary's use of private e-mail was seen as "alarming" and a "serious breach." Now it was being described as business as usual—and certainly not a breach of anything:

> Members of President Obama's cabinet have a wide variety of strategies, shortcuts and tricks for handling their email, and until three months ago there was no law setting out precisely what they had to do with it, and when. And while the majority of Obama administration officials use government email to conduct their business, there has never been any legal prohibition against using a personal account.

Meanwhile, we were learning that many, if not all, leading Republicans had held themselves to a far lower standard of transparency. Scott Walker's County Executive office used a secret e-mail system in order to avoid public records disclosure laws, which, investigators determined, allowed him and his staff to engage in campaign work on county time. Chris Christie's staff used private e-mails to conduct state business, and ignored reporters' requests to view them. John Kasich kept a list of his staffers' private e-mail addresses labeled "DO NOT DISTRIBUTE." Mike Huckabee physically destroyed travel records and calendars and, yes, e-mails.

And then there was Jeb Bush. Recall that, in the original *New York Times* story, Michael Schmidt had held him up as a paragon of transparency compared to Hillary:

> And others who, like Mrs. Clinton, are eyeing a candidacy for the White House are stressing a very different approach. Jeb Bush, who is seeking the Republican nomination for president, released

a trove of emails in December from his eight years as governor of Florida.

"Transparency matters," Jeb had tweeted; Hillary's "emails should be released."

But he had only released 250,000 e-mails, less than one tenth of the 3 million he had received on a server that, like Hillary, he owned himself.

And then, just eleven days after Schmidt's story, it emerged that, as the *New York Times* itself reported, "it took Mr. Bush seven years after leaving office to comply fully with a Florida public records statute requiring him to turn over emails he sent and received as governor, according to records released Friday."

In fact, he had forked over the latest batch—twenty-five thousand e-mails—only when he was beginning to think about running for the White House. And that, it turns out, actually *was* breaking the law:

A Florida statute governing the preservation of public records requires elected officials, including the governor, to turn over records pertaining to official business "at the expiration of his or her term of office."

"If they've been adding to it, it's a technical violation of the law," said Barbara A. Petersen, president of the First Amendment Foundation, a nonprofit, nonpartisan group in Florida that advocates access to government information.

She added, "The law clearly says you're supposed to turn everything over at the end of your term in office."

Jeb's lawyers explained that they had only just found these e-mails. But, as the expert quoted in the story said, that smelled funny: "I can see how it might take six months or so, a year maybe, to locate all these records. But we are talking, what now, seven years?"

Of course, even though Jeb Bush *had* actually, indisputably, broken the law, there was no rush to judgment, no rending of garments among his supporters, no antagonistic press conference. The headline on the *Times* story read, AN EAGER CRITIC TOOK TIME RELEASING HIS OWN RECORDS. It was buried on page A14. Never mind—except for Hillary.

⌒

So, what have we learned here?

We learned that Hillary Clinton's e-mail practices didn't break any rules—but Jeb Bush's did.

We learned that what at first appeared to be a deeply damaging new scandal was, in reality, just another failed attempt to create one—those of us who smelled a rat from the start were proven right, and those who ran for the lifeboats were proven wrong.

And we learned, as if we need to learn it again, that when it comes to the way the press covers these kinds of stories, the rules are always different for Hillary.

Indeed, even as the initial story was falling apart, it gave Washington reporters an excuse to reflect on how things always seem tumultuous when Hillary's around.

"The circus is back in town," wrote the *Washington Post*'s Karen Tumulty, complaining that "the spectacle of the Clinton White House years is unfolding again."

And, of course, that spectacle, according to the conventional wisdom of the media, was no one's fault but Hillary's.

## Chapter Twelve

# The Haters and the Enablers

It's impossible to talk about the right's case against Hillary without talking about sexism. Sexism is in fact integral to the right-wing attacks we've just delineated—on her record, her character, and her personal biography. And it's also integral to the Right's antiwoman ideology, which a Hillary candidacy is uniquely positioned to expose.

Two decades have passed since the *American Spectator* dubbed Hillary "the Lady Macbeth of Little Rock" on its cover. The magazine flew off the stands, and in subsequent years attacking powerful women—especially Hillary—proved both a durable business model for conservatives and a way of amping up in the right-wing base's hatred and fear of the social and cultural changes, and the shift from traditional gender power dynamics, they personify.

From practically the moment Hillary entered the national consciousness, there was never a price to be paid for pushing the envelope when it came to her, and so conservatives pushed it as far as their imaginations would allow. Hillary was the "the Winnie Mandela of American politics," she was imprisoned hotelier Leona Helmsley, she was criminal mastermind Ma Barker—she was even Eva Braun. Her 2008 campaign, in which she threatened to break the last and highest glass ceiling, brought the right's attacks on Hillary as a woman to the forefront.

On the campaign trail in New Hampshire, Hillary was met by hecklers yelling "Iron my shirt!" Conservatives sold LIFE'S A BITCH, DON'T VOTE FOR ONE T-shirts. A Facebook group called itself "Hillary Clinton: Stop Running for President and Make Me a Sandwich." And when a voter asked GOP candidate John McCain at a campaign rally in South Carolina, "How do we beat the bitch?" McCain just laughed it off.

On his radio show, Glenn Beck called Hillary a "stereotypical bitch" (and a year later, when he was confronted about the remark, he only walked it back so far as to admit that "probably a better word is *nag*.") That B word was in the air all campaign long—from conservative activist Ted Nugent, who at a 2007 concert called Hillary "a worthless bitch," to Fox's Neil Cavuto, who speculated that Hillary was trying to "run away from this tough, kind of bitchy image."

And time and again, whether it was Rush Limbaugh chuckling about Hillary's "testicle lockbox," Tucker Carlson ruminating that there's "just something about her that feels castrating," or pundit Cliff May suggesting that Hillary be referred to as a "Vaginal American," conservatives couldn't stop conjuring up images of Hillary as a man-eater in their campaign to demonize her.

Others found more subtle ways of calling Hillary Clinton a bitch. Writer Joel Achenbach suggested in the *Washington Post* that Hillary "needs a radio-controlled shock collar so that aides can zap her when she starts to get screechy." Conservative author Marc Rudov went on Fox News to proclaim, "When Barack Obama speaks, men hear, 'Take off for the future.' And when Hillary Clinton speaks, men hear, 'Take out the garbage.'" As he spoke, the chyron read, RUDOV: CLINTON'S 'NAGGING VOICE' IS REASON SHE LOST MALE VOTE.

When it wasn't Hillary's voice, it was her laugh. Bill O'Reilly discussed it with a "body language expert" who characterized it as "evil." Sean Hannity called it "frightening." O'Reilly also hosted a guest who warned of "PMS and mood swings" with Hillary in the Oval Office.

This is ugly stuff, and it reveals the unapologetic sexism and even misogyny that, unfortunately, still has a place in the modern conservative movement. These types of attacks obviously would never be leveled at a male candidate.

And, frankly, I doubt they would be tolerated against most female candidates. But the rules are different for Hillary. And in 2008, instead of calling out the right's personal attacks, the mainstream media joined in.

It wasn't just Fox making an issue out of Hillary's laugh, it was the *New York Times*, which—in a news article mind you—referred to it as "The Cackle" and suggested it may have been "programmed."

On MSNBC's *Morning Joe*, Mike Barnicle earned a round of laughter from the panel when he compared Hillary to "everyone's first wife standing outside a probate court." Dana Milbank and Chris Cillizza, political analysts for the *Washington Post*, made a "comedic" web video where, wearing silk bathrobes for some reason, they guffawed about Hillary drinking "Mad Bitch" beer.

The *Post* wasn't joking, however, when it published an article about Hillary's cleavage, asserting, "The last time Clinton wore anything that was remotely sexy in a public setting surely must have been more than a decade ago." Ten days later, MSNBC devoted six separate segments—a total of nearly twenty-four minutes of airtime—to talking about Hillary's décolletage.

Also on MSNBC, Chris Matthews compared Hillary to Nurse Ratched from *One Flew Over the Cuckoo's Nest*; NPR's political director Ken Rudin said she was Glenn Close from *Fatal Attraction*, comparing Hillary to a violent, psychopathic fictional character.

And when Hillary's voice broke during a campaign event in New Hampshire, it wasn't just Bill Kristol claiming, "She pretended to cry." It was mainstream outlets like *Newsweek* calling it her "most famous moment of trying to be like an average human being." Conversely, Dick Morris thought that the tears were real—and disqualifying: "I believe that there could well come a time when there is such a serious threat to the United States that she breaks down like that."

And it wasn't just Rush Limbaugh wondering whether "if her name was Hillary Smith, would anybody be talking about her as a presidential candidate?" ABC News anchor Charles Gibson asked Hillary point-blank, "Would you be in this position were it not for your husband?" And it was Chris Matthews (again) claiming, "The reason she's a U.S. senator, the reason she's a candidate for president, the reason she may be a front-runner is her husband messed around."

After that remark sparked howls of protest and even an old-fashioned protest by women's groups, led by Emily's List, outside NBC Studios, Matthews issued a brave apology—and since then has admirably cleaned up his rhetoric. Matthews said:

> Was it fair to imply that Hillary's whole career depended on being a victim of an unfaithful husband? No. And that's what it sounded like I was saying and it hurt people I'd like to think normally like what I say, in fact, normally like me.... On those occasions when I have not taken the time to say things right, or have simply said the inappropriate thing, I'll try to be clearer, smarter, more obviously in support of the right of women—of all people—the full equality and respect of their ambitions. So, I get it.

So are all these well-respected media figures raging misogynists? Of course not. But by playing to familiar, even at times seemingly harmless, sexist tropes, they enable attacks from the right-wing gutter, which has shifted the window of what is and isn't acceptable to say about Hillary.

⌒

And then, of course, there is the matter of Hillary's age. Despite the fact that on assuming office Hillary, at sixty-nine, would be younger than conservative icon Ronald Reagan—and is only five and a half years older than Jeb Bush—Republicans clearly think that age is a potent attack against a woman who would be president.

For example: Rush Limbaugh wondered, "Will Americans want to watch a woman get older before their eyes on a daily basis?"

For example: The *New York Post* reported that, appearing at a conference in California, Karl Rove "said if Clinton runs for president, voters must be told what happened when she suffered a fall in December 2012."

"Thirty days in the hospital?" Rove asked rhetorically. "And when she reappears, she's wearing glasses that are only for people who have traumatic brain injury? We need to know what's up with that."

It was a seemingly clever attack, combining a subtle suggestion that Hillary was too frail to be president with a more or less open accusation that she was lying about her health to gain political advantage.

Hillary, of course, was fine. She had been in the hospital only four days, not thirty. A Clinton spokesperson poked back, "Please assure Dr. Rove she's 100 percent," adding, "Karl Rove has deceived the country for years, but there are no words for this level of lying."

And even Rove seemed to walk his comments back: "Now, is this going to be the issue of the 2016 presidential campaign if she runs? No, it's going to be a minor thing."

But Republicans embraced the provocation. Matt Drudge spotted a picture of Hillary on the cover of *Parade* magazine where, he thought, it looked like she was using a walker—a ridiculous claim, but one he nevertheless trumpeted with his infamous siren graphic. The "walker" was a patio chair.

"I think that health and age is fair game," said Republican National Committee chairman Reince Priebus. "It was fair game for Ronald Reagan. It was fair game for John McCain."

"She's going to be old!" crowed *RedState* blogger and Fox analyst Erick Erickson, illustrating exactly what the GOP considers to be fair game. "I don't know how far back they can pull her face!"

❧

In his 2012 campaign, Mitt Romney frequently touted his eighteen grandchildren on the campaign trail. His comments passed without notice. But when the news broke that Hillary was becoming a grandmother, the reaction was entirely different.

The Hillary-as-grandmother story provided an opening for the media to speculate (once again) about Hillary's age—the *Drudge Report* blared "Grandma Hillary"—about whether her grandmotherly duties would provide too great a distraction for Hillary once in office, and about whether Hillary would use the new baby as a "stage prop," as Kyle Smith charged in the *New York Post*. "So play nice and don't projectile vomit. Grandma is not what grown-ups call maternal."

Steve Malzberg, host of an online TV show sponsored by *News-Max*, said, "Pardon the skeptic in me...but what great timing! I mean, purely accidental, purely an act of nature, purely just left up to God. And God answered Hillary Clinton's prayers, and she is going to have the prop of being a new grandma while she runs for president."

*Politico* ran a story speculating that Chelsea's pregnancy might even cause Hillary to forego a 2016 candidacy, asking, "Why beg donors for money at dozens of events a month when there's a happy baby to spend time with in New York?"

All of which raised the question, posed by Aliyah Frumin on MSNBC.com, "of how we would treat this news if Clinton were a man."

Debbie Walsh, director of the Center for American Women and Politics at Rutgers University, told MSNBC: "There's a disproportionate attention to her being a grandmother. Certainly, many men have run for president as grandfathers. And nobody worries if they can't do their job."

⌒

The right's motives in leveling such nasty personal attacks against Hillary are as obvious as they are predictable. Much more confounding is when women join in the sexist attacks.

For instance, columnist Peggy Noonan has also compared Hillary to the Glenn Close character in *Fatal Attraction*. Then again, maybe she wasn't Glenn Close. Hillary, Noonan wrote, "doesn't have to prove she's a man. She has to prove she's a woman."

Then there is Carly Fiorina, the failed former Hewlett-Packard executive and failed Senate candidate who seems to be running for president so that the GOP can launch gender-based attacks on Hillary while avoiding charges of sexism. Fiorina has accused Hillary of waging "a war on women" by using "identity politics to divide the electorate." One of her standard lines, "Hillary Clinton must not be president of the United States but not because she is a woman," is of course a not-so-subtle way of reminding audiences that Hillary *is* a woman. Fiorina also asserts that only a woman candidate, such as herself, can cut into Hillary's support among women. "And I will say this, if Hillary Clinton had to face me on the debate stage at the very least she would have a hitch in her swing."

But *New York Times* columnist Maureen Dowd is the woman who has made attacking Hillary her stock-in-trade for the better part of two decades.

Relying on thinly veiled sexism, Dowd's decades-long campaign not only reflects the misogyny of the right but also validates it.

By saying things about Hillary she would never say about a male politician, Dowd sanctions a double standard against her. And the fact that the *Times* gives Dowd such a prestigious platform for her anti-Hillary rants makes it that much harder to insist that there be consequences when right-wingers go overboard in their rancor. In this way, Dowd provides cover for crazies like Ted Nugent. And a great liberal paper like the *Times* becomes the top enabler of the Hillary haters.

If Dowd doesn't share the conservative movement's unhinged loathing for Hillary, she does a good job of faking it. In June 2014, Media Matters sought to quantify Dowd's obsession, looking back at every column Dowd had written since 1993 in which Hillary received a significant mention. Out of 195 columns we analyzed, only 8 percent cast Hillary in a positive light. Another 20 percent were neutral toward her. And an incredible 72 percent of Dowd's Hillary columns were negative.

In other words, over two decades, Maureen Dowd wrote 141 columns attacking Hillary Clinton. Media Matters concluded:

- In fifty-one different columns (more than a quarter of her total output), Dowd cast Hillary as power-hungry, often in gendered terms. Dowd has called her a "controlling blonde," a "debate Dominatrix," a "manly girl." She has written that "nothing but a wooden stake would stop" Hillary, and that she "moves like a shark." For Dowd, Hillary's "relentless ambition" dates all the way back to her 1969 commencement speech at Wellesley College.

- In forty-three different columns, Dowd attacked the Clintons' marriage, which she termed "warped," "rootless and chaotic," "transcendentally wacky," a "repugnant arrangement." "They seem," she wrote, "like a virus or alien that needs a host body to survive." The constant theme is that their marriage is a loveless sham, and that they won't simply go away like everyone (or at least Maureen Dowd) wishes they would.

- In thirty-five different columns, Dowd accused Hillary of betraying the feminist cause and trading on slights from men to get ahead. In 1999, she wrote that Hillary "was unmasked as a counterfeit feminist after she let her man step all over her." In Dowd's eyes, Hillary "got to be a senator playing the victim card": She "won her Senate seat only after becoming sympathetic as a victim" and "because men abused her." And as a senator? "[She] is now so eerily glazed and good-natured that she could be the senator from Stepford." Dowd summed up her sexist thesis in a 2008 column:

> She won her Senate seat after being embarrassed by a man. She pulled out New Hampshire and saved her presidential campaign after being embarrassed by another man. She was seen as so controlling when she ran for the Senate that she had to be seen as losing control, as she did during the Monica scandal, before she seemed soft enough to attract many New York voters.

- In thirty-four different columns, Dowd claimed that Hillary is insincere and fake: "The public," she wrote in 2007, "still has no idea of what part of her is stage-managed and focus-grouped, and what part is legit. It's pretty pathetic, at this stage of her career, that she has to wage a major offensive, by helicopter and Web testimonials, to make herself appear warm-blooded." In Dowd's eyes, Hillary is "shape-shifting" and "cynical," and she's made sure to use gender as a weapon here, too, comparing her to Sybil, the title character of a 1976 film about a woman with multiple-personality disorder, and on another occasion comparing her to Meryl Streep as a "master thespian."

- In nine different columns, Dowd explained why Hillary isn't likable. Her "smile," Dowd wrote, "is not connected to her face," adding, "you might admire her but you wouldn't want to hang out with her." Dowd claimed that Hillary's "abrasive and secretive management of health care doomed it." And, she opined, Hillary was now "paying a fortune to try to buy the secrets of likability."

In one 2015 column, headlined GRANNY GET YOUR GUN, Dowd addressed Hillary's apparent problem of not being able to "figure out how to campaign as a woman," chided her for "the foolishness of acting like a masculine woman," while at the same time exhorting Hillary to show that "bitch is the new black."

Go figure.

Clark Hoyt, the *Times* public editor in 2008, took Dowd's coverage of that campaign to task, writing, "by assailing Clinton in gender-heavy terms in column after column, [Dowd] went over the top this election season." He noted that Dowd was listed in a "Media Hall of Shame created by the National Organization for Women. The *Times* reported on the list in a front-page article but failed to mention that Dowd was on it, and her rampage continued.

After 141 often self-contradictory and unintelligible hit pieces over the course of twenty years, the readership of the *New York Times* has surely gotten Dowd's one point: She hates Hillary Clinton.

～

By now, however, some smarter conservatives are beginning to realize that blatant sexism can backfire.

As Republican strategist Katie Packer Gage told Hanna Rosin of the *Atlantic*, "Women have this feeling that the world—and particularly this town—is run by men, and if something comes across as mean or unfair, they want to rush to her defense."

Another Republican strategist, Kelly Ann Conway, was reportedly working with focus groups to perfect the attack on Hillary not as *a* woman but as "*that* woman."

So, clearly, such personal attacks are not off the table, and conservatives won't refrain from engaging in lines of attack that subtly remind their audience of their favorite stereotype.

The truth is the Republicans can't help themselves. As Jessica Valenti observed in the *Washington Post*, "When misogyny is part of your ideology, it's hard to muzzle." In other words, no matter how sly the Republicans are in making their sexist attacks, what they can't hide is that their anti-Hillary agenda is part and parcel of their antiwoman agenda—against abortion rights, birth control, equal pay for women, universal preschool, and child care. It's an agenda poised to alienate women voters especially.

And who better to underscore what's at stake for women in the next election than candidate Hillary Clinton?

A candidate who has spent four decades, from the Children's Defense Fund in the 1970s through her tenure as secretary of state, fighting for the disenfranchised, particularly women and girls.

A candidate who ended her last campaign for presidency by citing eighteen million cracks—the number of votes she got in the Democratic primaries—in "that highest, hardest glass ceiling."

A candidate who, in her first remarks after leaving the State Department, addressed "the untapped potential of women around the world."

A candidate who announced her 2016 bid, saying, "I may not be the youngest person in this race, but I'll be the youngest woman president in the history of the United States."

At Media Matters we will, of course, be on the lookout for examples of both blatant and more subtle sexism from the right during Hillary's 2016 campaign. Glenn Beck, for example, wonders whether Hillary shaves her face. But I'm less concerned with the Glenn Becks of the world and more concerned with the Maureen Dowds—less worried about some idiot with a talk show crossing the line and more worried about some widely-read columnist with a prominent position at a reputable outlet using it maliciously.

After all, while most Americans would probably recoil from the kind of grotesque attacks you can find if you wander into the fever swamps of the far right, many will see cable TV hosts and newspaper columnists refer to Hillary's coldness or calculating nature without a second thought as to the root of such stereotypes. They'll come to accept it as an article of faith that Hillary is overly ambitious, even though no one is saying that about the men who are running for president with far thinner résumés. They'll watch pundits debate Hillary's pantsuits instead of her policies, see her hair and makeup choices weighed as matters of state—and they may even participate in the conjecture without realizing how demeaning and ultimately damaging it can be for her candidacy.

That's why, as much as we need to call out and expose the revolting rhetoric of the far right, we need to be just as on guard against mainstream journalists who—knowingly or not—parrot those clichés. The press has a role to play in holding candidates accountable. But we have a role to play in holding them accountable. For twenty years, it has been acceptable to deploy sexism against Hillary Clinton, to attack her not because of what she's done or what she believes, but simply because of who she is.

The good news is that a new generation of online activists is poised to make a difference in 2016 with technologies that were still nascent in 2008. As Jessica Valenti noted in her *Washington Post* op-ed, today clips of Rush Limbaugh calling Sandra Fluke a slut, or Todd Akin talking about "legitimate rape" go viral and spur online outrage—and action.

Citing a *Time* feature story on Hillary's 2016 run that represented Hillary on the cover as a giant high heel crushing a tiny man and asking "Can Anyone Stop Hillary?"—which provoked a hugely negative backlash online—Valenti wrote:

> Perhaps the biggest change surrounding women's responses to political misogyny comes from the explosion of social media. Women on Twitter and Facebook shared their ire over the *Time* cover minutes after its release—much as they do every time something truly offensive happens, whether it's objectionable news media coverage, a politician's blunder or a new anti-woman law. But, unlike most Internet outrage, feminist Internet outrage gets results. And it will give the Clinton campaign—and Hillary supporters—a weapon they did not have last time around.

At long last, it's time for the hating and enabling of hatred of women—and of *that* woman—to stop. And Hillary 2016 *is* that time.

## Chapter Thirteen

# The Coming Battle

O ver the course of this book, we've explored the ongoing political arms race between the left and the right—detailing the evolution of the political and media landscape, exposing how the conservative movement plots to distort facts and smear its opponents, and explaining how we've built a progressive infrastructure that can effectively play both defense and offense.

We've met the billionaire Koch brothers who sponsor disinformation campaigns, the right-wing talking heads who serve as their puppets, and the truth tellers who toil in obscurity every day in an attempt to correct the record.

We've seen how sleazy scandalmongers in the conservative media push phony wares into the mainstream, and how even reputable members of the press are seduced into legitimizing them.

And we've looked at the likely strategies that Hillary Clinton's Republican opponents will employ as they jockey for advantage in the Twitter era.

There's only one actor whose role in this drama we haven't discussed: you.

~

There are a variety of ways in which you can choose to participate in the 2016 presidential campaign, from volunteering your time to donating your money. (And I won't be the first or the last to urge that, whatever else you do, you make your voice heard by voting—after all, the ballot box is the one place where you and David Koch have the same say.)

But whether you actively decide to engage in the campaign or not, you are a part of this story.

You watch TV. You read the news. You scroll through your Twitter feed and Facebook wall. And, as you do, you make countless decisions every day about what information to seek out, and how to interpret what you see and hear.

Meanwhile, even if you don't pick up a clipboard and hit the doors for Hillary or some other candidate, you will most certainly be a participant in the debate simply by virtue of having conversations with your fellow citizens at family gatherings, around the watercooler, and on social media.

Indeed, simply talking to the people in your life about politics is one of the most powerful forms of activism there is. And the first step in making sure you're using that power for good is becoming an educated consumer of political information.

This leads me to a common frustration among most voters—even those who don't engage much in politics at all: It's hard to know where you can go to find news you can really trust. As we've discussed, this isn't really a concern for conservatives, who largely tend to be interested in "news" that validates their existing worldview. But the rest of us want to know that we're getting the real story—not only are we concerned with whether a story is factually accurate, we want to know that it represents the truth, the whole truth, and nothing but the truth.

Trying to figure out what you should read or watch to be well informed, then, can be as aggravating as trying to figure out what you should eat to be healthy: You could read a million treatises on journalistic ethics in the digital age, when all you really want to know is whether or not it's okay to have eggs for breakfast.

Unfortunately, I don't have any easy answers for you. The Brock

News Diet, if you will, isn't a white list of sources you can blindly trust, but rather a way of approaching the information smorgasbord that confronts you every time you turn on the TV or open your browser. (Think of the writer Michael Pollan's advice: "Eat food. Not too much. Mostly plants.")

Of course, it's often easy to spot the worst of the junk. If it comes sandwiched between pieces of fried chicken, wrapped in greasy paper, and handed to you through a drive-through window, it's probably not good for you—like right-wing blogs or Rush Limbaugh. I'm not saying you should avoid right-wing media at all costs (it can be a great way to spot the next phony scandal before it breaks into the mainstream media), but moderation is advised, and, as with fast food, you should be mindful of what overexposure can do to your blood pressure.

The greater challenge comes in discerning the nutritional content of information you find in the mainstream media—and, as with food, you have to read the label carefully and know what to watch out for.

And that can be tricky. The *New York Times* is the most well-respected outlet in American journalism, the newspaper of record, but, as we've seen, they've proven to be wildly unreliable when it comes to the Clintons. With few exceptions, my rule of thumb will be to take nothing the *Times* reports about the Clintons during the 2016 race at face value. Some of the reporting will stand up to the extra scrutiny, but as we've already seen, a good deal of it won't.

While cable networks can be invaluable for staying on top of breaking news, when it comes to Hillary there is often limited or even negative value to the analysis that tends to fill up their broadcast day.

And the problem isn't just on Fox. Be prepared for even some avowedly progressive commentators to try to instigate a symbolic challenge to Hillary in the Democratic primary. Or, at least, to get airtime and attention for themselves at Hillary's expense. Know what this is when you see it, and don't take it as a reflection of widely held progressive views on Hillary, who remains formidable and popular across all sectors of the party.

This isn't exactly revolutionary advice—the Michael Pollan version might be: "Read widely. Trust your instincts. Ask questions." But the truth is that there's no best source for news, just best practices for consuming it. Reporters and editors take the facts and make choices about how to present them to readers—and sometimes, they make the wrong choices.

The more you know about the kind of journalistic flaws catalogued in this book—both malfeasance on the part of right-wing operators and misfeasance on the part of mostly well-intentioned reporters—and the more you read with a critical eye, the easier it will become for you to reverse engineer those choices, intuiting what's really going on behind the story.

⌒

This is especially true, and especially important, when it comes to Hillary Clinton.

As we've seen, the Clinton rules often lead to good journalists producing bad journalism—and if readers aren't aware of this factor and able to adjust their sensors to account for it, they can be suckered, too.

When the *New York Times* story about Hillary's use of a private e-mail account broke, it *seemed* like a solid and damaging hit. And while its central claims would eventually fall apart, how many people—how many of Hillary's supporters—drew the conclusion that she had done something wrong before the story could be subjected to critical scrutiny? How many shared that conclusion in the kind of casual conversations, both online and off, I mentioned earlier? How many of their friends and family members who weren't plugged in enough to read the follow-up coverage might still believe that Hillary was guilty of something?

And how much damage has been done to her image by negative

stereotypes that, had there been the progressive infrastructure to fight back against the lies that began to be spun about her back when I was a right-wing hit man, might never have penetrated into the American consciousness? As you talk about the election with people, you may hear them casually refer to Hillary as conniving, or manipulative, or aloof—where did that come from?

You also might hear the sexist jibe that Hillary is "too ambitious" to be president. Ask yourself: Who has ever won the presidency without the ambition to do so?

Your mission, then, should you choose to accept it, is twofold.

First: Help fight back against the lies we've already identified—the fake scandals, the false accusations, the groundless innuendo.

When your Fox-watching uncle cracks a joke about Hillary "wiping her e-mail server," remind him that she complied with every law and statute, that she went above and beyond the transparency obligations she had as a federal employee, that we still haven't seen one e-mail of Colin Powell's and likely never will, and that the entire story aided Republicans desperate for a new angle on the Benghazi hoax.

Speaking of Benghazi, don't be fooled by conservatives on Twitter who still think there's a bottom to be gotten to—it's nothing but the bottom-feeding of the Benghazi hoaxsters. After ten congressional committees, dozens of briefings, countless hearings, and millions spent on investigations, we now know for sure that there was no stand-down order preventing rescuers from saving the day, no "critical cables" proving that Hillary denied requests for increased security, no conspiracy to conceal the true motive behind the attack, no evidence of any wrongdoing whatsoever on her part. Hillary did what leaders should do: First, she took responsibility, and then she took action with an eye to preventing future attacks.

When your coworker insists that all Hillary did as secretary of state was fly around shaking hands, bring up her lengthy list of accomplishments: laying the groundwork for tough sanctions on Iran, that pressed the country to agree to the historic nuclear deal, negotiating the cease-fire in Gaza, the successful pivot to Asia and the opening of Burma, economic statecraft that brought hundreds of thousands of jobs to America, and her paradigm-shifting leadership on issues affecting women and girls around the world. Most of all, remind your friend just how low America's reputation in the world had sunk under George W. Bush and how high it soared on Hillary's watch.

When your neighbor rolls her eyes at the thought that Hillary might be able to identify with working-class Americans, remind her that Hillary grew up middle class, that she has worked her entire life since the age of thirteen, that she has focused on kitchen-table issues affecting children and families her whole career, that she and Bill weren't wealthy until late in their lives, and when they did become so, they devoted themselves to philanthropy.

And when that philanthropy comes under attack, don't be afraid to present the facts about the Clinton Foundation. You'll be in the company of Clinton Foundation supporters like Mitt Romney, the Bush family, John McCain, and other conservative leading lights—and you'll be able to talk about the good work the Foundation has done to cure disease, alleviate poverty, and promote the interests of low-income people the world over. And when you hear false attacks about a quid pro quo, you'll be able to say with confidence that Rupert Mudoch's *Wall Street Journal*, among others, has concluded that there's never been any evidence of impropriety.

When a progressive friend bemoans the lack of a challenge from Hillary's left, ask him what issue such a candidate could run on. Remind him that this is a woman who penned a progressive vision of the social compact, *It Takes A Village*—twenty years ago. Talk about how Hillary stood with Elizabeth Warren in creating a Consumer Financial Protection Bureau, how she had an aggressive plan to take on Wall Street and close tax loopholes for the wealthy long before it was cool, how she has fought her entire political career for equal pay and universal health care. Or just invite him to listen to her make the case for paid sick leave, immigration reform, LGBT equality, or any number of progressive priorities on the stump—including gun control.

And, for Pete's sake, don't put up with sexist attacks that would never be leveled against a male candidate—not from right-wing bloviators, not from smug cable pundits, and not from your friends and family.

Remind them that Hillary is so "calculating" that, against all political advice, she went to Beijing and declared that "human rights are women's rights, and women's rights are human rights." That was twenty years ago, too. And remember, these sexist attacks betray an ideology that seeks not just to hold back one woman, but to hold all women back.

Be bold. Be aggressive. Be confident. Be willing to step up—even if it means having Fox News make fun of your hair. As someone who has endured more than his fair share of slings and arrows because I've been willing to defend Hillary, I can tell you that there isn't one instance where I've regretted standing up for her.

Of course, by the time this book goes to print, there will no doubt be some "new" story about Hillary filtering up from the conservative oppo shop into the mainstream media. And, at first glance, it may well look damaging. You may be tempted to freak out. And then, soon enough, you will find that it was just another right-wing smear. Remember, you've seen it all before.

It's not too much to say that the never-ending barrage of misinformation and negativity directed against Hillary and Bill Clinton by the media could decide the 2016 election. Unfortunately I don't have much hope that the press will wise up to the propaganda it's being fed by the right; chasing the white whale of a real Clinton scandal is too irresistible. Indeed, as this book went to press, Dylan Byers, the astute media writer for *Politico*, reported that "the national media has never been more primed to take down Hillary Clinton (and, by the same token, elevate a Republican)."

Byers was echoing the observation of the *Washington Post*'s Dana

Milbank, who wrote during the 2008 primary season, when much of the media seemed to be openly campaigning for Obama, "The press will savage [Clinton] no matter what."

But how many times do we have to see the same media bias at play before we stop being fooled by it? It bothers me, of course, when I see Hillary's enemies parroting lies about her. But it bothers me even more when I see her supporters falling prey to the doubts that conservatives are hoping to sow by filtering their attacks through dupes like the *New York Times*.

That brings me to the second part of your mission.

If you're presently more fed up about 2016—or about the state of our democracy in general—than you are fired up, I suppose that's understandable after years of Republican-led gridlock and partisan bickering. But it's also dangerous; the right relies on cynicism and apathy. Conservatives don't just want you to give up on Hillary Clinton, they want you to give up on politics and changing the country for the better. When you leave the arena, that just leaves more room for them to operate.

And we just can't afford that. Not now. Others have written, and will write, more comprehensive analyses of exactly what is at stake in the 2016 presidential election: the balance of power on the Supreme Court, the fate of progressive reforms passed under President Obama but not yet fully implemented, the threat of conservative retrenchment on abortion and gay rights, the hope of addressing long-term issues like climate change and immigration reform, and so much more.

But I believe progressives would be doing themselves, and the Democratic Party's likely standard-bearer, a grave disservice if they sat this one out because conservatives had promised to make the road ahead so difficult and dispiriting. Hillary Clinton is more than simply the finest available leader for winning the election, advancing middle-class priorities, and defeating the extreme agenda of the far right.

As I wrote in my book about her almost twenty years ago, I still believe that Hillary truly is a historic figure with unmatched potential to change America's trajectory for the better. And the constant antagonism directed at her from the right over the last twenty years makes me more—not less—certain of that fact.

⌒

On Election Night 2014, I was privy to an intense scene. Senator Harry Reid sat with New York senator Chuck Schumer in a small conference room at the DC headquarters of the Democratic Senatorial Campaign Committee. The room was quiet as the returns from around the country rolled in. When the results were clear, Reid looked up and broke the silence, saying simply "the Kochs bought the Senate." Then he walked out.

In 2016, the Kochs are poised to buy the presidency—and the Supreme Court along with it. Independent of the GOP itself, the Kochs are building a polling, message-testing, and media-buying capacity that they own. They've already spent $50 million developing sophisticated voter profiles on 250 million Americans. The data is so good, Republican campaigns are buying it instead of cheaper data from the RNC. The Kochs are also orchestrating a permanent boots-on-the-ground campaign infrastructure in key states—outside the traditional party get-out-the-vote efforts that come and go with each campaign cycle—something that's never been done before. In short, Democrats are facing not only the Republican Party, but the Party of Koch.

So, the Democratic nominee for president will spend over $1 billion to get elected, the Republican will spend over $1 billion, and the Kochs will spend yet another $1 billion. You do the math. That's what we're up against.

Now, I've spent years monitoring, tracking, and analyzing the organized right. And what the Kochs are planning is the most audacious power grab I've ever seen—a wholesale takeover of our political system by just two men. If they succeed, what's at stake is bigger than progressive policy wins or the political fortunes of Democrats—it's democracy itself that will be in peril.

Democrats won't have access to anything like the Koch brothers' bottomless treasure chest, but they are going to have to raise and spend significant funds in order to stay competitive and win this election. With respect to third-party groups, Democrats are going to have to walk and chew gum at the same time. They're going to have to enthusiastically back Hillary's campaign plank against unaccountable money in politics while—maybe not so enthusiastically—opening their wallets in support of Democratic SuperPACs, money that Hillary herself has said is critical to the election's outcome.

One thing I'll say about the Kochs: They understand the power of building institutions for the long haul. Progressives have certainly made headway in this regard in the years I've been involved, but going forward we're going to have to do more to stay politically competitive.

Finally, Democrats have to keep the heat on the Koch brothers and their lackeys, exposing their radical ideas and greedy motives at every turn. Already, there are signs they can't take the heat. At one of the Kochs' famous closed-door donor conferences, Koch's general counsel, Mark Holden, warned the assembled right-wing tycoons of how "very effective" our organizations have been at exposing their self-serving political agenda.

If we keep it up, the Kochs might just pull back.

~

When Hillary declared her candidacy in April 2015, the "shadow campaign" period ended on a successful note. Powerful networks online and off had been built. A pro-Hillary grassroots volunteer and low-dollar donor infrastructure was in place. Ready for Hillary, the Super-PAC that did this work, declared "mission accomplished" and closed its doors after transferring its assets to the campaign itself.

Meanwhile, Correct the Record had repelled attacks on Hillary's record and reputation, and she appeared to have weathered the latest storm of pseudoscandals that beset her. Surveys showed Hillary's ratings as a strong leader rising in the wake of the manufactured e-mail and Clinton Foundation controversies, as Democrats rallied to her side in the face of partisan attacks, the Republican opposition hardened, and independents, for the most part, tuned out. And while the "shadow campaign" groups never said so publicly, their show of force in the precampaign period surely discouraged high-profile would-be Democratic challengers from jumping into the race.

With Hillary's campaign officially under way, Correct the Record made some necessary adjustments to its structure, splitting off from its parent group, American Bridge, into its own separate political committee. Most SuperPACs make "independent expenditures"—paid communications on a candidate's behalf—and thus are forbidden by law from coordinating their activities with campaigns. But since Correct the Record, a research organization that publishes its content online and distributes its content through free media channels, intended to do no paid advertising, it was able to set itself up as an entity that could coordinate its activities with the Clinton campaign. The rough division of labor was that while the campaign stayed positive and above the fray, Correct the Record would go head-to-head with the Hillary smear merchants—be they candidates, GOP party committees, congressional investigators, or Swift Boat–type third-party groups.

Our move to establish a SuperPAC that could raise unlimited funds in support of a candidate's campaign while coordinating with it was another first in presidential politics. Press reports called it "novel," "innovative," even "ground-breaking." And, as these things predictably go, the new Correct the Record SuperPAC immediately attracted a Federal Elections Commission complaint from a self-styled ethics watchdog fronting for the GOP falsely alleging that we are operating in violation of campaign finance laws.

Our fleet of organizations was growing, adapting, and revving its engines as we hurtled toward November 2016. Altogether, we had a staff of 250, and led by Mary Pat Bonner, the best fundraiser in the business, we were raising over $30 million a year to support our work from generous—and generally selfless—progressive donors. Media

Matters, the mother ship, was entering its twelfth year of operations. Dozens of researchers were not only engaged with the ongoing fight with Fox News but also with more important and more complex targets like the *New York Times*.

American Bridge had been researching the records of Hillary's potential GOP opponents and videotaping their events and local media hits for more than two years, putting it light-years ahead of where any Democratic Party–affiliated group had ever been this early in a presidential cycle. Most of what we learned we banked for future use, though if you saw the videos of Chris Christie telling a questioner on Hurricane Sandy relief efforts to "sit down, and shut up!" or of Scott Walker comparing union workers to terrorists, or of Jeb Bush looking like a deer in the headlights when asked his position on the Paycheck Fairness Act, you saw our handiwork.

Altogether, there were now twelve distinct legal entities in our domain working to level the playing field with the organized right wing. From these platforms, we were not only monitoring and exposing right-wing influence in the media and catching gaffes on the campaign trail; we were organizing and training an army of pro-Hillary media surrogates through the Franklin Forum; we were holding corrupt public officials accountable through Citizens for Responsible Ethics in Washington and the American Democracy Legal Fund, which sent tremors through the Republican National Committee when we sued it for illegally coordinating with GOP SuperPACs; and we were probing the shady business practices of the Koch brothers and GOP megadonor Sheldon Adelson through the American Independent Institute, an investigative journalism fund.

Of course, I'm already thinking ahead, to even filling more gaps in our progressive infrastructure. For one thing, we need a stronger crop of Democratic surrogates willing to stand up for our ideas, our values, and our candidates with the fearlessness that this critical moment dictates. Over the longer term, progressives need to think seriously about how to overcome the political advantages the Republicans have won in the states through better strategy, harder work—and the funds to do the job. And, before we know it, the redistricting battles of 2020—the next chance we'll have to take back the majority in the House—will be upon us. We need to start planning for that now even as we fight in 2016.

In addition to my own groups, I was also involved with the efforts of Priorities USA, the leading pro-Hillary SuperPAC that sought to raise hundreds of millions of dollars to run a paid advertising campaign against Hillary's Republican opponents, ads that would be based on the oppo research provided to it by American Bridge. Originally founded as a pro-Obama vehicle in the 2012 cycle, I joined Priorities' board in 2013 as it sought to morph into a pro-Hillary vehicle.

That road proved a bit rocky. In 2012, Priorities and my American Bridge organization had clashed repeatedly in a competition for SuperPAC dollars. Now under the leadership of Jim Messina, who had managed Obama's reelection campaign and was named cochair of Priorities, current and former Priorities officials had gone to the *New York Times* in early 2015 and told the story of that 2012 clash, in an apparent effort to get the upper hand against American Bridge in fund-raising for 2016. When I learned who was behind the front-page article that cast aspersions on my fund-raising shop, I immediately and publicly resigned from Priorities, which I charged had instigated "an orchestrated political hit-job" on my group. The ensuing media flap—which focused on a purported political rivalry between the Obama (Messina) and Clinton (me) camps that never existed—painted an ominous picture of dissension and chaos in Hillary's 2016 ranks. One donor aligned with Priorities publicly called me a "cancer."

In part to stem the tide of negative press reports, several Priorities board members asked me to reconsider and rejoin the board. Though some board members told me I should never have aired dirty linen in the media, in the numerous conversations I had with them, not one expressed any doubt that some in Priorities were capable of sanctioning the leaking of negative information on a potential competitor (though they did deny it)—even one that was fighting in the same cause.

Moreover, my resignation was catalyzing conversations both within and outside of Priorities about long-festering issues in the group that had nothing to do with the *Times* leak. Board members were voicing concerns that Priorities had no coherent plan to raise the level of funds required to do the job, and that it was operating with little regard for sound management practices or organizational transparency. In fact, since the board had been reconstituted in the spring of 2013, it had never once met.

I agreed to reconsider my resignation, which, publicly at least, would repair the rift and present a united front for Hillary's sake. I strongly believed that a successful Clinton candidacy needed a SuperPAC like Priorities to go up against the massive amount of cash Republican donors were expected to pour into their own SuperPACs for negative ads attacking Hillary's character. Although her overall favorables remained sound, Republicans were encouraged by press reports claiming that the drumbeat of scandal was taking a toll in her poll ratings for honesty and trustworthiness (even though the numbers hadn't really changed much since 2007). 57% SAY HILLARY IS A LIAR, screamed the *New York Post*. And Karl Rove announced that he was reorienting his American Crossroads group to be solely focused on more personal anti-Hillary attacks.

But I remained skeptical of some of the Priorities crew. Within a few months, there would be a shake-up in Priorities' leadership structure, with Guy Cecil, an official in Hillary's 2008 campaign, named to cochair the board and run its operations, as others were sidelined. As one of his first moves, Cecil asked me to rejoin the board, and with the organization in steadier and friendlier hands, I immediately agreed. The pro-Hillary groups needed to quit fighting each other and get down to business fighting the Republicans.

⌒

When Barack Obama was elected president in 2008, it seemed like a new chapter was beginning. Not only would he be the first African-American man to occupy the Oval Office, he brought with him the promise of a new approach to politics, a new opportunity to erase old partisan divisions, transcend our broken discourse, and unite the country around a progressive agenda.

Eight years later, the country is undoubtedly better off: Millions more have health care, most of our troops are home from Iraq and Afghanistan, Iran's nuclear ambitions have been thwarted, and the economy is once again roaring to life.

But, as President Obama himself has acknowledged, even his rare combination of charisma and intellect hasn't brought about the kind of political paradigm shift he and his supporters envisioned. The media culture is even more corrosive than before. The influence of money in politics has only grown. And, of course, Obama has faced fierce conservative opposition and obstruction at every turn.

So, I fear, will the next Democratic president. After all, if the right was motivated by a positive vision for America's future, then perhaps some grand bargain could have been struck.

Now, the Republican attacks on Hillary, entirely by contriving doubts about her personal character and integrity, once again reveal a GOP with no positive vision for the country. Instead of developing ideas to meet the challenges that face us, the negative personal attacks are a centerpiece of the Republican campaign of fostering fear, uncertainty, and doubt about that future.

While Hillary is leading with confidence, a clear program, and a steady grasp of the challenges ahead, the Republicans are attempting to cover their own confusion, disunity, and disorientation—and their true hidden agenda for the Koch brothers, et al.—by character assassination and smears. To the degree that the Republicans have opened their campaign with this character attack, they've exposed how little they have to offer.

Fear of the future. Running on empty. Looking backward. All negative, all the time. That's the GOP platform.

It won't work. That's because, just as it was when I was getting started back in the 1990s, the right isn't motivated by what it wants, but rather by who it hates.

Hillary Clinton's election as president is a political and moral necessity for many, many reasons. One is that we need a president who knows that our nation can't rise above the current deep divisions and partisan gridlock without first acknowledging the true aims of today's extremist wing of the GOP and accurately assessing its strengths and weaknesses. We need a president who will reach out to Republicans when she can, but will not hesitate to defeat the conservative movement when she must.

After all, 2016 may be the last battle of the Clinton Wars—but it won't be the last battle in the fight to determine America's future. There will be legislation to pass, nominees to confirm, more elections to win. And nobody is more battle-tested and ready for the change we need than Hillary.

# The House Select Committee on Media Matters

As this book went to press, Media Matters, the progressive media watchdog group I head, found itself in the crosshairs of the House Select Committee on Benghazi. How did the House Select Committee on Benghazi morph into the House Select Committee on Media Matters? And why were the Republicans on the committee suddenly more interested in *The Benghazi Hoax*—the title of an e-book I cowrote with a Media Matters colleague debunking the falsehoods and right-wing conspiracy theories about the attacks—than in Benghazi itself?

The farcical events surrounding committee testimony by Sidney Blumenthal, a former journalist and Clinton White House aide—and a longtime friend of mine—would have made for a fitting new chapter in *The Benghazi Hoax*. The Blumenthal saga was where all of the pseudoscandals of recent months—from the right's obsession with Benghazi, to the media frenzy over Hillary's e-mail habits, to the grotesque caricatures of the charitable Clinton Foundation as a shady political operation—converged.

Yet had they done some homework, committee Republicans easily could have learned about my relationship with Blumenthal, which was no secret. Both he and I had written about it in our respective memoirs of the 1990s, *The Clinton Wars* and *Blinded by the Right*.

Back when we first met in 1997 and became friends, we were an unlikely pair, to say the least. Blumenthal was a trusted advisor to President Clinton, well known for his political and personal commitments to the first couple, and also for having unusual insight into the right wing in his long career as a journalist. As such, he was scorned in some anti-Clinton media circles in Washington and despised by some in the conservative movement, which at that time had been engaged in a five-year campaign to destroy the Clinton presidency.

And me? Well, as you know, for most of those five years, I had been a leader in the far right's anti-Clinton operations. And after learning the hard way that I was complicit in campaigns of smears and lies under the guise of conservative journalism, I had just publicly broken with my political bedfellows in a confessional article in *Esquire*. "David Brock, the road warrior of the right, is dead," I declared.

However, my relationships and associations with my fellow partisan warriors did not end overnight. I remained employed at the *American Spectator* magazine, which was running the Arkansas Project, the reckless dirt-digging operation against the Clintons. I was friendly with lawyers working on Paula Jones's sexual harassment suit against President Clinton. That suit had come about in response to a deeply flawed *Spectator* article I had written in 1993 and by now was the vehicle through which the right was aiming to set up a perjury trap for the president by probing his sex life.

I still had sources in the office of Kenneth Starr, the former right-wing judge whose special counsel investigation of the Clintons' money-losing Arkansas land deal known as Whitewater had come a cropper. I knew that Starr, casting about desperately for a new angle to nail the Clintons, had been colluding with the Paula Jones lawyers to get personal dirt on Clinton.

And I remained close with anti-Clinton agitators in the right-wing media like Matt Drudge, Laura Ingraham, and Ann Coulter.

In part through my talks with Blumenthal, who reached out to me, I came to see that I had been fighting on the wrong side of the Clinton wars, and for a time I became an informant for the pro-Clinton side. Throughout the fall of 1997, I relayed the goals, contours, and details of this secretive anti-Clinton movement to Blumenthal at the White House.

Then, in one critical conversation on the day the Monica Lewinsky story broke in January 1998, I laid out for Blumenthal very specifically all I knew about the right-wing scheme to use Lewinsky to criminalize a private consensual affair and impeach the president for it. And I knew plenty.

If the Republicans had looked it up, they would have found the mystery of our relationship dispelled in several passages in Blumenthal's *The Clinton Wars*, including this one:

> I related to Hillary my conversation with Brock. I had been telling her about him all along. His revelations filled in the details of what was driving this new "acute" scandal phase. Having knowledge restored a sense of normality, even amid the storm. We could see the lines of influence underlying the scandal, the cause and effect, intent and action—and they were political and familiar. Thus, on the first day, both Hillary and I knew about what she would soon call the vast right-wing conspiracy.

As I similarly recounted the experience in *Blinded by the Right*:

> In the coming days, I decided to tell Sidney everything I knew that could help the Clinton White House defend itself against the effort to drive the president from office... The information helped the White House pull back the curtain and reveal the machinery behind the Lewinsky scandal. It enabled the Clinton defense team to identify the opposing players and connect the political and financial dots among them more swiftly than they otherwise

would have. And in an odd—one might even say surreal—historical footnote, given Sidney's proximity to the First Lady, it may have been the germ of the first line of defense: that Clinton was targeted, as Hillary Clinton soon charged on the *Today* show, by a "vast right-wing conspiracy."

Clinton, of course, defeated the unconstitutional impeachment crusade and remained in office for the remainder of his term, ending it with high approval ratings and a sterling list of accomplishments for the country. And Blumenthal and I would maintain a professional relationship and friendship for the next fifteen years.

⌒

Blumenthal became a target of the Benghazi investigators by a fluke. In 2013, a set of Blumenthal's e-mails addressed to then Secretary Clinton, Blumenthal's friend for more than thirty years, was stolen illegally through wire fraud by a hacker in Romania who went by the code name "Guccifer" and was working from a Russian server. He is now serving a seven-year sentence in a Romanian prison and was charged in a U.S. indictment last year. The hacker, who also purloined the e-mails of former president George W. Bush through his sister Dorothy's account and former secretary of state Colin Powell, was probably part of a Russian intelligence operation, according to the FBI. In the federal indictment, Blumenthal is listed as a "victim" along with Powell and Dorothy Bush.

At the time, the online gossip sheet Gawker posted the illegally obtained Blumenthal e-mails online, which, among other things, included private reports Blumenthal sent to Hillary on political events and security issues in Libya. Gawker also ran a story on them. It was hardly a surprise that the other media organization that posted the stolen e-mails simultaneously with Gawker was Russia Today, the official outlet for the Russian government. But there the story died.

Two years later, however, during the controversy this past spring over Hillary's exclusive use of a private e-mail account while she served in the State Department, Blumenthal's now-public e-mails were resurrected and recycled by the right-wing media, which promoted the fantasy that their bête noire Blumenthal had been the central figure in Hillary's "secret spy network," operating outside government channels.

The e-mails actually showed a friend and former colleague of decades forwarding on potentially useful information to a top U.S. policy maker about critical issues of national security. Certainly, Hillary wouldn't be the first public official to hear competing perspectives from outside official government sources. As James Fallows put in the *Atlantic*, "It is usually a sign of canniness in a public official, rather than the reverse, to keep channels open to friends who predate the official's time in office. This is something we celebrate in leaders from Lincoln to FDR."

Judging by her e-mail exchanges with Blumenthal, who sent them on his own, Hillary seemed happy to have the additional data points, and she sometimes forwarded them to senior aides for their consideration.

That was all. Would that George W. Bush had shown such intellectual curiosity in collecting differing opinions and consulting varied sources of information on security policy as he took the nation to war in Iraq under false pretenses.

But no matter. The right wing, entering a presidential contest divided, disoriented, and bereft of any positive ideas for the country, was determined to conjure up a scandal where none existed. In a column for the right-wing *Washington Times*, Monica Crowley, a former aide to the disgraced Richard Nixon, set down the conservative line: "Was Hillary Clinton running her own rogue intel operation?"

The right-wing *Wall Street Journal* editorial page went further, demanding a Justice Department investigation into the e-mails from one friend to another, which it posited was somehow "in violation of State rules."

But the right couldn't successfully scandalize the Clinton-Blumenthal e-mails without the complicity of others in the media, outside of its ranks.

Enter Jeff Gerth, the *New York Times* reporter who wrote the first Whitewater story. Gerth has since left the *Times*, but not, apparently, the anti-Clinton beat. In a March 2015 article for ProPublica, done, oddly, in collaboration with Gawker, Gerth sought to validate the Blumenthal conspiracy theory for mainstream reporters, writing, "The contents of the memos, which have recently become the subject of speculation in the right-wing media, raise new questions about how Clinton used her private email account and whether she tapped into an undisclosed back channel for information on Libya's crisis and other foreign policy matters."

In fact, there was a far-reaching and ongoing federal investigation into those e-mails, but not what the breathless Gerth reported. Those stolen e-mails were at the heart of the criminal federal indictment of the foreign hacker operating from a Russian server. And the FBI also was conducting an investigation of the involvement of the media organizations—Gawker and Russia Today—that had posted the illegally obtained e-mails.

As if on cue, Gerth, in a feedback loop with the right wing, soon delighted conservatives with an appearance on the far-right *Breitbart News Sunday* show, where he took his rhetoric up several notches, comparing the Blumenthal e-mails to the Iran-Contra scandal in the Reagan administration, for which officials "either went to jail or were convicted and got pardoned," he added, helpfully—or was it hopefully? He quickly passed from merely distorting the facts into partisan advocacy.

Like his bogus Whitewater reporting, the Gerth piece on Blumenthal fell flat as journalism, but it had a political effect because it was read closely by his former colleagues at the *Times*. And they soon got on the case to chase it.

To close observers of the paper's Clinton coverage, what came next was no surprise. Rather, it was part and parcel of a now predictable pattern of anti-Clinton scandalmongering, now being directed by the paper's Washington bureau chief and politics editor, Carolyn Ryan.

The Blumenthal assignment was the latest in a series of *Times* investigative pieces, all touted on the front page, aimed squarely at Hillary's presidential candidacy. As we've seen, there already had been Ryan-backed hit jobs on the Clinton Foundation and on Hillary's use of a private e-mail account while in government. Up at bat once more with the Blumenthal story, the *Times* swung furiously but whiffed again, publishing an innuendo-laden piece based on selectively leaked e-mail correspondence between Hillary and Blumenthal that had been turned over to the House Benghazi committee as part of its investigation.

"According to that story, the former journalist and Clinton confidant wrote a series of 'intelligence' memos about Libya that he sent to Hillary Clinton while she was Secretary of State—supposedly in the hope of advancing the interests of 'business associates' who wanted to undertake humanitarian enterprises in the country," as Joe Conason summarized the *Times* piece in the *National Memo*.

Yet according to Blumenthal's testimony to the House committee, the Libya memos the *Times* had attributed to him, and that he had forwarded to Hillary, had actually been written by his friend Tyler Drumheller, the highly regarded former CIA European chief now working in the private sector. The business "venture" repeatedly referred to by the *Times* never happened—it was nothing more than an inchoate idea to provide hospital beds and medicine in war-torn Libya that never got off the ground. And despite the *Times* huffing and puffing about imaginary conflicts of interest, no money ever changed hands with Blumenthal, he never made a nickel, and he had sought no favors from Hillary or anyone in the U.S. government for his mythical Libyan "business venture."

Who stated that the *New York Times* got it all wrong about Blumenthal? None other than Trey Gowdy, the Republican chairman of the Benghazi Committee. Of course, it was his Republican staff that had a hand in the story in the *Times*. But a week after Blumenthal testified under subpoena in a closed deposition with the public and press excluded, Gowdy wrote in a letter on June 22, 2015, to Congressman Elijah Cummings, the ranking Democrat on the committee, "It is...important that I correct certain misapprehensions that have, inadvertently I am sure, made their way into media accounts quoting Democrat sources." His feigned cluelessness of how those false stories with their "Democrat sources" appeared was rich. He went on to debunk the premises of the story the *Times* had published as fact—acknowledging that Blumenthal didn't write the reports he passed on to Hillary, and he didn't have a financial interest in Libya. Gowdy also conceded that subpoenaing Blumenthal was plainly absurd: "The Committee never expected Witness Blumenthal to be able to answer questions about the attacks in Benghazi."

Guess what? The *New York Times* never reported Trey Gowdy's public letter undermining its story point by point on Blumenthal. Apparently, it was not news fit to print.

What's the matter with the *New York Times*? Is it really that bad? It is. As it concerns Clinton coverage, the *Times* will have a special place in journalism hell.

❧

As we've seen, the House committee that the *New York Times* is so cozy with—the House Select Committee on Benghazi—is the tenth congressional committee to investigate the events surrounding the terrorist attack. None of them—including the Republican-led House Intelligence Committee—have found significant wrongdoing by the Obama administration or Secretary Clinton. Yet as of mid-June 2015, Gowdy's committee had been investigating the same issue for 409 days, longer than U.S. inquiries into Pearl Harbor or the Kennedy assassination or Iran-Contra, according to a statement by the committee's Democrats. They calculated the cost to U.S. taxpayers at $3.5 million—and counting.

If there was a scandal for the *Times* to investigate, this redundant waste of public money was it, but the paper was too busy running the committee's political errands to notice.

Even though the Benghazi inquiry had been under way for more than a year, on the day the *New York Times* published its piece about his e-mails to Hillary, Blumenthal became the very first witness subpoenaed by the committee. His wife, Jackie, was served by U.S. marshals at their Washington home.

In the past, Gowdy had said he would not subpoena a cooperative witness, and he also stated that "serious investigations do not leak information or make selective releases of information without full and proper context."

Yet the Select Committee's ranking Democrat, Representative Elijah Cummings of Maryland, blasted Gowdy for issuing the subpoena without first speaking to Blumenthal, with no committee debate or vote, and also for leaking news of the subpoena to the *Times* before it was even served. "The latest abuses by the Committee are just one more example of a partisan, taxpayer-funded attack against Secretary Clinton and her bid for president," Cummings charged.

But Gowdy was just getting started. Blumenthal was grilled in a closed deposition by the Benghazi committee for nine hours. And in all that time he was asked virtually nothing about... Benghazi.

That's right. Republicans asked him fewer than twenty questions about the terrorist attack in Benghazi, only four questions about U.S. security there, and zero questions about the U.S. presence in Benghazi, according to a fact sheet later circulated by Democratic committee staff.

Rather than asking about the ostensible subject of their investigation, the committee instead went on an odious fishing expedition into Blumenthal's professional and personal relationships.

Republicans asked questions about Blumenthal's political and personal history with Bill and Hillary Clinton. They asked questions about his work for the Clinton Foundation, a global charity, which Blumenthal advises. And they asked forty-five questions about Blumenthal's relationship with me, Media Matters, and a pair of SuperPACs I also founded, American Bridge and Correct the Record—a trio of groups that Blumenthal also advises.

"Gowdy was obsessed with Media Matters," Blumenthal told me on the night the ordeal ended. "They seemed more interested in my relationship with you than with Hillary."

Trey Gowdy had been elected to the House in the Koch-funded Republican wave of 2010. He had successfully challenged a Republican, Bob Inglis, for the seat in a primary. Inglis had a 93 percent rating of his voting record from the American Conservative Union, but he had angered the right with a factual statement that global warming is man-made, providing Gowdy with an opening.

Gowdy asked Blumenthal about his role in the production and promotion of four Media Matters research posts that were sharply critical of various false claims made by conservative media on Benghazi. Another Republican asked if Blumenthal had written or edited a recent statement from Correct the Record, a SuperPAC that defends Hillary against false attacks, that pointed out the partisan underpinnings behind the committee's ongoing investigation.

Blumenthal testified, accurately, that he had no role in any of it, though even if he had, what did that have to do with the avowed purpose of the committee?

This line of questioning led to a dead end. As it happens, Media Matters and Correct the Record source all of their research to publicly available information and verified reporting, and the groups make their work product public on their websites. If the Republicans want to figure out what we're up to, the answer is just a click away.

Nothing is amiss much less scandalous in the work of these groups; indeed, we're proud of what we publish.

I wish the same could be said for the Select Committee, which refused requests from committee Democrats and from Blumenthal to release publicly the transcript of his deposition. Clearly, Gowdy wants to suppress the evidence of his handiwork.

To be sure, the Republicans are sitting on the deposition—while leaking select parts to their friends in the media—to save themselves from political embarrassment. Sources who were in the room that day say the goings-on would be gold for the late night comics.

For instance, Blumenthal signed off one e-mail to Hillary with a joking reference to "Clio."

This led GOP Representative Mike Pompeo of California to demand to know, "Who is Clio?"

Blumenthal's answer? Clio is the Greek goddess of history. Nothing nefarious there.

At another point during the proceedings, California Republican Darrell Issa, who had chaired a prior failed Benghazi investigation, inexplicably tried to barge his way into the room where Blumenthal was being deposed before being turned away. "He isn't right," Gowdy said to a colleague, referring to Issa.

Blumenthal told me that the lead Republican lawyer for the committee told him and his lawyers at the end of a long day of questioning that "maybe we got five minutes' worth of something."

Yet while the inquiry was a pointless sideshow with respect to the committee's mandate, in fact it was not without a purpose. "So why was I subpoenaed at all before this committee? I am a longtime friend of Hillary Clinton," Blumenthal said in a statement after testifying. "It seems obvious that my appearance before this committee was for one reason and one reason only, and that reason is politics."

Indeed, the questions about Blumenthal's long-standing relationship with the Clintons, about his educational work at the Clinton Foundation and the Clinton Presidential Library, and about his work with our groups, were wholly illegitimate and out-of-bounds. But they were not without a design, and an insidious one at that.

By covering up the transcript, the Republicans are hiding the true nature of the Blumenthal deposition: their partisan attempt to both chill Blumenthal's right to freely express his own political views and, more broadly, to intimidate our organizations—organizations that have led the way in exposing the fraudulence of the Benghazi investigation itself.

If Democrats had hauled a politically active Republican before a congressional committee and spent hours hectoring the witness about his political and professional associations and activities—"Are you now or have you ever been a member of the Democratic Party?"—I can only imagine the hue and cry about the abuse of congressional power we'd have heard from the conservative echo chamber. Yet progressives for the most part stayed silent in the face of this blatant effort to suppress First Amendment rights.

And needless to say, none of the First Amendment champions at the *New York Times* found this travesty newsworthy.

Our groups have nothing to hide. After the deposition concluded, I publicly offered to give Gowdy a tour of our offices at his convenience. There he would find a hardworking staff committed to providing the public with fact-based information upon which to understand and judge the critical issues of the day—including the tragic deaths of four Americans in Benghazi that have been shamelessly politicized by the Republicans.

Gowdy would also meet people who won't be thrown off mission or harassed or cowed into standing down by desperate partisans who have nothing to offer voters in the coming election but tired pseudoscandals.

Staying silent in the face of outrageous right-wing misconduct just isn't our style.

July 8, 2015

# Acknowledgments

First and foremost, thanks go to Sean Desmond, my editor at Twelve, all of his colleagues there, and to Will Lippincott, my literary agent, for their wise counsel every step of the way to this book's publication.

In composing the book, I could not have asked for a sharper collaborator than Andy Barr.

Matt Gertz, Eric Hananoki, Hannah Groch-Begley, Isaac Wright, and Sam Ritzman worked hard to ensure the quality and accuracy of the manuscript. Thanks as well to the entire research teams at Media Matters, American Bridge, and Correct the Record, on whose superb published research I've drawn.

In my office, special thanks go to David Thau and Haley Link who went above and beyond the call of duty in ensuring a smooth and organized process.

This book is based in part on two speeches I've delivered in the past year, one at the Clinton School of Public Affairs in Little Rock, and the other at a Democracy Alliance conference in New Mexico. Those speeches were principally written by Jeff Nussbaum of West Wing Writers and Andy Barr. Eric Burns edited the Clinton School speech, and thanks as well to Skip Rutherford, the Clinton School's dean, for the invitation to appear. Gara LaMarche and the staff of the Democracy Alliance facilitated the DA address.

A number of friends and colleagues read drafts of the book and made astute suggestions and edits, large and small, including James Alefantis,

Bill Smith, Angelo Carusone, Michael Kempner, David Thau, Sidney Blumenthal, Mary Pat Bonner, Jeff Nussbaum, and Bradley Beychok.

I'd like to acknowledge the past and current teams and outside colleagues at Media Matters, American Bridge, and Correct the Record who contributed to the founding and subsequent success of the organizations over the years, especially former Media Matters presidents Eric Burns and Matt Butler, former American Bridge president Rodell Mollineau, Marcia Kuntz, Jamison Foser, Katie Paris, Jon Cowan, Kelly Craighead, Jill Alper, Eric Boehlert, Darrin Bodner, Tate Williams, Lida Masoudpour, Zac Petkanas, Ari Rabin-Havt, Allison Thompson, Matt Gertz, David Bennahum, Adrienne Elrod, Ilyse Hogue, Steve D'Amico, Jeremy Holden, Burns Strider, Phil Singer, Eddie Vale, Jessica Mackler, Sam Ritzman, Isaac Wright, Adrienne Watson, Maggie Williams, Phil Griffin, Sidney Blumenthal, Marc Elias, Jerry Hauser, and Bill Smith.

Special thanks to the current leadership of our teams: Bradley Beychok at Media Matters, Jessica Mackler at American Bridge, Brad Woodhouse at Correct the Record, and John Neffinger at the Franklin Forum; and to Mary Pat Bonner of the Bonner Group and her entire team.

None of these organizations would succeed in their missions without the critical support of a network of organizations and leaders in the progressive movement too numerous to single out. You know who you are.

Thanks to Senators Tom Daschle and Harry Reid, John Podesta, Rob Stein, and President Bill Clinton and Hillary Clinton for their early support of Media Matters.

Paul Begala, James Carville, Howard Dean, Stephanie Schriock, and Anita Dunn are always there for us. Susan McCue, Joe Conason, Marc Elias, Steve Bing, Susie and Mark Buell, Rob Dyson, Rob McKay, Michael Vachon, Paul Egerman, Patricia Bauman, and Rob Stein have also been important sounding boards over the years.

The boards of directors of these organizations comprise thirty-six stellar individuals committed to our mission. Special thanks to Kathleen Kennedy Townsend, the chair of Correct the Record.

These organizations are supported by more than four hundred generous donors without whom we simply could not do the work we do. I'd like to acknowledge, in particular, the ninety trustees who provide the core of this support on an annual basis. Peter Lewis, now deceased, is as responsible as anyone for our achievements.

Thanks to James Alefantis for his friendship.

And to Jack Bury, who kept my spirits up as I toiled away.

David Brock
July 2015

# Index

# About the Author

David Brock is a widely published author and Democratic activist. In 2004, Brock founded Media Matters, the nation's premier media watchdog. Following the 2010 elections, Brock founded the Democratic SuperPAC American Bridge, which is one of the largest modern campaign war rooms ever assembled using research, tracking, and rapid response to defeat Republicans. He is the author of five books, including his 2002 best-selling memoir, *Blinded by the Right: The Conscience of an Ex-Conservative.* His writing appears in *USA Today*, CNN .com, the *Huffington Post*, the *Daily Beast*, and *Salon*.

# ABOUT TWELVE

TWELVE

TWELVE was established in August 2005 with the objective of publishing no more than twelve books each year. We strive to publish the singular book, by authors who have a unique perspective and compelling authority. Works that explain our culture; that illuminate, inspire, provoke, and entertain. We seek to establish communities of conversation surrounding our books. Talented authors deserve attention not only from publishers, but from readers as well. To sell the book is only the beginning of our mission. To build avid audiences of readers who are enriched by these works—that is our ultimate purpose.

For more information about forthcoming TWELVE books, please go to www.twelvebooks.com.